SPEECH MATTERS

CARL G. HEMPEL LECTURE SERIES

SPEECH MATTERS

On Lying, Morality, and the Law

Seana Valentine Shiffrin

PRINCETON UNIVERSITY PRESS

Princeton and Oxford

Published by Princeton University Press, 41 William Street, Princeton,
New Jersey 08540
In the United Kingdom: Princeton University Press, 6 Oxford Street,
Woodstock, Oxfordshire OX20 1TW

press.princeton.edu

Jacket photograph: Subway Passengers, New York City: Two Women in
Conversation, January 27, 1941, Walker Evans (1903–1975). Film negative,
35mm. The Metropolitan Museum of Art, Walker Evans Archive, 1994
(1994.253.626.1). Image copyright © Walker Evans Archive, The Metropolitan
Museum of Art, New York, NY, USA. Image source: Art Resource, NY.

Library of Congress Cataloging-in-Publication Data

Shiffrin, Seana Valentine.
Speech matters : on lying, morality, and the law / Seana Valentine Shiffrin.
pages cm. — (Carl G. Hempel lecture series)
Includes bibliographical references and index.
ISBN 978-0-691-15702-3 (hardcover : alk. paper)
1. Truthfulness and falsehood. 2. Freedom of speech. I. Title.
BJ1421.S554 2015
177'.3—dc23   2014036621

British Library Cataloging-in-Publication Data is available

This book has been composed in Sabon

Printed on acid-free paper. ∞

Printed in the United States of America

1 3 5 7 9 10 8 6 4 2

For Vala

Contents

Acknowledgments

This book explores a variety of issues about the importance of sincerity and freedom of speech, in morality and in the law. It began as two lectures offered in honor of two inspiring women: "Lying and the Murderer Next Door," given in honor of Mala Kamm at New York University, and "Duress and Moral Progress," given in honor of Barbara Herman at Cornell University. The common themes of those lectures induced me to combine them and then to extend the arguments to the institutional context of the university for the Hempel Lectures at Princeton.

The Hempel Lectures emphasized philosophical, moral issues surrounding sincerity. In preparing them for publication, I decided to interweave three additional chapters that more directly concern theoretical legal issues about speech and its regulation. An earlier version of the third chapter, which advances a thinker-based defense of freedom of speech, was previously published in *Constitutional Commentary* (Fall 2011). I have substantially revised that essay, added new material on children and the mentally disabled, and incorporated some replies to critics. None of the other chapters draw on previously published material. I am grateful to Princeton University for the opportunity to present the Hempel Lectures, to Princeton University Press for publishing them, and to Rob Tempio for his patient encouragement.

I am humbled by the generous institutional, collegial, and familial support offered to me while working through these ideas. I can only make a partial attempt at voicing my appreciation. Discussions with Vincent Blasi, Tyler Burge, and David Kaplan, some quite long ago, encouraged my interest in these subjects and profoundly influenced the direction of my thinking. Later conversations with Joseph Almog, Asli Bali, Jennifer Dworkin, Gillian Lester, Tyler Meade, Michael Schrag, Neesa Levine,

Jacob Shiffrin, and Benjamin Shiffrin (sometimes charged) deepened my engagement with these themes.

More generally, I have been helped enormously by exposure to the stimulating, supportive, and dedicated intellectual culture at UCLA, both in the Philosophy Department and at the Law School, and especially its long-standing tradition of spirited dialogue about freedom of speech, testimony, and the conditions of a successful moral and political culture. I have been inspired by the wide array of colleagues and students who contribute to this dialogue and, in particular, those who have attended courses and seminars at UCLA about freedom of speech, contract theory, controversial communications, and truthfulness and promising. While thinking through these questions, I have been fortunate to work with and learn from extremely talented graduate students who have written on closely related issues, particularly Collin O'Neil, Robert Hughes, Jorah Dannenberg, Erin Taylor, and Jeffrey Helmreich. A small evening seminar of law and philosophy students, cotaught with Ronald Dworkin, discussed an early draft and offered stimulating and challenging resistance.

The research and administrative support at UCLA, particularly from the UCLA Hugh and Hazel Darling Law Library, is beyond parallel. Special thanks for research assistance are owed to Daisy Ding, Robert Double, Joseph Gilmore, David Schleider, Terry Stedman, Matthew Strawbridge, Stephen White, Lorien Whitehead, and Kevin Whitfield.

I am appreciative of the close care shown by Jill Harris, Eva Jaunzems, Kate Mertes, and Elyse Meyers in the preparation of the manuscript and index for publication.

I have also benefited from thoughtful, sometimes pointed, criticism from members of the September Group and from audiences in philosophy departments, law schools, and other fora at Boston College School of Law, Columbia University School of Law, Cornell University, Harvard Law School, King's College–London, Massachusetts Institute of Technology, New York University, Pepperdine School of Law, Queen's University, University of Colorado Boulder, University of Chicago School of Law, University of Sheffield, University of Virginia School of Law, Wayne State University, Yale Law School, and the IVR World Congress in Frankfurt, Germany. A grant from the Spencer Foundation and a Spencer Foundation conference on Justice and the Aims of Higher Education helped to make the work on the chapter on academic freedom and academic misrepresentation possible. My week at Princeton delivering the Hempel Lectures was especially fruitful.

On various chapters, I have received constructive advice, warm support, and detailed comments that altered my thinking from Jack Balkin, Netta Barak-Corren, Vincent Blasi, Joshua Cohen, Jorah Dannenberg, Ronald Dworkin, Richard Fallon, Claire Finkelstein, Mark Greenberg, Richard Holton, A. J. Julius, Frances Kamm, Leslie Kendrick, Alistair Macleod, Richard McAdams, Thomas Nagel, Collin O'Neil, David Owens, Joseph Raz, Mark Richard, Debra Satz, Thomas Scanlon, Frederick Schauer, Samuel Scheffler, Micah Schwartzman, Judith Jarvis Thomson, Catherine Wells, and Erik Olin Wright. Painstaking, detailed comments from Terry Stedman improved nearly every page. Chapter 3 arose from a multi-year e-mail discussion group on freedom of speech, spearheaded by Ed Baker and James Weinstein, that also included Vincent Blasi, Robert Post, Thomas Scanlon, Steven Shiffrin, Eugene Volokh, and Susan Williams. The products of our discussions were published in two collaborative symposia in the *Virginia Law Review* (2011) and *Constitutional Commentary* (2011). Each member's contributions prompted further development of and revisions to my own account.

Finally, a handful of people have offered a priceless combination of unstinting personal support, substantive assistance, and intellectual inspiration about these issues through lengthy conversations, more than generous feedback, their own writings, and their approach to life. Only a small fraction of my debt to them is evident in some footnotes. Largely, I remain speechless in gratitude toward Barbara Herman, Liam Murphy, William Rubenstein, Steven Shiffrin, Amir Vala Tavakoli, Joanna Valentine, and Mary Valentine.

SPEECH MATTERS

We cannot develop or flourish in isolation. Our mutual interdependence is not merely material but also, importantly, mental. The exchange of thoughts, beliefs, emotions, perceptions, and ideas with others is essential to each person's ability to function well as a thinker and as a moral agent. Sincere communication with others is, likewise, crucial to our ability to live together and to pursue our joint moral aims. Because we cannot peer into one another's minds, we depend upon others to convey their mental contents with precision and rich content through sincere communication. Sincere communication permits us, then, to share knowledge and hypotheses and to share needs, emotions, intentions, convictions, ambitions, desires, fantasies, disappointments, and judgments. Thereby, we are enabled to form and execute complex cooperative plans, to understand one another, to appreciate and negotiate around our differences, and to gauge, somewhat, the extent of our mutual ineffability. These achievements are important components of fulfilling the full range of our moral duties and ends, which involve mutual recognition, helping and respecting others, and responding to others as individuals—activities that often involve assessments of what others think, believe, and will.

Protecting this channel of mutual access must, therefore, be a substantial moral priority. My contention is that keener attention to the moral significance of communication would illuminate both the justificatory foundations of the prohibition against lying and the moral and legal prohibition against curtailing freedom of speech. Both prohibitions serve as moral protections of the reliability of communication and thereby preserve the conditions for moral agency, moral connection, and moral progress.

By probing the connections between discursive communication and moral agency, I hope to unify a variety of issues about communicative ethics and to motivate the outlines of a principled, nonconsequentialist approach to these issues—in particular to issues about lying, promissory fidelity, and freedom of speech. The approach I develop here complicates the case for making consequence-based exceptions to communicative duties in exigent circumstances created by bad agents. I argue that a nonconsequentialist case for sincerity and promissory fidelity has strong application outside of ideal theory, even in circumstances where immoral agents refuse to behave reciprocally and where insincerity and promissory infidelity are entertained because they would serve substantial moral purposes.

My aim is to provide a richer set of resources for deontological approaches to communicative duties and freedoms, by elaborating on the values communicative duties are structured to serve and by illustrating the connections between our communicative capacities and the cooperative project of developing and exercising our moral agency. Fleshing out these resources should clarify why making exceptions to communicative duties in exigent circumstances is not a simple ethical matter, and why yielding to consequences is in tension with the values these duties protect.

In short form, my claims revolve around the following ideas: Moral agency is a cooperative matter that depends on reliable channels of communication (among, of course, other things) for its development and realization. Every person matters, even those who go astray. In particular, every person's moral agency matters, even when they behave criminally. To preserve meaningful opportunities for the proper realization of our moral agency, we must protect the freedom to communicate. We must also protect the reliability and trustworthiness of communication as a window into one another's minds. The duties of sincerity and promissory fidelity play a large role in that scheme of protection. To abridge freedom of speech or to carve exceptions to these duties is, to a significant extent, to isolate thinkers from one another. This isolation is in tension with the cooperative and collaborative project of fostering everyone's moral agency. The arguments for restricting the scope of communicative duties and rights often seem insufficiently sensitive to the general role of communication in enabling moral agency, securing our moral ends, and facilitating moral connection and moral rehabilitation, even with, and perhaps especially with, wrongdoers. Being able to forge moral progress together without resorting to violence depends upon enabling and protecting somewhat fragile lines of communicative trust.

My more detailed plan to elaborate on these ideas is as follows. First, I will address some issues about our individual duties of sincerity and promissory fidelity. I will defend a qualified absolutism about lying that distinguishes the wrong of the lie from the wrong involved in deception (when it is wrong). My account emphasizes the role the stricture on lying plays in maintaining reliable channels of communication between moral agents. Then, I will investigate whether, how, and why it should matter that one's interlocutor is a moral criminal, the infamous Murderer at the Door.

The second chapter turns to the question of whether promises made under duress have moral force. Extending themes from the first chapter about the importance of maintaining reliable channels of communication and trust, I consider whether and why it should matter that one's promisee is a moral criminal, the proverbial highway robber. I will defend the surprising conclusion that some promises made under duress may indeed have moral force. Both chapters connect sincerity and promissory fidelity by individuals in nonideal circumstances with the social conditions that enable moral progress.

From there, I turn my attention to law and social institutions. In the second part of the book, I address the foundational connection between the grounds for the moral prohibition on lying and the moral and political protection of freedom of speech. Connecting the foundations of the duty of sincerity with the foundations of freedom of speech yields implications for free speech doctrine and for our legal treatment of lies. Making this connection also has critical implications for exceptionalist arguments advanced on behalf of institutions like the police, public employers, and universities, for institutional exemptions from the prohibition on lies and from free speech requirements.

Specifically, in the third chapter, I contend that the connection between discursive communication and moral agency also provides the foundations for what I call a "thinker-based theory" of freedom of speech. This theory defends freedom of speech for both political and personal speech by locating the foundation of freedom of speech in the needs of the individual thinker. I then turn to explore how a unified approach to sincerity and freedom of speech bears on the philosophical issues associated with the legal regulation of lies. This discussion spans two chapters. Chapter Four argues that, despite the common wisdom, legal regulation of lying poses no intrinsic threat to freedom of speech, although various regulations may, in context, pose a contingent threat by enabling governmental abuse. Chapter Five argues that although legal regulation of some autobiographical lies may not offend freedom, it may offend equality. I argue that our moral equality rests on a conception of each of us as imperfect moral agents that counsels for legal accommodation of the moral failure that (merely) autobiographical lies represent.

In the final chapter, I turn to the ethics of misrepresentations that are offered within institutional roles for institutional purposes. It is sometimes suggested that institutional values and roles provide special authorization both for controlled forms of misrepresentation to advance significant social purposes and for constraints on freedom of speech. I argue to the contrary, focusing on misrepresentations by academic researchers in the pursuit of truth and hierarchical justifications for speech restrictions. Because the university operates as a substantial epistemic resource, the success of which depends both on its credibility and intellectual independence, universities and their members have special obligations not to engage in misrepresentation and, at the same time, to protect a wide scope of academic freedom.

Two final notes about style: This volume began its life as three lectures, which appear, in somewhat revised form, as Chapters One, Two, and Six. Although the lectures addressed interconnected themes, each was meant to stand alone. To fill in the arguments about freedom of speech that appear in Chapter Six and to address the legal theoretical questions that grow out of Chapter One, I added the chapters about freedom of speech and the legal treatment of lies. Although the chapters build on one another and there are some cross-references between them, I have tried to retain their rough independence from one another so that readers may dip into subsequent chapters without having read the preceding ones.

Second, I write to an audience interested in theoretical and practical issues concerning morality, politics, and law. At times in the text, I advert to legal doctrines or to philosophical or legal literature that may be more familiar to specialists in those fields. Given my own background and expertise, my discussion of legal doctrine concentrates on U.S. law and often on the framework of free speech protection embodied in the First Amendment, our constitutional provision dedicated to the strong protection of free speech. I have attempted to make these references accessible to those outside the discipline in question but, in any case, I try quickly to return to more general and approachable themes.

CHAPTER ONE

Lies and the Murderer Next Door

In human social life, the principal object is to communicate our attitudes, and hence it is of the first importance that everyone be truthful
in respect of his thoughts, since without that, social intercourse ceases
to be of any value. Only when a person voices his opinions can another tell what he thinks, and if he declares that he wishes to express
his thoughts, he must also do it, for otherwise there can be no sociality
among men. Fellowship among men is only the second condition of
sociality; but the liar destroys this fellowship, and hence we despise a
liar, since the lie makes it impossible for people to derive any benefit
from what he has to say.

—**Immanuel Kant, from his** *Lectures on Ethics*[1]

Benjamin Constant famously complained about a "German philoso-
pher" who implausibly maintained that "it would be a crime to lie to a
murderer who asked us whether a friend of ours whom he is pursuing
has taken refuge in our house."[2] In response to this allegation, Immanuel Kant notoriously rejected Constant's contention that one has a duty
to tell the truth only to a person who has a right to one's sincerity,
declaring:

Truthfulness in statements that one cannot avoid is a human being's
duty to everyone, however great the disadvantage to him or to another
that may result from it; and although I indeed do no wrong to him

---

[1] IMMANUEL KANT, *Of Ethical Duties Towards Others, and Especially Truthfulness*, *in* LECTURES ON ETHICS 200, 200–01 (Peter Heath & J.B. Schneewind eds., Peter Heath trans., 2001) (27:444).

[2] IMMANUEL KANT, *On a Supposed Right to Lie from Philanthropy*, *in* PRACTICAL PHILOSOPHY 611 (Mary Gregor ed., trans., 2005) (8:425) (citing Benjamin Constant, *Von den Politischen Gegenwirkungen*, 6 FRANKREICH IM JAHR 1797, at 99, 123 [1797]).

who unjustly compels me to make the statement if I falsify it, I never-theless do wrong in the most essential part of duty *in general* by such falsification which can therefore be called a lie . . . ; that is, I bring it about, as far as I can, that statements (declarations) in general are not believed, and so too that all rights which are based on contracts come to nothing and lose their force; and this is a wrong inflicted upon hu-manity generally.[3]

Kant's notorious refusal to dissociate himself from the Murderer-at-the-Door example often serves as the fulcrum around which critical paro-dies of him, and of deontology more generally, pivot. Although a spate of recent work suggests both that Kant's nuanced position has been misun-derstood and that a plausible position on lying may be constructed from Kantian materials, much of it has focused on showing that the Kantian position need not be as extreme as critics and the Murderer-at-the-Door passage suggest.[4] Less of it, I think, has made sense of why lying as such exercised Kant so strongly and why, despite the strong temptation to dismiss his position about the Murderer at the Door, that passage exerts a magnetic attraction on critics and friends alike.

Here, I aim to address that gap and to sketch a theory that provides some plausible ground for a qualified form of Kant's absolutism about lying, building upon the themes Kant adduces in the opening passage of the selection from the *Lectures on Ethics*. Although I draw inspiration from some of Kant's texts and from some Kantian interpreters, my main interest is in what we may glean from Kantian or neo-Kantian *themes*. I do not claim that my worries are, in the end, the same as Kant's, and I do not aspire to an accurate exegesis of Kant's text.

Investigating the resources of the Kantian position has contemporary relevance because a tension in our moral attitudes toward lying remains

---

[3] *Id.*, at 611–15 (8:425–30).

[4] I have particularly in mind recent work of Christine Korsgaard, Tamar Schapiro, David Sussman, and Allen Wood. *See* CHRISTINE M. KORSGAARD, *The Right to Lie: Kant on Dealing with Evil, in* CREATING THE KINGDOM OF ENDS 133 (1996); Tamar Schapiro, *Kantian Rigorism and Mitigating Circumstances*, 117 ETHICS 32, 32–45 (2006); David Sussman, *On the Supposed Duty of Truthfulness: Kant on Lying in Self-Defense, in* THE PHILOSOPHY OF DECEPTION 225 (Clancy Martin ed., 2009); ALLEN WOOD, KANTIAN ETH-ICS 240–58 (2008). I am closer in spirit to Barbara Herman's treatments of Kant on lying and deception, as will become evident, but I will flag the moments where our approaches may diverge in some important respects. *See* Barbara Herman, *A Mismatch of Methods, in* 2 DEREK PARFIT, ON WHAT MATTERS 83 (Samuel Scheffler ed., 2011).

unresolved. On the one hand, with respect to everyday cases, few people subscribe to consequentialist accounts of the wrong of lying. Whether one should lie for personal gain does not seem to turn upon the question of whether the benefits to oneself outweigh the costs to others. Even when large benefits to oneself would eclipse the costs to others, most people are persuaded that more principled, nonconsequentialist arguments explain why the lie is impermissible. To lie for personal convenience seems to violate fundamental norms of equality and interpersonal respect by wrongfully treating oneself as more important than one's interlocutor, whether because one thereby makes an exception for oneself to crucial rules of communication, because one thereby attempts to gain an unfair epistemic advantage over another, or because one attempts to manipulate another's trust for one's own private ends. The deontological view that the duty of sincerity regulates one's behavior for reasons independent of the overall value of the consequences of its fulfillment or violation seems plausible. Considerations of this sort suggest that deontological accounts of sincerity are planted on solid ground, at least when the temptation to violate a prohibition arises from self-oriented motives.

Deontological positions often seem to lose their firm footing, however, when the temptation to violate a prohibition arises from moral motives, especially when the immediate beneficiary of the prohibition would be a moral criminal. When the murderer comes to one's door asking for the whereabouts of his intended victim, it does not ring true to insist that lying would involve carving out an exception for oneself or manipulating trust for one's private ends. One's ends here could not be more publicly oriented: to save the innocent and to frustrate a terrible criminal endeavor. Even those who regard dishonesty as a serious moral offense often begin to hedge when the subject of exigent circumstances arises. If an innocent life is at stake, surely the strictures against misrepresentation substantially relax. Many find it hard to resist the idea that in exigent circumstances, when one's aims are public-spirited, and particularly when the circumstances are created by a wrongdoer, the consequences should determine what one communicates—most famously, that one should lie to the Murderer at the Door about the location of his intended victim to save that victim's life.

I feel the pull of these ideas about exigent circumstances, but, upon reflection, I think they are overly simple. In particular, they seem insufficiently sensitive to the role of communication in enabling moral agency, securing our moral ends, and facilitating moral connection and moral rehabilitation, even with, and perhaps especially with, wrongdoers. The conditions of forging moral progress together seem to depend upon securing and protecting the lines of communicative trust. In what follows, I try to offer a deontological account of the wrong of lying that distinguishes the wrong of the lie from the wrong of deception (when it is wrong) and that resists complete (theoretical) capitulation to the Murderer at the Door.

I do not contend that one may never intentionally misrepresent anything at all to the Murderer at the Door. In fact, although many recent accounts try to reconcile Kantian principles with the permissibility of misrepresenting to the Murderer at the Door, I believe they do not venture far enough. They endorse untruthful representations to the murderer at one's own door, but they have a difficult time justifying what seems an equally clear case: the neighbor's intentionally false representation about the intended victim's whereabouts to the murderer *next* door.

In other respects, however, recent efforts to recast the Kantian position go too far and, in essence, endorse an overly broad range of misrepresentations to wrongdoers. We need not represent truthfully when our representations would constitute cooperation with a criminal aim, but at the same time, the fact that the murderer has a nefarious aim does not suffice to authorize any manner of misrepresentation. Some intentional misrepresentations told even to the Murderer at the Door are wrong. I suspect the over-breadth of some recent reconciliations emanates from some larger presuppositions that I reject about our relations to wrongdoers and how and when we may reasonably expect moral transformation and reconciliation to occur.

To elaborate these ideas, I will begin with some preliminary thoughts about what typifies the lie and what I take the distinctive wrong of lying to be, as opposed to the wrong of deception (when deception is wrong). Although lies are often used to achieve deception and often a part of the wrong of such lies is their deceptive use, I contend that lying is distinct from deception. Further, the wrong of lying differs from the wrong of deception. I will then proceed to the problem of the Murderer at the Door and connect it to other issues about our moral relations with wrongdoers and the process of their moral evolution. My overarching aim is not to defend an absolutism blind to the circumstances of communication, but to try to reframe how the consequences of communicative actions matter by advancing a more contextual and content-based approach to the question of when one may misrepresent.

Lying and Its Wrongfulness
Why Truthful Communication Matters

I will start with what I take to be the central, but relatively neglected, good that Kant stresses as promoted by truthful communication.[5] Its fuller appreciation helps to explain his profound animosity toward untruthfulness.

As Kant emphasizes in his *Lectures on Ethics*, we lack direct access to the content of one another's minds. We must rely upon communication for mutual understanding and cooperation, which are compulsory ends for human rational agents living together.[6] As human beings, we have foundational interests in knowing the contents of one another's minds.

Given our mutual epistemic limitations and the complexity of the environment in which we find ourselves, we depend upon one another's beliefs, knowledge, and reactions to our beliefs to construct a reliable picture of our world, so that we can navigate through it and understand who we are and where we are situated. This mutual epistemic dependence encompasses not only our ability to apprehend the material and social world, to learn history, and to apprehend the wide realm of *a priori* truths.[7] It also includes our ability fully to understand our moral and political duties. As imperfect rational agents in a complex and evolving social world, we need one another's help to understand what morality requires. Moreover, as is explicit in democracies, because our political duties demand responsiveness to what other agents believe is right, we need to have a clear and reliable understanding of their will in order to be appropriately responsive to it.

In addition to relying upon one another's understanding of the moral environment to form a coherent, accurate picture of our general moral and political duties, we have other moral reasons to seek knowledge of the contents of one another's minds. Many moral duties require responsiveness to other people as particular individuals, which demands a good sense of others' thoughts, beliefs, feelings, and perceived needs. To respect

---

[5] Charles Fried's remarks in *Right and Wrong* about how the lie abuses the mechanism of communication seem correctly sensitive to this good. CHARLES FRIED, RIGHT AND WRONG, 64–68 (1978).

[6] KANT, *supra* note 1, at 200–01 (27:444).

[7] Burge stresses the general fact that "most of our knowledge is dependent on others," and addresses important epistemological issues raised by that fact in Tyler Burge, *Content Preservation*, 102 PHIL. REV. 457, *passim* and especially 466–68, 485 n. 23 (1993). *See also* C.A.J. COADY, TESTIMONY (1992).

their autonomy, we need to know what their capacities are, what information they have access to, and, most important, what they will. Further, our ability to assess when others have behaved well or badly, whether they have acted in or out of character, whether they have and exercise virtues and vices of character, and whether they have acted freely or under coercion will often depend on our knowing what beliefs, reasons, emotions, and other motives propel their behavior. Because our full moral assessments of their behavior depend upon some understanding of others' mental contents, so will our apt moral reactions to their behavior. Relatedly, we care for one another and both need and care to be known and cared for by others. Relationships of recognition and close relationships—both necessary for full self-development and flourishing—depend upon access to the contents of one another's minds. For me to be an object of particularized respect and appreciation requires others to know me for who I am, although it is important that I have some control over who has access, to what, and when. The fulfillment of these foundational moral interests requires a mechanism for accurate, discretionary self-revelation.

Speech, which I will use as shorthand for "linguistic communication," plays a special role in allowing us access to this necessary information, helping us overcome the opacity of one another's minds. Although we can often observe behavior, including facial expressions, and make inferences about what that behavior reveals about others' mental contents, that behavior provides only a rough guide to the variegated and nuanced territory of the mental. It is difficult to read behavior accurately and to grasp the subtleties of mental content through just our external actions.

Communication by one mind to another, particularly through speech, provides the only precise mechanism by which one's mental contents may be conveyed to another mind, with all their subtlety and detail. Intentional communication is also the only *authoritative* source of one's own mental contents. Only I have direct access to the contents of my mind. My representations about what I think, believe, feel, experience, have decided, and so forth, have an authoritative status that other sources of information about me lack.

Of course, individuals may not fully know themselves and, further, may be self-deceived. Hence, they may not be fully equipped to share (should they decide to do so) all of the contents of their minds with others and to enable others to know themselves directly through testimony.

The phenomenon of self-deception does not diminish my point. Even when people are self-deceived, what they consciously take to be their beliefs, emotions, and other mental contents is a vital aspect of who they are and composes part of their mental contents.[8] Sharing these contents, confronting the reactions of others, and learning of any observations of one's behavior to the contrary are often crucial both to others' understanding of oneself and to resolving and eliminating one's own self-ignorance and self-deception. That process is an important part of being taken seriously as a rational agent, albeit one who is flawed and partially self-deceived. It enables one to confront one's imperfections as a rational agent in a rational, self-conscious way.

Together, our need to convey our mental contents and to have access to others' mental contents, combined with the unique role speech plays in addressing that role, underpin the view that we have duties to promote truthful understanding about our beliefs and other mental contents, and that there is a default moral presumption of truthfulness in communication.[9] I take this presumption to encompass a requirement of sincerity, namely that one believe what one says when one solemnly affirms it,[10] as well as a requirement to exert some effort to be accurate about what one says.[11] Because, as will emerge, my concern in what follows is the sincerity element of this presumption, I will use "presumption of truthfulness" and "presumption of sincerity," interchangeably.[12] I suggest these needs also help to explain why lying might be a special way those duties are subverted and why lying might constitute a form of harm to self and to

[8] See also Stuart Hampshire, Sincerity and Single-Mindedness, in FREEDOM OF MIND AND OTHER ESSAYS 232, 236–38, 253–55 (1972).

[9] I borrow the language of a presumption of truthfulness from Herman, supra note 4, at 107.

[10] I bracket some of the complications associated with characterizing what sincerity involves when making sarcastic or ironic remarks or when implicating. Many of the relevant wrinkles are discussed in Andreas Stokke, Insincerity, Noûs in doi: 10.1111/nous.12001 (Early Online View, 2012).

[11] As Stuart Hampshire observes, there is another sense of sincerity associated with whole-heartedness or single-mindedness—one that I will put aside. See Hampshire, supra note 8. One's regret over an action is thought to be sincere in this other sense, for example, if one does not also harbor small twinges of guilty pleasure that one had the audacity to perform it.

[12] Thus, I will put aside the extremely interesting issues of what levels of effort and success at accuracy, both in self-understanding and in understanding of the world are required. I take it that agents are not always required to succeed in being accurate and that the level of effort they must exert to try to achieve accuracy may reasonably depend upon contextual factors, such as the degree of difficulty, the subject matter, the agent's level of expertise, the role of the agent in the epistemic division of labor, and the resources and vulnerabilities of her audience. These fascinating issues belong predominantly to the topic of deception.

humanity, as well as an insult and, potentially, a harm to the recipient in particular. Let me now sketch those moves.

What Is Lying?

I will use the following working characterization of the lie, which is meant to capture the core cases of lying that matter from a moral perspective. My characterization of lying is unique in some respects that, I think, help to highlight why it is a distinctive wrong. But, my account of the distinctive wrong that lying represents ultimately does not depend on any of these respects and is compatible with other characterizations.

I propose that, as a working characterization, we understand a lie to be:

An intentional assertion by A to B of a proposition P such that[13]

1. A does not believe P,[14] and
2. A is aware that A does not believe P,[15] and
3. A intentionally presents P in a manner or context that objectively manifests A's intention that B is to take and treat P as an accurate representation of A's belief.

This characterization reflects three crucial desiderata. First, the proposition (P) that a lie transmits may be false, but need not be false.[16] Rather,

[13] I use the term "assertion" to cover propositional utterances or statements, whether believed or not and whether presented in a somber or jocular context. I do this for ease of expression, although I am aware that some restrict the term to propositional statements that *are* in fact believed by the speaker, presented as to be believed, or both. Those who object to my use might instead substitute "utterance" or "statement" where I use "assertion." For convenience, I focus on explicit assertions. I bracket the question of whether and when one may make an assertion (and lie) through an exclamation, facial expression, or bodily gesture. I also intend to bracket some interesting problems about whether one may lie without using assertion, e.g., whether exclaiming "ouch!" when one has not been hurt both does not advance an assertion but nevertheless is a lie, or is, instead, a related form of misrepresentation.

[14] I assume that the content of an assertion may depend upon the context in which it was uttered. Different contexts may demand or impute different levels of precision in the use of graded adjectives, such as "square," "low-fat," and "level." In Chapter Four, I discuss some difficult questions posed by conscientious objections to the implicit criteria for some concepts embedded within some conversational contexts.

[15] For ease of discussion, I will assume that the assertion is unqualified. Qualified assertions may also be lies where the speaker knowingly misrepresents her degree of conviction or uncertainty.

[16] For a different view, *see* Thomas L. Carson, *Lying, Deception, and Related Concepts,*

as Harry Frankfurt has rightly emphasized, what the lie *necessarily* transmits is a false representation of the (conscious) contents of the speaker's mind.[17] But since the speaker may herself have false beliefs, in falsifying the (conscious) content of her mind, she may inadvertently transmit the truth about what she states.

Also, I eschew an alternative formulation that requires the liar to "disbelieve" the content of what she asserts,[18] because that alternative formulation excludes idle fabulists. If, in reaction to your question "What happened in the world today?" I spontaneously invent that the volcano in Iceland erupted again, I have lied even if I have no opinion one way or the other whether in fact it did. Agnostics about the truth of their assertions who nonetheless assert them without qualification tell lies, on my view. I will use the term "falsification" to refer to the liar's utterance, connoting that the liar says something she does not believe to be true. Her utterance thereby falsifies the contents of her mind, even if it does not necessarily falsify the facts about the world represented in P.

Second, although lies and wrongful deception are related ways of subverting duties to promote truthful understanding, they are not coextensive. Nor are lies a strict subset of the category of deception. A lie does not depend upon its recipient being deceived or upon its issuer intending to deceive the recipient.[19] It is very odd to think that whether a speaker lies *hinges* upon the persuasiveness of the speaker or the credulity of the listener (especially when this feature of the listener is unknown to the speaker). To illustrate this point further, as well as a related point about intent, consider these two examples: A witness on the stand may perjure himself even if he knows that everyone in the court knows that what he

---

in THE PHILOSOPHY OF DECEPTION, *supra* note 4, at 153, 154–55. Carson also takes a somber assertion to be a promise that its contents are true, whereas, strictly speaking, I regard promises as moral devices used to transfer rights about decision-making power and not as devices of warranty or guarantee. *Id.* at 165.

[17] Harry Frankfurt highlights the central role of this feature in the wrong of the lie, although he regards the intent to deceive as a central feature of the lie, rather than as its frequent companion as I do. Harry Frankfurt, *The Faintest Passion*, 66 PROC. & ADDRESSES AM. PHIL. ASS'N 5, 6 (1992).

[18] *See, e.g.*, Larry Alexander & Emily Sherwin, *Deception in Morality and Law*, 22 LAW & PHIL. 393, 395 (2003) (defining the lie as a "statement, verbal or non-verbal, of a proposition that the speaker believes to be false, but that the speaker intends the audience to take as a proposition the speaker believes to be true"). As I discuss in Chapter Four, the stronger criterion that the liar actively disbelieve what he asserts may be a more appropriate requirement when lies by individuals are subject to *legal* regulation.

[19] The requirement of the intent to deceive is, however, a common feature in the literature on lying. *See, e.g.*, SISSELA BOK, LYING 13 (1978) and *infra* note 28.

is saying is false and knows that he couldn't believe it.[20] Or, an under-graduate may come to you five consecutive weeks in a term, each time asking for still another paper extension, because she has to attend (yet another) grandmother's funeral. Even accounting for the complexities of the modern extended family, this scenario defies credulity, as any under-graduate would know. Yet she may still offer this story as a reason, know-ing full well you will not believe it, but still offering it to be taken as true. In these cases, I submit, there is a lie performed without the intent or likelihood of deception. The perjurer and the undergraduate do not think they will be believed. They are not even credibly described as making a desperate attempt at the hopeless. The aim of both parties seems better described as evading the truth rather than attempting to implant the false. Neither wants to face, or to face in front of others, what happened or how they failed. Nonetheless, because they are under pressure to com-municate and to give an account, they offer an assertion they do not be-lieve, although they have no reason to believe that you will believe it.[21]

The undergraduate and the perjurer represent somewhat common-place, if episodic, examples of lies told without the achievement, intent, or expectation of deception. The pathological liar represents a familiar, if not commonplace, figure for whom the practice of lying may regularly become decoupled from the pattern or aim of deception. For the patho-logical liar, "material reward or social advantage does not appear to be the primary motivating force, but the lying is an end in itself; an inner dynamic rather than an external reason drives the lies, but when an ex-ternal reason is suspected, the lies are far in excess of the suspected exter-nal reason."[22] The pathological liar may repeatedly utter falsifications, even when it is known by the liar and his audience that they are untrue,

---

[20] Carson, *supra* note 16, at 159–61 also uses a perjury example to make the same point.

[21] In a case holding that the False Statements Accountability Act, 18 U.S.C. § 1001, did not immunize false self-exculpatory statements, the Supreme Court registered a similar skepticism about the suggestion that one might be innocent of the commission of the crime of deliberate misrepresentation to a federal official if one's statement were disbelieved by one's audience. Such a doctrine "would be exceedingly strange; such a defense to the analo-gous crime of perjury is certainly unheard of . . . ." Brogan v. United States, 522 U.S. 398, 402, 402 n. 1 (1998) (quoting United States v. Abrams, 568 F.2d 411, 421 (5th Cir. 1978), "Grand jurors . . . are free to disbelieve a witness and persevere in an investigation without immunizing a perjurer."). Although I agree with the Court on this question of whether dis-believed misrepresentations may nonetheless qualify as lies or forms of perjury, I should register that the terrain of self-exculpatory misrepresentation is complex. To federal offi-cials, claims of "innocence" and denials of "guilt" should not be understood as factual deni-als of wrongful involvement in a crime, but as invocations of a right to further due process; thus, I do not classify them as lies.

[22] *See* Charles C. Dike et al., *Pathological Lying Revisited*, 33 J. AM. ACAD. PSYCHIATRY

and even when their utterance poses a threat to the liar's social and professional status.[23]

The third clause of the characterization clarifies that not all assertions the speaker does not believe are lies.[24] The disbelieved statements imbedded in jokes, fictional stories, and the magician's patter are not properly understood as lies. Neither are speculations or devil's advocacy that are not really believed by the speaker but offered to further an exploratory conversation. A lie is not merely a statement the speaker does not believe, but is rather a falsification presented in a context that objectively conveys that the statement is to be taken as a *true* representation of the speaker's beliefs (usually transportable to other contexts) and not merely to be used within its discrete context of presentation as though it were true.[25]

L. 342, 343 (2005). Unfortunately, as Dike et al. discuss, the topic of the pathological liar has receded from academic attention over the past fifty years. *Id.* at 342.

[23] Charles C. Dike, *Pathological Lying: Symptom or Disease*, PSYCHIATRIC TIMES (June 1, 2008), http://www.psychiatrictimes.com/articles/pathological-lying-symptom-or-disease (describing a "not uncommon" case of a pathological liar who often "told blatant lies, and even when confronted, and proved wrong, he still swore they were true.") There seems both to be evidence that the pathological liar may buy into his or her lies at certain moments, but also that the pathological liar shows guilt reactions when lying under polygraph. Graham E. Powell, Gisli H. Gudjonsson & Paul Mullen, *Application of the Guilty-Knowledge Technique in a Case of Pseudologia Fantastica*, 4 PERSONALITY & INDIVIDUAL DIFFERENCES 141, 145–46 (1983). More important, under pressure, the liar will acknowledge his or her lies as lies. Other evidence suggests many pathological liars have a normal grip on reality. *See* Dike, *supra*; Dike et al., *supra* note 22, at 342–43; B.H. King & C.V. Ford, *Pseudologia Fantastica*, 77 ACTA PSYCHIATRICA SCANDINAVICA 1, 1–2 (1988).

[24] Sensitive to the same concerns, Carson suggests that a lie involves a knowingly false utterance in a context in which the speaker *warrants* its truth. Carson, *supra* note 16, at 170. This condition excludes too much. A speaker may, for example, *know* that a shop is closed but say, in response to an inquiry, "I have been wrong in the past and I'm not sure I should be trusted again, but the shop is open." Those prefatory remarks disclaim a warranty, but they nonetheless constitute a lie.

[25] Strangely, this condition is not respected in the prominent study that pioneered the commonly used Sheffield Test for (purportedly) tracking the brain activity of people who lie. The study's authors define lying as "the process by which the perpetrator (of a lie) deliberately attempts to convince their victim of the truth of a proposition they themselves know to be false." Sean A. Spence et al., *Behavioural and Functional Anatomical Correlates of Deception in Humans*, 12 NEUROREPORT 2849, 2849 (2001). This definition is overly narrow in excluding deliberate misrepresentations that do not aim to convince the recipient of their content. It is overly broad by including other forms of deceptive activity, such as mere failures of disclosure without active misrepresentation or truthful statements that may mislead given the listener's prior beliefs. Ironically, despite the authors' definitional stress on the intent to deceive, what the test actually registers as a lie differs. To "lie" within the experimental constraints, the subject had to press a button in response to a computer prompt that corresponded to what the subject regarded as the wrong answer. Because the subject had, in advance, submitted the correct answers to the administrators of the exam, and because the "lie" was prompted by the administrators flashing a specified color on the screen and solic-

SUSPENDED CONTEXTS

I want to expand on this third feature at greater length. Let's refer to contexts like those of joking, fiction, plays, and devil's advocacy as communicative contexts in which the truthfulness presumption is *suspended*.

To refine this terminology further, I will use the term *epistemic suspended context* to cover contexts in which ascertainable facts about the situation itself, or the actions or utterances of one or more participants, deprive the listener of the epistemic warrant to presume, in a predictive sense, that the speaker will tell the truth. For example, a declaration by the speaker that she will sprinkle fictions and fantasies into her utterances over the next hour would, in this sense, create an epistemic suspended context with respect to her immediate subsequent utterances. That a context is epistemically suspended does not entail that the speaker definitely will speak insincerely, but rather merely that a predictive expectation of sincerity is not warranted.

I will use the term *justified suspended context* to refer to contexts in which the speaker's (potential) insincerity is reasonable and justifiable. Here, the normative presumption of truthfulness is suspended because these contexts serve other valuable purposes whose achievement depends upon the presumption's suspension and the fact and justification of the suspension are publicly accessible.

Because one variety of suspended context is an epistemic notion and the other variety is a normative one, the two varieties may not always overlap. Usually, a justified suspended context will also be an epistemic suspended context, but not necessarily. Suppose that the practice hour of a community theater's improvisational group constitutes a justifiable suspended context: within their improvisations, it is entirely justified that members may pretend and utter insincerely within assumed characters or even, apparently, without assuming a special character role but seemingly, in their own voice. Sufficient experience with one of the group's members, though, has revealed that this member has a reflexive and inflexible attachment to literal truth-telling. She is invariably and rigidly the "straight person." She would like to learn how to pretend and improvise,

---

iting the "wrong answer," the situation was as far as it could be from trying to *convince* a *victim* of anything. *Id.* at 2849–50. Operationally, these researchers and the plethora of other researchers who use this test treat a solicited, deliberate, and transparent inaccuracy as a lie. Classifying a deliberate inaccuracy as a lie is questionable when its recipient *instructed* the speaker to speak inaccurately. It is therefore unlikely that the speaker offered the falsification to be taken as a true representation of his beliefs. Hence, the test seems poorly designed to track the brain activity involved in lying.

but years of effort have proven fruitless. She may operate within a justified suspended context, but her informed interlocutors retain their epistemic warrant to presume that her utterances are sincere. Such cases are,
while philosophically conceivable, rather esoteric. So, I plan to put them
aside and, for the most part, assume that, generally, justified suspended
contexts operate as epistemic suspended contexts as well. My focus will
be on justified suspended contexts and the conditions that activate them.

   Notably, not all epistemic suspended contexts are justifiable suspended
contexts. That division arises in less esoteric ways. For example, interactions with a person who regularly lies for convenience may generate an
epistemic suspended context by virtue of the liar's habitual practice. Yet
the liar's habits do not render his insincerity justifiable—only predictable.
Since the truthfulness presumption represents a default *moral* requirement, then as with other morally grounded expectations, a mere intention or declaration of an intention not to respect the truthfulness presumption is not itself a justified reason for the failure to conform to it.
   Only where there is a normatively justified reason for the suspension
of the presumption of truthfulness is there a "justified suspended context." The improvisational group may represent such a context, because
that communicative opportunity allows members a well-defined arena in
which to express their creativity and imagination and to play. Or, to take
another example, to teach a language effectively, within the confines of a
language class, and to provide critical feedback about a student's accent
and fluidity, a language teacher may ask him to deliver a first-person narrative using a range of vocabulary that may have no veridical basis in his
life story.
   Both the examples of the pathological liar and the foreign language
class bring out that, with respect to both varieties, the suspended context
may not be reciprocal, epistemically or normatively. That is, although
suspended contexts often extend to all the members of a communicative
context (as with the improvisational group), in some communicative situations, the context may be suspended only for some, but not all of its
participants. Returning to the language class case, although the students
are expected and justified in giving insincere monologues in the language
under study, the language teacher would not be justified in speaking insincerely when giving feedback, and the students would not expect this
either.
   My claim that a suspended context may not be reciprocal may at first
seem more controversial in the pathological liar case than in the case of
the language class. How one thinks of the pathological liar case may de-

pend, a little, upon whether one affirms the strong reciprocity thesis, to wit that, generally, the normative expectation of sincerity is contingent upon either a reciprocal commitment to, or reciprocal practice of, sincerity by one's interlocutor. Presumably, the members of the language class have this commitment, but the pathological liar does not. Although the pathological liar lacks a commitment to speaking sincerely when sincerity is called for, I do not think it is obvious that therefore her interlocutors are exempt from either epistemic or normative expectations that they will speak sincerely to her. For example, I am not at all confident that we would regard the liar's doctor as in an epistemically suspended context or a justified suspended context with respect to the doctor's own speech about the liar's medical condition. The doctor's responsibilities to his patient require sincerity. Those responsibilities are not undone by the patient's failure to meet her epistemic and moral responsibilities. (Although, depending on the nature of the patient's lies and the nature of the doctor's medical practice, the lies may justify the doctor's termination of the relationship.)

Likewise, our moral responsibilities to each other when we choose to communicate also require sincerity, and it is not clear how the liar's irresponsibility undoes them. The liar's failures to be sincere may justify reticence on our part for those topics on which forthcomingness is merited or made meaningful by reciprocal sharing (e.g., many disclosures of a personal nature), but it is not clear why those failures would, as a general matter, justify insincerity when we elect to communicate or when we are bound to communicate to the liar. Further, even those who affirm a strong version of the reciprocity thesis may instead think that although the liar and her interlocutor are in an epistemically suspended context with one another, still there is an asymmetry here. If the strong reciprocity thesis holds, it only suggests that the interlocutor is in a justified suspended context, activated by the liar's unjustified practice or unjustified and unexcused breach of the implicit commitment to sincerity. The liar is still unjustified in speaking insincerely.

A final note about terminology. I have characterized the lie as an assertion the speaker does not believe but offers anyway and presents in a context that objectively manifests the intention that the assertion may be taken to reflect the speaker's belief. I have been arguing that justified suspended contexts are contexts in which the speaker's utterance does not, objectively, manifest that intention. It follows then, on my view, that falsifications offered within a justified suspended context do not fit the characterization of lies. This, I think, is the correct way to think about the false statements within a novel, by an actor in a play, or by the neighbor who says just what etiquette demands. These false statements are falsifications but not lies, because they issue from a justified suspended context. As I go on to argue, some misrepresentations offered to the Murderer at the Door, e.g., about the location of his intended victim, occur within a justified suspended context and are not lies at all. Others will prefer to classify them as justified lies. They may find the notion of a justified falsification that is not a lie semantically awkward. I concede it is sometimes awkward. I tolerate the awkwardness because I fail to see a principled line of difference that distinguishes etiquette, for example, from other justified falsifications. (Some, I note, acknowledge the same symmetry but are prone to resolve the tension in the other direction, calling polite falsifications "white lies.") I don't think much hangs on whether we label these "falsifications in a justified suspended context" or "justified lies emerging from a justified suspended context."

Instead, the truly interesting issues about lying, I submit, have to do with what contexts are justifiably suspended and why. Tackling the questions of what makes for a justified suspended context and whether the strong reciprocity thesis is true constitute the major tasks of this chapter. I will turn to them when we confront the Murderer at the Door.[26]

DISTINGUISHING LIES FROM DECEPTIONS

Before doing so, however, I need to say a little about how lies differ from deception and why lying is wrong. I take the wrong of lying to inhere in the production and expression of a lie. I have claimed that the lie does not require successful or attempted deception. Indeed, deception differs, conceptually, from the lie in at least three respects.

First, lies need not affect the listener's mental contents with respect to the proposition the liar affirms or with respect to the liar's beliefs about that proposition; lying need not involve the intent to affect the listener's mental contents about those matters either. By contrast, deception must impart a false belief to the listener or confirm a preexisting false belief of the listener. That false belief may either concern the content of the speaker's assertion or the speaker's own beliefs concerning the content of what he asserts. (There are nuances here. "Deception," "deceit," and "deceived" all imply the listener's mental content was actually affected. A "deceptive" remark may just be one that might reasonably deceive or that re-

[26] I explore other issues about identifying justified suspended contexts in Chapter Six.

flects an intent or likelihood to deceive. A "deceiving person" may be one who succeeds at deception or may be one who intends deception and thereby intends to affect the listener's mental contents but fails.)

Second, speakers do not believe the propositions expressed by their lies. By contrast, speakers may believe the explicit propositional content of (some) of their deceptive assertions. They may be deceptive because they leave a misleading impression on the listener that causes the listener to draw a false conclusion. Purportedly, when Athanasius of Alexandria was hiding on a boat, his hostile pursuers approached the boat and asked where Athanasius was. Athanasius allegedly replied, "He is not far," a statement he believed. Its false implicature (that he was not also "here") deceived its recipient into believing the speaker was not Athanasius and that Athanasius was not on the boat.[27] Both lies and deception, as classifications, turn on a particular sort of mental content, but the crucial mental content of the lie is the disbelief of the *speaker* in what she says; the crucial mental content picked out by deception is the *listener's* formation or confirmation of a false belief.

Third, lies involve assertions or utterances of propositions. Deception need not. For example, deception may involve mere activity, such as Kant's example of packing a suitcase in front of a neighbor, leaving the false impression he was about to travel, or it may take place through the omission of communication, as when one party fails to correct another party's assertion about the former's whereabouts and the latter concludes, falsely, that her assertion was confirmed by the silence.[28]

[27] The example is discussed in Alastair MacIntyre, *Truthfulness, Lies, and Moral Philosophers: What Can We Learn from Mill and Kant?, in* 16 THE TANNER LECTURES ON HUMAN VALUES 309, 336 (1994), *citing* F.A.M. FORBES, ST. ATHANASIUS 102 (1919).

[28] The failure to distinguish carefully between lies and deception represents a defect in the empirical literature about lying; the other major defect is the failure of researchers to adhere to their own definitions within their studies. See also *supra* note 25. For example, a routinely cited statistic alleges that most people lie at least once a day, but the study from which that statistic originates is unreliable both because the researchers used an implausibly capacious definition of lying and because they did not apply their own definition consistently. *See* Bella M. DePaulo et al., *Lying in Everyday Life*, 70 J. PERSONALITY & SOC. PSYCHOL. 979 (1996). That study tracked lies through self-reporting, but the subjects were instructed that "a lie occurs any time you *intentionally try to mislead someone*. Both the intent to deceive and the actual deception must occur." *Id.* at 981. Of course, if *any* form of deception counts as a lie, then the result that "lies" occur daily is substantially less meaningful because it would encompass failures to disclose information that allow an observer to proceed with a false impression. On this definition, it would count as a lie to fail to tell one's neighbor that one had dyed one's hair yesterday when that allowed her to believe that one had not yet begun to gray. Another difficulty, albeit one more associated with underreporting and inconsistent results, is that it is unclear whether the research subjects consis-

Of course, not all mistaken inferences by an observer or listener involve deception, in the morally relevant sense, by the observed agent or speaker. Although one might say something like "I thought he was a police officer. I forgot it was Halloween and I was deceived by his uniform," that sense of "deceived" only refers to the origin of the error but does not refer to the morally relevant form of deception. The morally relevant form of deception seems either to involve a directed effort to influence another's mental contents or the frustration of an epistemic expectation of the listener or observer that the speaker or observed agent will not permit or facilitate, whether directly or indirectly, a false impression of the facts. When the latter form of deception is not merely morally relevant but wrong will depend upon whether the pertinent epistemic expectation is also normatively justified.

This description may point to a fourth difference between deception and the lie. The normative reasonability of the epistemic expectation that makes deception possible (when it does not use a lie as its mechanism) and that grounds its wrongfulness when it is wrongful may vary, depending, e.g., on the content of the false impression conveyed and on the relationship between the parties. Whereas, as I will now argue, the underlying moral expectation that grounds the wrongfulness of the lie does not vary in these ways.

The Distinctive Wrong of the Lie

Although lies may but need not deceive their recipients, I have assumed that lies without any connection to deception are nonetheless wrong and that their moral defect is shared with those lies that also involve deception or its attempt. If that is correct, the wrong of the lie should be distinct from the wrong of deception. Providing the resources to make this distinction should be a desideratum.[29] Rather than directly arguing for the desideratum and against the skeptical arguments against it, I hope to

---

tently applied the broad definition rather than their own, more common-sense understanding, e.g., that lies at least involve some sort of linguistic discourse. Indeed, the researchers did not consistently apply their own definitions within their research. Although the study's definition (communicated to the subjects) stressed that for a lie to transpire, "actual deception must occur," the study's questionnaire allowed for the possibility that the lie's recipient was not deceived, but still classified the event as a lie. It appears, then, that actual deception was not a prerequisite of what they counted as a lie. *Id.* at 982, 989–90.

[29] Not everyone takes this view. *See, e.g.,* T.M. Scanlon, What We Owe to Each Other 317–20 (1998).

vindicate the desideratum by showing how it might be satisfied in a way that reveals an interesting ethical distinction.

Nonetheless, many accounts of the wrong of the lie fail to satisfy it. Many accounts of the wrong of the lie emphasize the wrong of manipulating or aiming to manipulate the will of the recipient; such accounts implicitly imagine that deception is an aim or product of the lie, for otherwise no such manipulation could occur. They then have to struggle to explain why lies differ from less direct methods of deception. Perhaps that may be done on a manipulation-oriented account, but it is tricky. The lie may be more effective at stimulating a false thought in the target in some cases, but in others it may be less effective because, by contrast, indirect methods of deception obscure the origin of the false belief and may therefore suppress critical reflection. In this way, indirect deception may in some cases be more manipulative and disrespectful of another's will than the lie, because the indirect deceiver's effort to influence another's mind is opaque.[30]

I propose instead that the wrong of deception, when it is wrong, properly focuses on the violation of a duty to take due care not to cause another to form false beliefs based on one's behavior, communication, or omission. Where one's violation is intentional, one thereby attempts to interfere with or control another's rational processes for one's own purposes.[31] A full account of wrongful deception obviously would have to spell out what communications and what omissions fall within this duty of care. I do not offer such an account here (nor does my treatment of the lie depend upon any particular account). I will merely note that many interactions in which a listener understandably forms a false belief or impression from a speaker's communication do not violate the relevant

[30] For an insightful discussion of the problem of distinguishing between the wrong of lying and the wrong of deception and a different, creative solution, see Collin O'Neil, *Lying, Trust, and Gratitude*, 40 PHIL. & PUB. AFF. 301 (2012) and, generally, Collin O'Neil, "The Ethics of Communication" (2007) (unpublished Ph.D. Dissertation, UCLA).

[31] Many discussions of deception focus, usually without explicit mention, on intentional deception and the special wrongs of manipulation that intentional deception entails. My understanding of the wrong of deception allows for the possibility of a range—of negligent, reckless, and intentional forms of wrongful deception. That position accords with much of the law of deceptive advertising that recognizes that some forms of deception may be inadvertent but irresponsibly so. *See* LOUIS ALTMAN & MALLA POLLACK, CALLMANN ON UNFAIR COMPETITION, TRADEMARKS AND MONOPOLIES § 5:28 (4th ed. 2013); Richard Craswell, *Regulating Deceptive Advertising: The Role of Cost-Benefit Analysis*, 64 S. CAL. L. REV. 549, 590 (1991); Richard Craswell, *Interpreting Deceptive Advertising*, 65 B.U. L. REV. 657, 697 (1985). *Cf.* JAMES B. ASTRACHAN, DONNA THOMAS, GEORGE ERIC ROSDEN & PETER ERIC ROSDEN, THE LAW OF ADVERTISING § 18.02(1)(b)(iii) (Matthew Bender ed., 2013).

duty. In other words, we do not have a comprehensive duty to avoid or correct all misunderstandings and mistaken inferences by our audiences. Consequently, not all deception need be wrongful. But, when it is wrongful, it is because it violates a duty not to cause, reinforce, or in another way allow inaccuracy in others.

The wrong of lying, by contrast, is not essentially that it risks implanting or leaving false beliefs in the recipient's mind. Rather, the wrong of lying is that it operates on a maxim that, if it were universalized and constituted a public rule of permissible action, would deprive us of reliable access to a crucial set of truths and a reliable way to sort the true from the false. Deception is wrong because it unduly hazards the false for the deceiver's own purposes, whereas lying is wrong because it places the certainty of truth out of reach for the liar's own purposes.

How does the liar's willing his maxim of insincerity place the certainty of truth out of reach? The liar represents his declaration as fit to be taken on his say-so as true and as at least representing the contents of his mind. If what I said earlier was apt, there are no alternative, precise, and authoritative avenues into the contents of each other's minds; there is only testimony. To use this avenue of knowledge for a contrary purpose is to render it unreliable and to taint it. If universalized, one's maxim transforms a mechanism for exclusively conveying the truth into a mechanism for conveying both the false and the true. In this case, versatility is a vice. By doing so, one has eliminated a fail-proof, trustworthy mode of access to one another. Because there are no external methods of verification—no means by which others may peer into one's mind—to lie is to sully the one road of authoritative access to oneself and thereby cut oneself off from community with others. Doing so frustrates achievement of the compulsory moral ends associated with mutual understanding and cooperation.[32]

So, independent of deceptive intent or effect, the lie has wrong-making features that surface in three dimensions. First, the lie wrongs the listener by deliberately presenting unreliable testimonial warrants to her. By warranting distrust in his testimony, the liar creates an epistemic gap between the speaker and the listener. This gap precludes, among other things, full moral relations between them by obstructing the sort of mutual understanding that must be based on rational communication and justified be-

---

[32] The contradiction involved in deception, when universalized, involves defeating the very purpose one pursues through the deception. The contradiction involved in the lie is that one disables oneself from pursuing one's more general compulsory end to convey one's beliefs and oneself (through conveying one's beliefs) to others.

lief. The liar fails to treat the listener, therefore, as an equal moral partner and as a rational agent who deserves to receive warrants that she may accept as representing the listener's beliefs. Second, the liar wrongs himself by isolating himself from a moral relationship with the listener based on rational communication and rationally justified beliefs. Because the liar's maxim affirms a principle of treating others in this way, the liar does not merely insult and create distance between himself and the particular recipient of his lie, but affirms a principle that does damage to the rational basis of relationships between him and the community of possible recipients of his speech. Finally, the liar wrongs humanity by acting on a maxim that could not serve as a public principle of action, because it would undermine the rational reliability of warrants altogether and with it, our ability to pursue our joint moral ends. The liar's maxim shows disrespect to our collective interest and duty to maintain reliable channels of communication and the liar's action begins, concretely, to sow seeds of doubt in one another's testimony.

To identify these three facets of the wrong of the lie does not yet confront the special issues raised by communication with those who intend to do wrong. To those issues I will now turn.

Metaphorically, I regard the wrong of the lie as a generalization of the wrong of perfidy and, in particular, of the abuse or misuse of the white flag in war. The white flag, as you may recall, is a special signal used between warring parties to convey a willingness to negotiate or to surrender. Once the white flag is raised, it is prohibited to attack the messenger who carries it or to use it as cover to gain access for a surreptitious attack.[33] Indeed, it is considered a high war crime to use the white flag to surprise and sabotage. Even between parties who are authorized in some sense to kill one another, the white flag is regarded as sacrosanct. One may try to kill one's enemy, but one may not abuse the white flag, not even to defeat an evil enemy who is one's wrongful opponent in a just war.

What I take to be the moving idea behind this convention is that it is essential—even when we are at each other's throats and even when we

---

[33] See 1 JEAN-MARIE HENCKAERTS & LOUISE DOSWALD-BECK, CUSTOMARY INTERNATIONAL HUMANITARIAN LAW 205–07, 219–33 (2005); 2 JEAN-MARIE HENCKAERTS & LOUISE DOSWALD-BECK, CUSTOMARY INTERNATIONAL HUMANITARIAN LAW 1259–69, 1360–414, 1467–501 (2005). See also J. Ashley Roach, Ruses and Perfidy: Deception During Armed Conflict, 23 TOL. L. REV. 395, 407, 407 n. 44, 411–12 (1992). John Deigh writes illuminatingly about the connection between the white flag convention, the power to promise under coercion, and the use of conventions in making promises possible in Promises Under Fire, 112 ETHICS 483, 489–90, 493–95 (2002).

are grappling with evil (i.e., with each other's evil)—to preserve a way out. We must preserve an exit through which we could negotiate an end to conflict and move toward reconciliation using rational discourse rather than relying solely upon the crude tools of violence, domination, and extermination. To avoid the horrors of devastations and massacres and to protect the possibility of peace, an absolutely trustworthy method of communication must be preserved. Without it, the possibility of escaping chaos and reestablishing moral community with one another turns into a possibility that rests on mere chance and contingency rather than a possibility predicated on choice.

Although the stakes are higher for warring parties than for us everyday citizens, their need is no greater. We must cooperate far more extensively despite our often disparate and competing interests. Although we need not reveal all to one another at all times, we must be able to cooperate fully and to know and be known by others. Further, we must always preserve the possibility of repairing moral relations that have been ruptured. But if moral relations require understanding and appreciating others' mental contents, then we have to preserve the reliability of those mechanisms that give us access to information about one another and the world (which we cannot fully comprehend alone). We cannot emerge from moral solitude, confusion, and chaos into fellowship, if *the* channel or compass dedicated to reliable direction and orientation may be scrambled.

In what follows, I will try to redeem (or at least expand upon) some of these sermonizing sentiments and distinguish this account of lying from others by reflecting on the Murderer at the Door. But first, let me review and clarify the structure of the argument I am developing. The means of successful communication are crucial, but fragile mechanisms for the most valuable human endeavors—from establishing and conducting personal relationships, to engaging in cooperative activities, to understanding and developing the self. Preserving and protecting these means therefore figure among our fundamental moral priorities. On occasion, however, it may be tempting to misuse our means of communication and to risk some diminution of their effectiveness when other substantial moral priorities are under threat, especially when lives are at stake.

My concern about yielding to this understandable temptation, as described, is that when we lie for a morally good end, we are not merely balancing the risk of damage to one moral priority for the heightened chance of securing another. Our ability to assess our moral ends and to make tradeoffs to secure them presupposes an operative, functional form of moral agency. My basic argument is that the fundamental responsibility to secure and protect the individual and social conditions under which we possess this agency and under which we may understand and acquit our moral duties exerts a lexical priority. To satisfy this responsibility, our reasons for action must take a form that, if known and regarded as permissible, would maintain the epistemic conditions and presumptions that enable successful moral agency, rather than jeopardizing them, calling them into question, or rendering their existence merely accidental.

Understanding and acquitting the full range of our moral duties depends upon having reliable forms of precise communication. To deliberately misrepresent in a standard context of communication in order to further another morally substantial end is to wrong the recipient and yourself by contaminating the warrant the recipient should have that would enable her to relate to you fully as a moral agent. Further, the maxim on which you act is defective, because its publicity would compromise the conditions of enabled moral agency for others. It could not function as a public maxim for action generally without frustrating our compulsory end of ensuring that communication remains reliable and produces the right sort of warrants.

Although this argument requires delving into the moral purposes and value of communication, that does not render it a consequentialist argument. My argument is not that we must attempt to maximize the realization of moral communication. Nor is my argument that the permissibility of misrepresentations hangs on the test of whether they in fact do or do not increase or diminish episodes of moral behavior. The lie does not merely threaten the achievement of one of many moral ends but it (and the principle its affirmation stands for) degrades the foundation of our moral agency, including that aspect of our agency that requires interpersonal communication and coordination and rationally justified relations of belief and trust in one another's representations.

Let's now consider the Murderer at the Door.

The Murderer at the Door and the Murderer Next Door

As I remarked at the outset, Kant is often pilloried for his hard, implausible line about lying. Somehow he thought that a lie, even to the Murderer at the Door who asks you where his intended victim is hiding, would undermine human dignity and the dignity of the liar.

The modern Kantian response has pursued two major tacks in response. The first corrects the record on Kant's actual view and the second shows that Kantian philosophy need not be tied to the claimed implausibilities of Kant's actual view.

Kant

First, as Allen Wood and others have argued, Kant's position is considerably more nuanced than the caricature suggests.[34] Kant's view is not that one has a duty never to utter any proposition one does not believe. Rather, one's duty is to refrain from making false *declarations*, i.e., statements "that occur in a context where others are warranted or authorized . . . in relying on the truthfulness of what is said, and make the speaker liable by right . . . if what is said is knowingly false."[35] As I remarked earlier, any remotely plausible view of truthful utterances must, of course, take *something* of this shape. To achieve all we can through the vast resources of language, we must be able to establish contexts in which our utterances are necessarily supposed to be truthful as well as contexts in which they are not, such as in fiction, where listeners are not warranted to rely on their contents either being true or representing the utterer's beliefs.

Such a view, of course, makes it crucial to answer the question of when an utterance should count as a declaration. Wood does not offer a complete account of Kant's take on when an utterance counts as a declaration, but Wood reminds us of two major points. First, Kant recognizes many contexts in which an utterance is not and should not be understood to be a declaration, some of which are ordinary, while others are extraordinary. One is not expected to give a *declaration* off the cuff when casually asked, "How do you like my work?" Nor is the listener warranted in relying on the truth of the reply.[36] Further, one is not expected to make a declaration in response to a robber's inquiry about the location of one's wallet.[37]

Second, the determining factor is not, Kant thinks, whether the particular listener in question expects or should expect a true declaration rather than a mere utterance, but whether, in my terms, the context authorizes a mere utterance because it is justifiably suspended. Wood's ex-

---

[34] *See* WOOD, *supra* note 4, 240–51.

[35] *Id.* at 241.

[36] KANT, THE METAPHYSICS OF MORALS 184 (Mary Gregor ed., 2007) (6:431).

[37] KANT, *supra* note 1, at 203 (27:447).

ample is that of testimony in court. A self-conscious malicious prosecutor who knows I lie in the face of evident malice may have no particular warrant to rely on the truth of what I say. Further, his particular malicious purposes may cast doubt upon his normative authorization to demand information from me, but the context is one in which others are present who, given the social role courts serve, are warranted and authorized in relying on what I say. That is, they may reasonably expect and demand declarations. My particular interrogator, as a person, may have no such warrant, but that fact does not render my utterance a mere utterance.[38]

Wood suggests that the dispute between Kant and Constant turns on this second matter. They are both thinking of Kant's prior example in an earlier work of a guard coming to the door and asking for the head of the house. Constant has in mind corrupt political officials. To understand their exchange, we should imagine that the Murderer at the Door is a political official pursuing a campaign of unjust persecution. In this light, Kant's position is best understood as something like the view that utterances to officials in their official capacity are, generally, declarations. What matters is the role of the official and not the particular justice of the official's mission.

In response, one might be tempted to disagree with that conclusion if applied to *every* official, but there is something fairly reasonable lurking in the vicinity; e.g., one may not perjure oneself in court (at least if the system is reasonably just), even if one believes that the testimony may be misconstrued and may substantially injure an innocent or convict a person of a crime that the positive law recognizes but should not.

So Kant's view may be best understood as the conjunction of the claim that utterances to government officials on duty are *ipso facto* declarations and the claim that one must be truthful even to officials engaged in nasty business. Let's put that interesting but narrow issue aside and focus on the case as it is usually discussed: a wise-guy comes to the door and demands to know the location of a person whom he intends to harm. He has no authorization of any sort, perverted or no, to perform this deed. One has to say something or else, *ex hypothesi*, one's silence will be revealing. The claim about officials, even if true, need not suggest that one must regard one's reactions to the common Murderer at the Door as declarations about which one must be truthful. Perhaps this is what I called above a justified suspended context in which one's utterances are

not subject to the objective normative expectation that they are assertions advanced to be taken as true. Indeed, it seems obvious that one need
not answer truthfully. But the deontologist cannot merely stipulate that
declarations need not be true when truth-telling will harm another or
cause poor consequences.

Recent Kantian Reconstructions

The standard reasons offered by contemporary deontologists for depart-
ing from the presumption of truthfulness in this context take three forms:
(1) the demander is acting coercively and one may defend oneself from
coercive intrusions into one's store of information that would otherwise
be private;[39] (2) the demander is attempting to elicit (or force) one's testimony for an immoral purpose and one may resist being so used to further
an immoral purpose;[40] (3) the demander is misusing the practice of communication directly by deceit[41] or indirectly as part of his general immoral plan; one need not follow the rules of a practice with a party who
is attempting to abuse it or manipulate it.[42] All of these rationales contain
a large grain of truth, but they are either or both under-inclusive and
over-broad.

THE UNDER-INCLUSIVITY OF SELF-DEFENSE APPROACHES

All three of these rationales have a certain flavor of reactive self-defense
to them. One may respond defensively to coercive efforts to invade one's
privacy; one may respond defensively to efforts to recruit one into furthering an immoral cause; one may respond defensively to efforts by
immoral agents to exploit one's compliance with the moral rules of the
practice of testimony. Most such accounts make it central to the case
that the murderer interrogates you and that you are put on the spot,
provoking defensive measures. I agree that being thrust into a defensive

---

[39] See, e.g., KORSGAARD, The Right to Lie, supra note 4, at 144–45. On different versions
of this view, the coercion may involve explicit or veiled threats to one's well-being or may
be more subtle, placing the interlocutor in a position in which his speech is compelled,
whether by additional threat, concern about the inference to be drawn in the absence of
speech, or other features of the conversational context.

[40] Id. at 145–46, 153; Sussman, supra note 4, at 233–34, 241–43; Herman, supra note 4
at 113–14. Herman stresses both the forced speech and the abetting evil aspects of the encounter with the Murderer at the Door. It is somewhat unclear whether either factor on its
own would, in her view, justify deliberate misrepresentation.

[41] KORSGAARD, The Right to Lie, supra note 4, 136–37, 145.

[42] Schapiro, supra note 4, at 49–56.

posture matters morally, but I disagree that it is the central salient fact in this case.

Imagine a variation on the case in which the thug does not act coercively in the slightest. He tentatively inquires, ignorant you are aware of his purposes. You know you will not be hurt if you decline to answer and that he will not in fact draw dangerous inferences about the location of the victim from your silence. Still, I think you may falsely utter.

Or, suppose that you are the next-door neighbor of the party upon whose door the murderer knocks. He does not know you are home so you are under no threat. You are not even the recipient of his inquiry. Perhaps he has not even knocked yet on your neighbor's door so he's instigated no inquiry in the slightest. You are more of a bystander to his coercive behavior than an object of it. Still, I think it is just fine to poke one's head out the window and say (untruthfully): "Hey! Did you see what I just saw? I think Victim was running a four-minute mile toward the beach! She could run in the Olympics!" It is hard to claim this action is necessary as a matter of personal *self-defense*, resistance to forced speech, or a refusal to be part of a nonreciprocal communicative relation or a party to immorality. One could just have closed the window sash and accomplished those worthy aims. If my imagined utterance is just fine, then the self-defense claims are interestingly under-inclusive.

THE OVER-BREADTH OF APPEALS TO RECIPROCITY

But, in another respect, I worry that those accounts, such as Tamar Schapiro's,[43] that stress the moral corruption of the miscreant risk over-breadth. Although I regard the active, entirely volunteered misrepresentation of the location of the victim as entirely permissible, a number of other false representations to the Murderer at the Door and to other miscreants seem like a different matter, to wit, the legal misrepresentation, the strategic misrepresentation, and the moral misrepresentation. Suppose the murderer does not reveal his intention in asking for the victim but pretends to have an innocuous purpose; he is a census taker, trying to locate unaccounted-for residents. After discovering you are a law-

---

[43] Schapiro, *supra* note 4, at 49–56. Although Schapiro rightly insists that the murderer may not be grossly manipulated or tortured, her claim that he is not committed to the "common deliberative standpoint" that constitutes the point of the practice of truth-telling, a practice demanding reciprocal wills (if not also reciprocal behaviors), seems to authorize a wide swath of deliberate misrepresentations, and it is hard to see whether and where her account would draw a line between them.

yer, he notes the recent controversy over the death penalty and asks what the penalty for first-degree murder is in this jurisdiction. You believe that misrepresenting the penalty will deter him and falsely avow that the death penalty is regularly applied. Or suppose he is open about his plans and asks you, in light of the other crimes he has committed on his recent spree, whether it would make any difference to the *legal* disposition of his situation if he turns himself in now rather than proceeding on his way to commit one final murder. It would not. But, knowingly, you falsely say it would. I believe these are wrongful lies. So too I am terribly troubled by the negotiator misrepresenting to the hostage-taker whether his requests have been or will be met, to effect a release of hostages.[44] I believe these strategic lies are out of bounds. Finally, I condemn moral misrepresentations by negotiators who express false sympathy with the hostage-taker's cause and methods, as well as misrepresentations by the police, when they attempt to elicit a confession through false expressions of solidarity and normalcy by reporting to suspects that the crime was not so bad or that the officer has engaged in it himself or herself on occasion.

You may or may not part company with me about some of these examples. To the extent some of them trouble you, though, you may worry about the over-breadth of the standard deontological defenses of misrepresenting to the Murderer at the Door. Accounts that stress the miscreant's hidden purposes, his willingness to do wrong and his distance from the moral project, and particularly those that stress his willingness to manipulate or his failure to engage in open, reciprocal dialogue run the danger of authorizing one or more of these morally tricky misrepresentations. For those views seem, roughly, different ways of defending the idea that the murderer's lies or wrongdoing disqualify him from treatment according to standard moral norms. The views have something of a procedural tenor. Because the wrongdoer does not follow the rules, the general rules do not apply to him and therefore, we can lie in order to constrain him, not because of the content of our misrepresentation but

---

[44] For a sensitive treatment and discussion of a variety of historical cases, see Joseph Betz, *Moral Considerations Concerning the Police Response to Hostage Takers*, *in* ETHICS, PUBLIC POLICY, AND CRIMINAL JUSTICE 110 (Frederick Ellison & Norman Bowie eds., 1982). Interestingly, although police training manuals actively encourage lies and deception as normal operating procedure for interrogation, crisis negotiation manuals discourage lying and deception, although they do not articulate an absolute bar on either and emphasize the importance of maintaining credibility and the risks of being caught in a lie. *See, e.g.*, FREDERICK J. LANCELY, ON-SCENE GUIDE FOR CRISIS NEGOTIATORS, ch. 6 at 13–14, ch. 8 at 8 (2003); THOMAS STRENTZ, PSYCHOLOGICAL ASPECTS OF CRISIS NEGOTIATION 69 (2006).

because his interactions with and among us do not comply with the rules that render him eligible for truthful communication, or something of this flavor. This position, however, strikes me as dangerously overbroad.

A Content-Based Approach

By contrast, I think the *content* of what one misrepresents here largely determines whether one may misrepresent. It is because information about the victim's location will either assist the murderer or obstruct him in carrying out a crime (understood as acting on an evil maxim) that one may misrepresent, whether in defense of oneself or in defense of another.

To defend this more content-oriented view, I propose that we return to the question of what distinguishes contexts where the truthfulness presumption is in place from those in which it is suspended. In justified suspended contexts, we may justifiably use communication for valuable purposes other than to convey believed assertions, *and* listeners have sufficient reason to know that they are in such a context, so they have no reasonable normative expectations that a truthful representation is being or should be conveyed. Fiction, for instance, furthers moral purposes by allowing us to explore alternate possibilities and social arrangements and to contemplate the details of other sorts of lives and human interactions without the invasions of privacy that would be involved if the accounts were veridical. Fiction also allows a speaker to exercise the imagination and to explore various thoughts in a noncommittal way. These opportunities facilitate intellectual and emotional growth and mutual understanding. In fiction, assertions are made not to convey the truth of their content (or of the author's belief in their content) but to paint a picture that allows for the apprehension, appreciation, and contemplation of other truths that might otherwise be out of reach. It also permits certain sorts of close-up views of the false and the wrong through depictions that it would be immoral to create in reality for the purposes of study or whose scrutiny in reality might violate privacy. The reasonable reader can recognize fiction as such and has no warrant to take representations in fiction as true. The false assertions embedded within a fiction give the reader no reason to doubt the truth of assertions made in more somber contexts, because the former assertions are not offered as true, and this fact is or could be available to the reasonable reader.[45]

[45] This is an oversimplification. Even within a fiction, not all factual misrepresentations may be ethical, and the reasonable reader would not suspend belief with respect to all fac-

The false assertions permitted and sometimes required by etiquette or privacy also submit to a similar treatment. In certain social contexts, people who encounter one another need to acknowledge one another, welcome one another, and engage in other activities fostering social inclusion. Communicative acts are essential to these aims, and certain assertions play a ritual role in their accomplishment. "It's nice to see you," "I'm doing fine," and "I like your new haircut," may be the sorts of statements demanded by the social context and its function, but which the competent listener has reason to think are not offered in order for their content to be absorbed as true.[46]

It seems that we may create justified suspended contexts in situations where we have other worthwhile purposes for communication that involve or are consistent with suspending the presumption of truthfulness, where their creation does not stymie the purposes served by the presumption or other commitments, and provided participants have reason to know that the presumption is suspended (whether or not they realize it). With respect to information that would further the recipient's seriously immoral end as such, an end like murder, I contend we should regard the presumption of truthfulness as justifiably suspended. Given the compulsory ends morality supplies us, we could not reasonably use communication to further an evil end, and we cannot reasonably expect others to supply us with the reliable warrants necessary to do so. More generally, the listener's compulsory end to comply with morality limits that she may

tual representations within that fiction. This is one way to understand the legal doctrine of fictional libel. I myself think that statements about characters and their behaviors are *exactly* the sort of things that operate in a epistemic and justified suspended context within a fiction; for this reason, I am a critic of fictional libel and believe it should not be a cause of action. Nonetheless, I contend that other embedded false facts within a fiction may be unethical to insert and might reasonably provide the basis for liability were a reader to suffer harm because she believed them. For instance, it is not evident that the reasonable reader would have reason to doubt embedded false factual claims about matters orthogonal to the fiction and its form. Suppose in a contemporary realist family drama novel featuring a reliable narrator, one that is not a mystery, thriller, or science fiction, a doctor character who is lauded in the fiction for his care and precision (falsely) declares, "It's perfectly fine to take 3000-milligram doses of ibuprofen daily if the pain persists." Or, suppose in passing a renowned mycologist character gives a lecture full of false information (represented in the novel as true) about how to identify a poisonous mushroom. Although it would be linguistically inappropriate to say the author "lied," it would be reasonable to hold the author morally accountable for the misrepresentation. The fact that it appeared within a fictional work should not (fully) exonerate her.

[46] See Thomas Nagel's discussion of related cases in his CONCEALMENT AND EXPOSURE 3–26, 31–52 (2002).

expect from others and the speakers' similar ends limit what she may say. One in hot pursuit of an evil end should have no reasonable expectation that the world or other people cooperate with her evil enterprise. She has no entitlement to those warrants about the world that would materially further those ends.

Two further points. First, a full account should specify what sort of information falls within the scope of "furthering an evil end." I do not have a full theory, but I take it that telling a parched and, therefore, morbidly weakened Murderer at the Door where the water fountain is located is not providing information essential to furthering an evil end *as such*, even though it is information essential to his being able to further his own ends, which happen to be evil. So, I have something in mind like information the intentional supply of which (if it were offered to aid the endeavor) would count as a form of assistance constituting accomplice liability. Second, this justification for misrepresenting to the Murderer at the Door would distinguish not only what the content of the misrepresentation is, but also who the recipient is. That is, this justification provides an argument for misrepresenting to the murderer, but not for misrepresenting to a bystander who one hopes will innocently pass on the false information to the murderer. I regard the bystander case as importantly more difficult, because the bystander may have no reason to know she is in a justified suspended context, and because the bystander is not pursuing an evil end that displaces her legitimate interest in truthful communication on the relevant topic.[47]

There is an analogy here between this content-based account of the permission to misrepresent and promises to engage in (deeply) immoral activity, such as a promise to tie down a victim.[48] I take such promises to be void *ab initio*. The recipient has no moral basis to complain if performance does not occur, because the promisor had no right to decide to perform the activity and so could not transfer any such right to decide to

---

[47] For a more confident expression of the permission to misrepresent to the bystander, see FRANCES KAMM, INTRICATE ETHICS 13 (2006).

[48] There is an important difference, though: in giving a false promise, one misrepresents one's moral situation (that one has a right to engage in the relevant activity). As I will discuss *infra*, I have particular concerns about moral misrepresentations and so, although I think the immoral promise is void *ab initio*, I am more worried about whether one may ethically block or impede another's criminal activity by making a (false and unreliable) immoral promise to assist. I discuss immoral promises at greater length in *Immoral, Conflicting, and Redundant Promises, in* REASONS AND RECOGNITION: ESSAYS ON THE PHILOSOPHY OF T.M. SCANLON 155, 159–63 (R. Jay Wallace, Rahul Kumar & Samuel Freeman eds., 2011).

perform it to the recipient. Any reasonable recipient should know this. Generally, the murderer has no moral right to expect assistance, and you have no moral right to provide it. These facts limit what epistemic rights and warrants, as well as what moral rights and warrants, you may convey and what the recipient may reasonably take you to be giving. Hence, the murderer has no moral expectation that communications on *this* subject will be reliable, trustworthy, or otherwise provide a warrant.

So, in my view, you may offer a false assertion about the location of the victim as part of your worthy end of impeding the efforts of the Murderer at the Door, because the criminal's aim to use the information as a means to commit a criminal act renders the context justifiably suspended between the two of you with respect to that information. Properly understood, one's aim in misrepresentation is not to manipulate the murderer but only to impede or obstruct his illegitimate plan, albeit using communicative means.[49] By contrast with defensive accounts, one may impede these efforts whether or not the Murderer at the Door acts aggressively or in some other untoward way toward oneself. Notably, the Murderer at the Door has reason to understand that this is a justified suspended context and that your assertions are not warrants offered to be taken as true. Of course, the murderer may not in fact realize that you know this is a justified suspended context with respect to this content. This does not render your falsification a lie, however, any more than the mistaken inferences of those who tuned in late to the broadcast of War of the Worlds transformed Orson Welles' radio-theatrical speech into a pack of lies. Significantly, though, one's falsification and the interaction more generally do not depend upon the murderer's ignorance of the relevant context in which he finds himself. There may still be a point to the communication, even if the murderer understands that the context is justifiably suspended.

This last point may be reinforced by turning again to Kant's case of a mugger who forcibly demands to know where one's wallet is. Kant declares that it is permissible to falsify in answering, and that the mugger could hardly expect otherwise. But why would the mugger ask if he had the expectation that he was not owed a truthful response? He may hope that from fear or from habit, you will answer truthfully or that in some

---

[49] Notably, one need not think the permissibility of falsifying depends on a justification for manipulating the criminal's will. *See also* Herman, *supra* note 4, at 109. This is worth mentioning because I worry that thinking of the misrepresentation here as a manipulation may sometimes drive the move toward defensive accounts (to provide a limiting principle for justified manipulation) that in turn court under-inclusivity.

other way (perhaps through a tell), you will reveal the wallet's location. Even if you are not afraid, you may answer the question, hoping that the mugger will accept your answer either from habit or from a false hope that the question, although not deserving a warrant, may nonetheless elicit one in response, or because he has no other alternative. Or, you may answer not to convey information on the hope it will be accepted, but rather to stall. My point is that the obstruction may succeed without depending on deceit by means of apparently authoritative testimony. The mugger may know that your statements need not reflect your thoughts as in the case of testimony, but yet may rely on them because, reasoning under uncertainty, he suspects that reflexive truthfulness is the most likely sort of utterance.

I have begun to sketch an account of why it is permissible to falsify in speaking to the Murderer at the Door, one that treats the murderer next door as on a par, and one that does not render its permissibility contingent upon the murderer first making an improper communicative overture that in turn then legitimizes a defensive response. This may promise to handle the under-inclusivity problem, but, it may be objected, places the account in an even worse position to handle what I have called the over-breadth problem, because it permits active misrepresentation and not merely reactive misrepresentation.

That is, one might object that my account fails to condemn a wide variety of the misrepresentations I suggested were morally problematic. So long as the murderer is engaged in his nefarious plans to commit a murder with impunity, why can't we use communication to impede these illegitimate efforts, whether it be about the location of the victim, the conditions of safe haven, or the state of the law; whether we sympathize or not; and whatever the evidence we have amassed against him? Some may regard this objection as showing a flaw in the account, while others will regard it as showing a flaw both in my desiderata and in one of my criticisms of the more standard defensive accounts.

My answer is to distinguish misrepresenting information that would constitute assistance in the commission of a crime (even if one offers it to impede and not merely to refrain from assisting), from misrepresenting information that would, in another way, stop or solve a crime. Let me start with my concern about what seems to underlie the case for a broader permission to misrepresent; namely, a general suggestion that the criminal himself carts a justified suspended context along with him wherever he goes (something like an ethical analog to Pig-Pen's private dust-storm). This suggestion seems propelled by the argument that because he is involved in pursuing an evil deed, he should expect the world to be unco-operative in every way, and so he should not harbor normative expecta-tions that any communications will be reliable, at least until he unilaterally surrenders.

Something like this view, I believe, lurks behind the Supreme Court's shocking decision in *Holder v. Humanitarian Law Project*, which upheld a Congressional prohibition of assistance to designated terrorist organi-zations against a First Amendment challenge. Within the context of the statute, assistance was construed to include mere speech providing advice about how to petition the U.N. for relief and how to use legally permis-sible means to resolve conflicts peacefully. In essence, the statute isolates those considered to be terrorists from communicative assistance, even assistance aimed at using peaceful and lawful methods to petition and implement social change. The U.S. Supreme Court agreed that freedom of speech could be restricted to exclude interchange between members of terrorist organizations and any one else, including constructive exchanges instructing such members how to use peaceful and nonviolent methods of petition.[50] Those organizations classified as "terrorist," therefore, were ineligible to receive a wide range of reliable warrants, to the extent that those tried to offer them became liable.

Communication and Preserving the Possibility of Redemption

To explain my discomfort with the idea that the criminal carries a com-prehensive suspended context with her at all times, I want to advert back to the white flag. That convention demands sincerity in its invocation, even between mortal combatants. It preserves an avenue of rational means by which those at severe odds may nevertheless come together to discuss the conditions of conflict resolution. It does not first require com-plete surrender by one party, before the conditions of surrender are dis-cussed, but rather insists upon the need for a reliable avenue of commu-nication, even when the dispute remains lively and at least one party remains in the wrong.

There are important values contained in this tradition that are not confined to the wartime arena, namely: that a peaceful avenue to social and moral reconciliation and redemption always be open even to those who have strayed; that even those who engage in wrong remain members

[50] 561 U.S. 1, 36–40 (2010).

of the moral community, often still embedded in other moral relations; as members of the moral community, not all forms of constraint and respect owed to agents are inapplicable to wrongdoers; and that the availability of this opportunity should not be confined to those who have fully repented, in large part because achieving such repentance and recognition is usually a process that requires assistance from others.

One thematic way to put what troubles me about the idea that the murderer becomes a truth-free zone is that, were it a rule, it would place him in something like solitary confinement, without reliable access to a decent means of understanding the external world and human relations, and, further, without a compass for finding the exit. Solitary confinement is one of the cruelest forms of punishment, eliciting mental illness, emotional deterioration, a loss of the ability to interact with others, and the loss of a stable sense of reality.[51] Placing someone in this predicament, I think, is inconsistent with continuing to see him as a member of the moral community, albeit one in poor standing. Although I argue the murderer cannot expect veridical statements that would constitute cooperation with his nefarious enterprise, the arguments for that limited justified suspended context do not justify placing him in a wider arena of epistemic isolation.

Exiting Suspended Contexts and the Truth in Absolutism

So here's where we are in the dialectic: I metaphorically suggest that a permission to misrepresent *tout court* to the Murderer at the Door would place him in something like solitary confinement without a marked exit. I make the assumption, not defended here, that we cannot do just anything to wrongdoers on the grounds that they have strayed, even seriously strayed, from the moral path, and that we cannot entirely abandon them as members of our moral community. This claim holds even while the wrongdoer is engaged in wrongdoing.

A natural reply is that all he would have to do is abandon his immoral plan in order to become an eligible member of our epistemic cooperative scheme. I regard that counter-suggestion as imposing an overly strong

---

[51] *See, e.g.*, Bruce A. Arrigo & Jennifer Leslie Bullock, *The Psychological Effects of Solitary Confinement on Prisoners in Supermax Units: Reviewing What We Know and Recommending What Should Change*, 52 INT'L J. OFFENDER THERAPY & COMP. CRIMINOLOGY 622, 627–30 (2008); Craig Haney, *Mental Health Issues in Long-Term Solitary and "Supermax" Confinement*, 49 CRIME & DELINQUENCY 124, 130–32 (2003); Atul Gawande, *Hellhole*, NEW YORKER, Mar. 30, 2009, at 36.

condition for reentry into the moral community. My dissatisfaction stems, in large part, from the sense that even supposing morality's main contents are *a priori*, our cognition, absorption, and ability to act upon moral truths often depend upon epistemic cooperation and social support.

Morality's content, although largely *a priori*, is not easy to discern. Plenty of cognitive errors and personal and relational interests may distort our judgment as well as our capacity to act. Further, it is often unclear how principles apply in new situations. We often need one another's counsel to help us perceive and appreciate salient moral features and apt moral principles, and to better understand and reform our moral shortcomings. Further, some aspects of morality's legal and democratic manifestation are not and could not be *a priori*. We need to know what each other thinks because of our democratic meta-commitments to govern ourselves, at least in part, in ways that reflect deference for each other's independent judgment. If this were true, it would be strange to shut wrongdoers off from access to all of our epistemic resources until they had the sort of moral epiphany or transformation that we, in other circumstances, acknowledge as usually depending upon the epistemic assistance and support of others. Often enough, the wrongdoer has gone wrong, in part, by not using and benefiting from the resources of the moral/epistemic community as he should have. That fact, however, does not entail that now he can do without them or should have to do without them. Expecting a sudden, solo transformation is both unrealistic and unreasonable. Should it transpire, moreover, it may prove to be shallow and based upon less than a full understanding of the complexity of the moral domain.

I have been stressing the unreasonableness of demanding that a wrongdoer have a thorough moral epiphany and undergo a complete transformation of character on his own and that he renounce his malign aims as a condition of any access to our epistemic and testimonial wisdom. His isolation, of course, is not all that is at stake. The stance that one may intentionally falsify to the evildoer about any matter whatsoever (at least so long as one's motive is otherwise innocuous) or about any matter helpful in impeding his wrongdoing, covers a very wide swath of material— possibly touching on any aspect of his well-being, or any person or thing he cares about. Such a broad authorization to misrepresent threatens to isolate moral agents in good standing from those wrongdoers with whom they may have interests and to whom they may have a duty to try to establish relations on nonadversarial terms. If we act on maxims that authorize intentional misrepresentation on any matter that may help us frustrate, capture, or convict the evildoer, we may cut ourselves off from him and from our pursuit of our compulsory ends with respect to him.

So, I have thus far offered some account of why lying matters *in particular*, why one might nevertheless intentionally misrepresent to the murderer whether at home or next door, and why that justification may nonetheless have limits that preclude any and all intentional falsehoods that would be useful. I want to go one step further. Thoughts of the kind I was just developing may illuminate some otherwise puzzling remarks of Kant in his passage about the conversation with the mugger and the damage that lying inflicts on the dignity of the liar, even when her interlocutor has no right to the truth.[52] That in turn may put us in a position to redeem the sense that even in the Murderer-at-the-Door case, something in Kant's official position (and not just the Kantian reconstruction) may have been right, even if that murderer were an ordinary criminal and not a wayward official. Something there morally fascinates us.

As I mentioned earlier, Kant takes it that the mugger's demand that you tell him the location of the wallet may be permissibly met with an untruthful response, because "the other knows that I shall withhold the information, and that he also has no right whatever to demand the truth. . . ." But, Kant then goes on to say that if, nonetheless, you take the initiative to declare that you will speak your mind and volunteer information even when "the other is perfectly well aware that he has no right to require this of me," then, if you falsify, you "violate the right of [humanity by acting] contrary to the condition, and the means, under which a society of men can come about."[53]

Notice the passage suggests that what *justifies* (as opposed to "excuses") the misrepresentation in the first round of exchange is not *merely* that one speaks under circumstances of unjustified coercion. If that were Kant's position, it would seem as though any misinformation one offered the mugger would be morally indemnified since the mugger exerts coercion throughout the conversation and not merely in the first exchange. But this would not make sense of what he says.

Why, then, is falsifying at first permissible and then impermissible, despite the continuous pressure of coercion? The mugger's unjust purposes and techniques are sufficient to create a justified suspended context for his victim with respect to the location of one's wallet. The mugger has no right to the information and, especially, cannot expect its provision

[52] They also offer an opportunity to return briefly to the relevance of coercion in justifying misrepresentation.
[53] KANT, *supra* note 1, at 203 (27:447).

through the use of demands or threats. Nonetheless, the fact that the victim is in a justified suspended context does not end the matter. At least sometimes, one may exit a suspended context and redirect the communicative context back onto its truth-bound rails.

For instance, when attending a play, we do not expect the actors to utter their lines sincerely or, in any general or reliable way, to convey the literal content of their lines directly to the audience. When an actor unexpectedly and suddenly shouts "Fire," we may startle, but we are unlikely to look around for smoke; we are more likely to groan that the play was not *advertised* as theater of the absurd. Rationalization within the confines of the pretense of the play is likely to be our first response. Still, while it may reasonably be hard to convey sincerity, it *must* be possible for the actor to be able to break out of character, to insist, and successfully to convey that *actually, there really is a fire in the theater*. An actor cannot be stuck in character for the duration of the performance, *no matter what*. His and our safety may depend on preserving the possibility of exiting the context and exiting the theater in response to a perceived threat. Were he falsely, on a whim, to insist that he was in fact stepping out of character and alerting us to a danger, he would behave very badly, even though he began in a justified suspended context in which the heavy presumption is that he offers no warrants. If he resists the presumptions of that context, declares he will speak truthfully, and then does not, he threatens the safety of all of us, because he has rendered his word unreliable and given us reason to distrust people's word more generally.

To this example, one may object that one function of art is to supply a space for deliberate ambiguation and play with the boundaries of the real. Sometimes this play aims to question the boundaries of the moral and sometimes it aims to underscore morality's importance by offering a bracing glimpse into the phenomenology of its absence. Repeated false claims of fire and actors who remain stubbornly in character, no matter what the circumstance, may well figure into either enterprise. The success of some artworks may depend on the difficulty of penetrating the actors' personas. The players and the audience must be sufficiently engrossed to facilitate an appropriate suspension of disbelief.

In these canonical alternative spaces, as well as in some everyday conversational contexts (especially those touching on the private), participants may permissibly remain immersed in their (nontestimonial) role for some time. Certainly, emergence from the justified suspended context need not always be simple to achieve, invoked merely by the utterance of a magic word. Prolonged exchanges may permissibly transpire while interlocutors ascertain whether the purposes of the suspended context are being fully exploited or whether, in fact, a reasonable, sincere effort or request is being made to exit the suspended context. The first word on the subject need not be the last word.

Granting these points, my modest contention is that, nonetheless, it must be possible for there to be a sincere last word that can be reliably conveyed as sincere and that this exit should be available to any player. Each person has unique needs and distinctive vantage points about both their own needs and others'. This makes me skeptical about activities that threaten to isolate *individuals* through mechanisms of impenetrable insincerity, even when they are members of collectives that often represent their interests well. In a suitably confined, well-defined art-space, perhaps that rule holds only with respect to certain matters where the truth is essential in the moment, such as the safety of the staff, the participants, and the audience. Even so, this stance may place some limits on what art may strive for and achieve; I do not think those limits are so severe as to strangle art's potential, but some extreme works may be morally unavailable. In everyday life, where suspended contexts are common but less transparently bounded than in art and therefore more likely to bump into other significant moral ends, the imperative to preserve a reliable exit from insincerity seems all the more imperative.

With the principle in hand that an exit from insincerity must be possible, let us return to the case of the mugger. We begin our encounter with the mugger in a justified suspended context, at least with respect to the location of our wallet and perhaps with respect to our later whereabouts and intentions with respect to the police. If we actively attempt to break out of this context and to try to deliver a *declaration* to the mugger, then we do wrong to misrepresent, because we then implicitly affirm a principle that, if public, would undermine our ability to exit the suspended context. An ethical permission to misrepresent would obstruct the believability of all of us to achieve such an exit.

The sort of example I have in mind is this. Suppose that after the mugger demands to know the location of your wallet and you deliver your permissible falsehood that your friend borrowed it, he then begins to brandish his knife, threatening to cut up your car cushions to find where you've hidden the wallet. To buy time, you falsely *volunteer*: "Stop looking. I will *really* tell you this time if you leave the cushions alone. The wallet is in the locked glove compartment. I don't have the key so you'll have to jimmy it." What troubles me about this case is not the false content of what you convey, but that you *actively* misrepresent your moral situation and *actively* invoke the capacity to dissolve a justified suspended context and to return to a context of utter reliability, while acting in a way that undoes the possibility of a reasoned exit to veridicality.

But, one may object that one always had the right to give one's wallet to the mugger. One does no one but oneself harm when one reveals the location of one's wallet. But how could this story possibly vindicate Kant's remarks about lying to the Murderer at the Door? How could it be that one would ever be bound to tell the Murderer at the Door the truth about his victim's whereabouts?

I agree there is no plausible story that could lead to *that conclusion*. One is categorically prohibited from voluntarily offering the murderer concrete and material assistance in the commission of his crime. But, still, one would go very wrong by *volunteering gratuitously* to the Murderer at the Door that one does not regard the context as justifiably suspended and that one really is telling the truth. (To be sure, there may be cases where the assurance is not gratuitously volunteered but necessary to avoid direct exposure of one's initial misrepresentation or of that which one's misrepresentation legitimately concealed. Those cases may differ.)

To volunteer the intentional misrepresentation of the nature of the context one is in or to misrepresent one's intention to extricate oneself from a justified suspended context is to isolate oneself from the potential to operate in community with others.[54] Intentional misrepresentation about our moral location and whether we are in or whether we are disconnecting from a justified suspended context threatens to remove (or at least to damage) the linchpin of the possibility of community, sociality, and full moral life.

We often find (and place) ourselves in ambiguous locations where it is not clear whether the context is suspended or not. Such deliberate and nondeliberate ambiguity contributes to art, play, privacy, and interpersonal self-exploration. Ambiguity may also be the product of moral disagreement about the boundaries of suspended contexts and the reach of the legitimate expectations of audiences to somber (non-suspended) discourse. I don't deny these valuable uses and understandable causes of

---

[54] See also Harry Frankfurt's discussion of Adrienne Rich's observation that the "liar leads an existence of unutterable loneliness." Frankfurt claims that because the liar hides his thoughts actively in a way that tends to obscure that they are hidden, this form of refusal to be known to others is part of the insult to the victim of the lie, whether the victim believes its content or not. Harry Frankfurt, *On Truth, Lies, and Bullshit, in* THE PHILOSOPHY OF DECEPTION, *supra* note 4, at 39, discussing ADRIENNE RICH, *Women and Honor: Some Notes on Lying, in* LIES, SECRETS, AND SILENCE 191 (1979).

ambiguity. (In some related situations, it is unclear whether a misrepresentation is serious or deliberate. Sometimes people say things in the spur of the moment and it is unclear whether they *really* affirm what they have said or whether their speech was accidental, exploratory, or the regrettable product of momentary, spontaneous weakness.)

What is appalling is the deliberate abuse of the method of dissolving such ambiguity and of confirming one's precise communicative coordinates.[55] I suspect outrage at the abuse of this method is partly what fuels the sense that often the "cover-up is worse than the crime," even when the initial crime was itself a misrepresentation. Abuse of the method of confirming one's precise communicative coordinates, whether to further an admirable end, a private end, or a corrupt end, transforms ambiguity from an option to a mandatory default. Hence that lie, whether to the Murderer at the Door or anyone else, seems indefensible. By threatening the ability to achieve moral communion, it also threatens the dignity of the liar.

Conclusion

It is hard to argue for any constraint when a life is at stake, especially when an "innocent" life is in jeopardy. It is always tempting to think that the constraint may be put on hold for a moment, while we attend to the urgent matter of saving that innocent life. Once the crisis is averted, we can return to our standard methods of respectful interaction.

---

[55] An interesting example of the outrage that misrepresentation about one's moral location inspires appears in *This American Life: Retraction* ([Public Radio International radio broadcast Mar. 16, 2012], *available at* http://www.thisamericanlife.org/radio-archives/episode/460/transcript). Mike Daisy misrepresented some facts about his trip to China reporting on factory conditions for the manufacture of Apple goods in a segment of "This American Life" and to the producers of the show. He explained the misrepresentation as, in part, stemming from his view about what level of creative license is appropriate in a theatrical presentation (even one that is framed as veridical, akin to a theatrical documentary) and from the fact that the radio act was a version of his theatrical show. The producers disagreed with his ethical view about what level of creative license is appropriate in theater. What really galled the producers was that, putting that disagreement aside, when they asked for confirmation that the segment conformed to journalistic standards, i.e., when they attempted to dissolve any ambiguity about whether Daisy was treating the show as a restrained, semi-suspended context, Daisy misrepresented how he viewed the context in which he was communicating. He proported to agree that it was a straightforward journalistic context rather than his version of a creative semi-suspended context. *That* misrepresentation was what, for the producers, constituted a deep betrayal.

Emergency-propelled thinking is both tempting and morally dangerous. As is well known, if one looks hard enough, the prospect of physical
harm is always lurking, and the argument for the exceptional can transform into the apology for what becomes routine. Not only must we guard
against that error, but our methods of preventing harm must be consistent with our retaining our own moral agency and dignity and with our
continuing to respect the agency and dignity of others, even those who
have gone profoundly astray. For that reason, there are actions we think
we cannot perform and rights that are not forfeited, even by wrongdoers,
although our abstention from these actions may represent a missed opportunity to prevent harm.

For example, despite the actions of many governments over the last
decade, horribly including my own,[56] most of us still believe that we may
not torture a suspect or a prisoner. There are communicative actions we
may not take, such as manufacturing evidence to convict an innocent
person, even if we have confidence that we will thereby elicit live-saving
information or avert a life-threatening riot. At the same time, there are
necessary accommodations to the enjoyment of civil freedoms that we
must make in exigent circumstances. For instance, *with sufficient evidence*, suspects' mobility rights may be interrupted and they may be tem-
porarily detained.

So, why might lying to avert a murder (when truth-telling would not
actively abet the murder) by falsely *swearing* that one is telling the truth
differ from acceptable forms of temporary detention? To be sure, the
standard communicative expectations of the parties toward one another
are disrupted by the lurking threat posed by the murderer, whether to his
interlocutor or to his intended victim. Further, I have, here, defended uses
of speech in exigent circumstances that resemble the temporary detention
of suspects. We may refuse to answer the demands of the Murderer at the
Door and we may even deflect those demands through misrepresentations, as we may misrepresent where our wallet is when the mugger demands it.

What seems out of bounds is to go further and, affirmatively, to deny
that one has put one's communicative practice in a holding pattern and
falsely volunteer that one has renewed full communicative relations. This

[56] For one comprehensive report of renditions, secret detentions, and torture organized
by the U.S. but involving at least fifty-four other governments, *see* Open Society Initiative,
GLOBALIZING TORTURE: CIA SECRET DETENTION AND EXTRAORDINARY RENDITION (2013),
available at http://www.opensocietyfoundations.org/sites/default/files/globalizing-torture
-20120205.pdf.

misrepresentation of one's moral location (rather than the misrepresentation of the victim's location) is what poses the fundamental difficulty in
exigent circumstances. It is less like placing someone in justified temporary custody and more like secretly taking someone into custody and
then denying her detention.[57] In some cases, the temporary detention itself may be permissible, but the Kafkaesque denial that it has happened
renders the behavior impossible to contest, to evaluate, or to monitor. In
other words, the *denial* aims to render impossible the ongoing operation
of moral accountability, the background possibility of which is a nonnegotiable condition of all justifiable action. *That* is an impermissible aim.
In this way, the denial that a person has been taken into custody morally
resembles torture, the aim and (often long-term) effect of which is to obstruct the possibility of moral interaction and moral accountability by
eclipsing the moral agent, albeit in another way—by reducing the victim
from her status as a person to that of a merely reactive creature.

My contention is that somberly to affirm but yet deliberately to misrepresent one's moral location is also to aim to obstruct moral accountability for one's communicative activity, an impermissible aim. Moreover,
by giving the wrong coordinates, one puts the possibility of moral interaction out of reach in the situation and jeopardizes future moral interaction because full moral interaction depends upon our believing and
knowing that we are reliably communicating. For these reasons, what
seems at stake with the lie, and particularly with the active, affirmative
misrepresentation that one is telling the truth rather than operating in a
suspended context, is not merely the sacrifice of one of our important
moral ends but also the basic conditions of interpersonal moral agency.

---

[57] *See, e.g.*, Dana Priest & Barton Gellman, *U.S. Decries Abuse But Defends Interrogations*, Wash. Post, Dec. 26, 2002, at A01 (describing the CIA's secret detention centers at
Bagram, Diego Garcia, and elsewhere, at which suspects were subject to aggressive interrogation methods that many regard as torture and where they were held without the release
of their names and without oversight by human rights organizations).

Duress and Moral Progress

The dominant view about duress holds that, generally, unjustified or wrongfully exerted coercion entirely exonerates the party subjected to undue pressure from responsibility for whatever actions the duress produces.[1] This is a powerful and attractive view. It makes sense, other things being equal, that one should not be held responsible for what results from the bluntest forms of coercion, coercion so blunt that some do not count it as coercion at all.[2] If I wrench your hand and force a scrawled signature on a real estate contract, the consequences of that endorsement should not be laid on your doorstep. Your signature in such a case reflects nothing whatsoever about your will or your responsibility. It does not differ importantly from a forgery.[3]

In other cases, duress may exert such strong psychological pressure that we may regard the responding agent as, in essence, out of her right mind for reasons not ultimately attributable to her. Hence, responsibility seems inappropriate here too. Fair enough—at least where such duress is atypical, a surprise, or not the sort of thing we should expect the mature psychological agent to be able to manage. Note, however, that here duress triggers something like temporary insanity. It is the diminished capacity that does the moral work, not directly the duress.

---

[1] *See, e.g.,* David Owens, Shaping the Normative Landscape 231–49 (2012) (noting, however, that there may be exceptions); Eric Chwang, *Coerced Promises, in* Promises and Agreements 156, 157, 161 (Hanoch Sheinman ed., 2011); Judith Jarvis Thomson, The Realm of Rights 310–13 (1990).

[2] *See, e.g.,* Robert Nozick, *Coercion, in* Philosophy, Science, and Method: Essays in Honor of Ernest Nagel 440, 441–45 (Sidney Morgenbesser, Patrick Suppes & Morton White eds., 1969). A strong account of the opposing view appears in Scott Anderson, *The Enforcement Approach to Coercion,* 5 J. Ethics & Soc. Phil. 1, 1–26 (2010).

[3] Justice Holmes' opinion in *Fairbank v. Snow,* 13 N.E. 596, 598–99 (Mass. 1887), however, distinguishes cases involving agreements with forced signatures that "turn the ostensible party into a mere machine" from agreements made under threat or fraud.

Further reflection quickly complicates what the dominant view portrays as simple. When duress does not unhorse the agent—when she retains her composure and her compass[4]—duress may surely alter *what* she is responsible for doing. It may, for instance, partly excuse. But, it does not always *entirely* exonerate. Think of disproportionate responses to duress, say, in a case of blackmail. Unless B steals $10,000 from their mutual employer, A wrongfully threatens to reveal B's embarrassing secret, which will lead to B's expulsion from her treasured, elite backgammon club. (Perhaps B consults a copy of *Backgammon for Dummies* during bathroom breaks.) Through A's threat, A exerts duress over B, but this surely would not justify or excuse B's stealing the $10,000 in capitulation or engaging in violence toward A. Nor would it be permissible for B to retaliate by falsely impugning A's credibility, e.g., by initiating a false rumor that A, a reporter, fabricated sources, or that A committed a heinous crime. A's threat may undo some of B's obligations to A, especially those conditioned on A's reciprocity, but it is unclear that it undoes independently generated duties or obligations.

My aim here will be to explore what obligations, if any, remain or are incurred when one promises under duress. If, under duress, B offers a bargain or makes a promise to the coercer, it is unclear whether B may blithely issue a false promise or, later, view herself as entitled to ignore the commitment she undertook, solely on the grounds that the formation condition was deeply defective. Suppose that, in response to A's blackmail threat, B instead offers to do something B already has strong reason, but no prior commitment, to do, e.g., B agrees to provide a needed raise to B's struggling supervisees, who include A among their number. Even though A's threat may be wrong, it is not clear that the moral remedy is to excuse B from performance or to regard the promise as utterly void, as though it never happened.

Indeed, on further reflection, it becomes a little mysterious what inclines us toward the dominant view. It is not hard to see that we might condemn the party exerting duress, but it does not follow that the party subject to it is off the hook for how she reacts and the choices she makes. I suspect the dominant view gains false momentum off the fumes of our third-party condemnation of the duress. As third parties, we may criminally punish the coercer. Within contract law, we decline to lend our efforts to help a coercer enforce agreements extracted using the technique

---

[4] See MARGARET GILBERT, A THEORY OF POLITICAL OBLIGATION 79 (2006) for an argument that "there is neither a conceptual nor an empirical connection between coercion and witlessness."

of duress.[5] That we decline to take the side of the coercer, however, does not (I think) serve as a reliable guide to the full moral terrain.

Although the choices a party makes under duress are not made under conditions she has chosen or circumstances she should, rightfully, be under, that does not really settle the case about whether her choices should be fully exonerated. Indeed, the idea that we aren't at all responsible for the choices we make under conditions *we do not choose* seems like an element of the worst sort of libertarian fantasy. The idea that we are not responsible for the choices we make under conditions we *should not have been under* seems like an element of the worst sort of utopian fantasy. Many of the moral situations that are the hallmarks of responsibility are ones we have not chosen, would not choose, and should not be in (had others behaved well).[6] Many cases of poverty that call for individual and social choices motivated by beneficence and justice are ones we have not chosen, would not have chosen, and, had others behaved well, would not be in. Yet we are responsible to make choices and honor commitments undertaken to address such poverty.

Perhaps duress is special. It does not merely deposit us in circumstances we did not choose and should not be in. With duress, the pressure of the unchosen is not merely part of our ambient environment, but involves specific and direct pressure intentionally exerted on a victim to circumvent her rational agency or unjustly distort her choice situation. In most cases, the leading beneficiary of the coerced promise is the coercing party. I am sure that these factors matter. Yet, I am not sure *how* they matter and whether the way they matter ramifies into a full justification or excuse for the victim's responsive behavior.

This is all by way of preface to my general state of unease about duress and its relation to excuse and justification for nonperformance and for promissory misrepresentation. Here, I want to pursue an alternative to the dominant view about promises made under duress, an alternative inspired by some remarks of Immanuel Kant and of Adam Smith.

As I discussed in the last chapter, Kant contends that you may initially misrepresent to the mugger who, illegitimately threatening physical harm, demands to know the location of your wallet. But, if after that farcical cycle of communication completes, you then go on affirmatively to volunteer and represent yourself as volunteering truthful information, you

[5] *See, e.g.*, RESTATEMENT (SECOND) OF CONTRACTS §§174–77 (1981).

[6] This is a powerful theme in Barbara Herman's work. *See, e.g.*, BARBARA HERMAN, THE PRACTICE OF MORAL JUDGMENT (1996) [hereafter, HERMAN, MORAL JUDGMENT]; BARBARA HERMAN, MORAL LITERACY (2007) [hereafter HERMAN, MORAL LITERACY].

are bound not to misrepresent.[7] Something resonates here for me. I also find myself sympathetic to Adam Smith's claim that one's promise to a highwayman to send him money if he spares your life generates some obligation to fulfill the promise or to do something in its direction.[8] I want to try to make sense of the judgment Adam Smith registers that one may create obligations under illegitimate duress, by further exploring the move Kant makes with respect to misrepresentation under duress. Both take the view that the mugger has no right to the truth or to what you promise, but, all the same, you may generate an obligation through your volunteered affirmations. I believe there is something to both ideas.

In brief, I will argue that there is an asymmetry between cases in which the party exerting duress dictates your response, e.g., directs that you "do this," "say that," or "promise this," whether explicitly or obliquely, and cases in which the victim of duress genuinely initiates or creates the response, e.g., a victim volunteers that if the robber surrenders to the authorities, the victim will call a lawyer on his behalf or help his family pay their rent. The former orchestrated cases fit more comfortably with the dominant view, but the latter do not. Victims of duress may not be required to exert creative agency when operating under duress, but when they do so, I will argue, it is a morally charged activity.[9] As others have argued about beneficence, once agents embark upon morally important but elective activity, they may then be embroiled in further duties, even though they needn't have exposed themselves in the first place to that particular sort of accountability.[10] Although I will focus on the case of promises made under duress by and to individuals, some points that

[7] IMMANUEL KANT, Of Ethical Duties Toward Others, and Especially Truthfulness, in LECTURES ON ETHICS 200, 203 (Peter Heath & J. B. Schneewind eds., Peter Heath trans., 2001) (27:444–48).

[8] ADAM SMITH, THE THEORY OF MORAL SENTIMENTS 327–42 (D.D. Raphael & A.L. Macfie eds., 1982) (1759).

[9] In an important article, John Deigh also defends the position that some promises made under duress are binding and emphasizes the connection between that position and the peaceful settlement of war. John Deigh, Promises Under Fire, 112 ETHICS 483, 485–96 (2002). His position, however, depends upon and is in the service of vindicating conventionalism about promises, a view I reject, and does not draw the distinction between initiated and scripted promises.

[10] See, e.g., HERMAN, MORAL JUDGMENT, supra note 6, at 63–72. This idea is also reflected, to some degree, in the law, which occasionally imposes duties of responsibility to take due care when engaging in elective, uncompensated activity. See, e.g., RESTATEMENT (SECOND) OF TORTS § 324 (1965), and the discussion of this doctrine in Dov Waisman, Negligence, Responsibility, and the Clumsy Samaritan: Is There a Fairness Rationale for the Good Samaritan Immunity? 29 GA. ST. U. L. REV. 609 (2013) (arguing that most indemnity for mere negligence of Good Samaritans is unjustified).

emerge have broader significance for larger political issues about the possibility of social moral progress in nonideal circumstances.[11]

To vindicate the asymmetry, I will begin with some further clarifications about the relevant terrain. Then, I will draw a connection between honoring initiated promises under duress and the conditions of moral progress. I will end by considering some objections to the moral appropriateness of honoring promises made under duress.

Terminological and Moral Clarifications
Moral Progress

Although the term does not exactly litter the pages of legal or philosophical journals, I mean something fairly intuitive by "moral progress." For an individual, to make moral progress would involve: a greater level of success in apprehending, understanding, and responding correctly to moral reasons, including greater compliance with one's moral duties; further moral development and maturation in one's character, attitudes, and habits; forging, maintaining, and deepening appropriate cooperative and other moral relationships with others characterized by mutual support, understanding, management of differences and conflicts through respect, appropriate sympathy, and the application of the techniques of reason rather than the use of force; and, the recognition and repair, where appropriate, of unremedied moral wrongs. In other words, moral progress involves improving one's moral life and forging and sustaining a morally good and just character.

I assume that, for most people, substantial moral progress is robustly possible under the right conditions, even if challenging, episodic, and perhaps only occasional. Of course, in each individual case, there may be more and less propitious times and circumstances for personal growth. To say moral progress is robustly possible is not to say that it could happen in an instant or in a brief period, at any point in a person's life, merely through simple resolutions and without social support. By stressing its robust possibility, I mean merely to reject the idea of utter irredeemability or profound incorrigibility.

[11] Some of the arguments, especially those criticizing opponents of compromise and those stressing the need for a reliable mechanism of forging peace, directly apply to agreements between corporate bodies, including nations. Other arguments draw on moral psychology and so do not directly extend to nations and other forms of government, although I suspect that quite similar points may be made about how diverse social groups come to establish ongoing forms of trust and cooperation.

Moral progress by a society would involve progress by its individual members on these dimensions; the provision of a supportive environment for members to progress in these ways; greater satisfaction of our joint, collective commitments to justice and other joint moral projects; and advancing the pursuit of appropriate moral, cooperative relations with other societies. It is a more complex issue whether every society can make moral progress. I take it that its members can, both as individuals and as a collective of individuals. But whether their society as a corporate body is capable of making progress may depend upon whether deeply unjust structural features define its identity. We might, for instance, think that a society structured around apartheid cannot make progress without becoming a different society. Nonetheless, because all that matters for my argument is the idea that the members of a society may individually and collectively change, I will leave aside the question whether an unjust society could alter dramatically while retaining its identity over time.

Duress

As with "moral progress," I do not have anything special or precise in mind by "duress." I will work with core cases of transparent duress, as contrasted with duress by fraud, in which the coerced party does not know the circumstances of her choice and so is unaware that those circumstances are tainted or morally sub-par.[12] In the cases I am concerned with, a clear threat is exerted against a party who then responds. I mean to encompass promises made both under threats manifested by quid pro quo coercive offers (such as, "your money or your life") and those offered in response to pure threats not ostensively presented or meant to elicit action or commitments from the threatened party (such as declarations like "I'll get you" or "I plan to harm you").[13]

---

[12] For an insightful discussion of what unifies transparent duress and duress by fraud, see THOMSON, *supra* note 1. Thomson argues that both forms of duress involve the illegitimate diminishment of a party's eligible alternatives and that this fact deprives the coercer of a claim to redeem the promise. This core commonality seems correct. In other respects, the two differ. Transparent duress will often trigger fear in the victim, but it also orients the victim to the nature of the transaction. Transparent duress may inspire a painful sense of overt subordination and powerlessness. Duress by fraud, by contrast, deprives the victim of the opportunity to apprehend and respond in real time to the crime against her. Also, because trickery is involved, duress by fraud may later trigger a distinct feeling of humiliation by the victim for being duped.

[13] *See* KENT GREENAWALT, SPEECH, CRIME AND THE USES OF LANGUAGE 90–92 (1989).

Morally, I will take for granted that in the dictated cases, the mugger who demands your wallet acts wrongly and has no entitlement to the wallet when and after he takes it from you; he should give it back. Third parties should not respect any claims the mugger makes to the wallet and, indeed, may owe you assistance in recovering it. Furthermore, where the mugger *demands* that you promise not to report him as a condition of your leaving unscathed, I concur with the dominant view that your scripted promise has no force as such.[14] Moreover, whether scripted or initiated, promises to perform intrinsically wrong actions or to give something that is intrinsically illegitimate for the coercer to have are not binding because (as I have argued elsewhere), in general there is no power to promise intrinsically immoral performances, whether under duress or not.[15] So, when the bank robber threatens to shoot a guard in order to get the guard to lower his weapon, but the guard instead promises to join forces with the robber and to provide the combination to a safe, that promise has no force. Promises to violate duties to self, such as agreements of indentured servitude, also fall into this category.[16]

My thesis is that matters may differ, at least from the moral point of view of the promisor, when she genuinely volunteers something that she possesses the normative power to volunteer and to commit to. There are better and worse such promises. There are pedestrian mugging cases in which bodily harm is threatened and resources are given or promised

[14] Although I argue that scripted promises are not binding as such on individuals, there may be some circumstances where there are other, non-promissory reasons to perform the promised act, e.g., that nonperformance may prolong a conflict but performance would bring an end to an incredibly destructive conflict. Such non-promissory reasons may exert special force for state actors who have special responsibilities for their citizens and for ensuring peace.

[15] Seana Valentine Shiffrin, *Immoral, Conflicting, and Redundant Promises, in* REASONS AND RECOGNITION: THEMES FROM T.M. SCANLON 155, 159–63 (Jay Wallace, Rahul Kumar & Samuel Freeman eds., 2011). Focusing mainly on agreements between states, Avishai Margalit offers a searching account of which sorts of agreements one should not make, even for peace, in AVISHAI MARGALIT, ON COMPROMISE AND ROTTEN COMPROMISES (2010).

[16] In addition, there may be actions that are permissible to perform but that cannot be the valid object of a promise: that is, cannot be the sort of thing that one may commit to not changing one's mind about or not exercising fresh autonomy over at the moment of action. I have in mind cases such as "promises" to have sexual intercourse or "promises" to take a lethal pill on one's death bed. Treating such things as promises would be inconsistent with honoring one's duties to self even if the activity promised were perfectly permissible. This category also encompasses promises that, functionally, perpetuate a relationship of unjust subordination or violence, such as promises made by abused partners in order to end an episode of domestic violence but that do not fundamentally alter, and instead, perpetuate, the dynamics of the relationship, e.g., by later serving as a rationalization by the abuser for further violence when the promise is later perceived to be breached.

instead; e.g., in exchange for release, you will not scream, or report the mugger, or offer your ring instead of your wallet, representing the jewelry as more valuable. There are also nonpedestrian cases in which the agreement itself has a more substantially morally charged content. For instance, when the robber issues the standard threat and the coerced party remonstrates with him to give up his life of crime and instead to enter rehab, promising to help him gain entry to a program the next day. In considering these promises, what matters, I suspect, is not the content of what is represented to the mugger alone, but also the victim's role in the interaction. The victim's role as the initiator of the solution, I think, makes a difference in whether he or she may misrepresent and what he or she should do thereafter. My challenge is to say a little more about why.

Before I do so, I need to offer further clarifications. First, I will assume that, by and large, we can distinguish which category actual cases fall into, although, in reality, the boundaries are not sharp. In part, the elusive line between the boundaries is due to the fact that a scripted promise may not wear its status explicitly on its sleeve. For instance, I mean to put in the dictated, compelled speech category cases in which the duress scenario is choreographed to elicit a predicted offer in response, even though it does not explicitly detail the terms of that acceptable offer: e.g., Bob files a frivolous law suit whose stakes threaten to ruin Sal. Although Sal could prevail as a legal matter, the suit will both embarrass Sal and cost too much to defend. Bob intends and structures this harassment to elicit a predictable settlement offer of $50,000 by Sal to make the suit go away. That is a scripted case, although Bob makes no explicit demand. Were Sal later to change her mind and attempt to set aside the settlement on the moral grounds that the settlement was induced only through illegitimate intimidation, I posit her resistance would be morally unremarkable.

I take a contrast case of an "initiated" promise to be one in which Sal responds, off-script, by offering and then promising, instead, to settle by donating $50,000 to Bob's favorite charity *and* to attend counseling with Bob to work out their personal differences. Here, completely reneging seems more problematic. More common initiation cases are ones in which the victim negotiates with the robber terms in which she can keep some of her property, she and others may walk away safely or, in more satisfying cases, in which the robber will forego his aim and the victim will help him ensure fair conditions of surrender or, in less morally successful cases, unobstructed passage.

Second, I focus only on cases in which the good or the action that is promised retains (some) of its value, even if offered and given under circumstances that are not free or that involve illegitimate inducements. Water, money, phone calls, and legal assistance all seem like goods of that sort. On the other hand, there are some goods (or actions) whose internal integrity is compromised when they are given under or promised in response to illegitimate pressure, such as promises to give honorary awards; the honor they convey seems tainted (at best) when what induced it is not the underlying quality of the honoree's bravery, writing, or what have you, but rather the promisor's effort to resolve and escape duress.[17]

Third, my contention concerns only cases in which what is promised is not only a generally legitimate object of promise, but also not independently owed to the coercer as a matter of right. That is, I exclude cases in which the coerced party promises to redeem the coercer's independent, valid claim of right. Certain forms of rebellion that elicit promises of reform may represent such cases, as when agents resort to force before it is justified, e.g., before exhausting peaceful methods of recourse, or when they deploy greater force than is justified as a remedy to recover or gain what is rightfully theirs. In other cases, the coercer may wield the prospect of disproportionate punishment and thereby inspire pledges of good behavior, or may issue an illicit threat to which the coerced party responsively promises something to which the coercer has a prior, but unredeemed, right. The disgruntled worker threatens the life of the abusive manager unless the manager steals $10,000 from the company for the worker, but the manager instead proposes to stop paying all the workers' wages out of tips. Or, rightfully imprisoned but badly mistreated prisoners strong arm the warden and threaten to kill her from anger; she reacts by acknowledging their grievances and promising adequate meals and an end to guard abuses.

---

[17] I also have in mind confessions of wrongdoing, as well as legal testimony in general. Not only does it seem as though the recipients of confessions should not use them when they are the products of or a response to duress, but those who promise to confess or to provide testimony against others should not regard those promises as having force, however diminished, when they were elicited under duress. Of course, any reasonable listener should downgrade the epistemic reliability of such testimonies or confessions due to their origins, but my point is the further one. It is more that, given the significance and the consequences of incriminating testimony, it seems important that the reason for offering it should be responsive to the general, direct reasons for offering such testimony (e.g., that it is true, that public knowledge of and accountability for this truth is an important aim, and that legitimate authorities elicit it through appropriate channels); the reason for its production should not trace to contingent, improper inducements. So, the state should not use or demand testimony against others elicited from circumstances of illegitimate duress for both epistemic and due process reasons; further, those who promised should feel no obligation to honor said promises because that testimony would be tainted by its inducement.

I put these cases aside because they do not seem especially interesting. Unless there is a good reason why good behavior is a condition of the right's validity, the duress should be treated as a wrong and the perpetrator subjected to an appropriate remedy, but the right should be satisfied nonetheless unless there is some special reason to think the appropriate remedy to address the duress just happens to be the denial of that right. The prisoners should, perhaps, have their sentences extended, but their behavior does not justify failing to keep a promise to protect their safety and supply them enough food. Whether the promise does any work, or the underlying right carries the full load,[18] what seems important is that even when what is promised was the object of the coercion, the fact that duress is used does not invalidate all claims to the object of the promise.

With these clarifications in hand, we can now turn to the central question: When a coerced party *initiates* a promise to act that is neither intrinsically wrong nor independently required, why do I think that *that* promise may have moral significance, even if its scripted, coerced counterpart does not?

Promises as a Moral Resource

Prominent accounts of why duress justifies nonperformance isolate convincing and serious defects in the transaction between the coercer and the victim. These defects are used, in turn, to explain why the coercer lacks a claim to the victim's later performance. For example, Judith Jarvis Thomson argues that the coercer illegitimately diminishes the victim's eligible alternatives, and this illegitimate inducement disqualifies the coercer from making a claim on the victim. The argument has the structure of a claim of unjust enrichment.[19] David Owens' account also focuses on how duress deprives the coercer of the ability to make a claim. His argument is that promises have special, distinctive normative force because they allow the promisee to direct the promisor's activity in a way that she could not prior to the promise and to do so on the basis of an authority interest that is as of right. The value of the authority interest encapsulated in a promise is that it permits one to direct another person to do something through a mechanism distinct from brute force or an illegitimate command. Duress is therefore "self-undermining," because it deprives the

---

[18] I discuss related issues in Shiffrin, *supra* note 15, at 165–71.
[19] THOMSON, *supra* note 1, at 310–14.

promise of its essential character and purpose.[20] If the reason I prefer a promise from you that you will pay me money over forcing your hand to sign a check is that it is normatively preferable to be able to request the money as of right, as opposed to exerting the brute power to make it happen, then using brute power to extract the promise undermines the distinctive point (and power) of a promise. Threatening the use of brute power inherits this same problem. In Owens' terminology, duress is sufficient to invalidate a promise because, for him, a valid promise is just a promise that imposes obligations on the promisor that are owed to the promisee and promissory obligations cannot be induced through wronging. Thus, by wronging the victim, duress cannot induce the obligations sought by the wrongdoer from his victim.[21]

Both of these accounts offer plausible reasons why a party exerting duress cannot demand performance on a promise thereby extracted. Both, to their credit, are also well-positioned to explain why promises may bind when legitimate threats of force are wielded and elicit a promise.[22]

Let us assume that one of these accounts, or something like them, succeeds with respect to divesting the promisee of any valid claims. Notice, however, that these accounts only address the (moral) point of view and the direct moral powers possessed by the attempted promisee. They do not settle the question of whether the absence of a claim by the promisee exhausts the moral significance of the promise if we instead consider the point of view of the promisor. If there are facets of a promise's moral significance in addition to its value to the promisee, then some of its significance and perhaps its bindingness may survive even an illegitimate inducement.

---

[20] Owens, *supra* note 1, at 231–49, especially 241–43; *see also* David Owens, *Duress, Deception, and the Validity of a Promise*, 116 Mind 293, 312 (2007).

[21] Owens, *supra* note 1, at 236–39.

[22] Think of the plea bargain, one component of which includes a promise to plead guilty, to reveal information about a crime, to evince remorse. That promise may be elicited by well-behaved prosecutors who threaten prosecution carrying a reasonable probability of prolonged incarceration in a just state with fairly obtained evidence that is ample to convict the accused of something that is and should be a crime. Where legitimate force (or its threat) induces a promise, the point of the promise may not be undermined because, in that case, force is not an illegitimate inducement used to circumvent legitimate modes of interaction. Therefore, it might be thought to be as acceptable as any other legitimate inducement to transfer a normative power. On this sort of view, what is wrong about the unjustified use of force to elicit a promise is not the deployment of force per se but that it is the attempt to use an illegitimate method as a complete substitute for the legitimate method of gaining normative power.

A promise not only offers the promisee something, it also offers the promisor an opportunity. A promise divests a power from the promisor, but that divestiture is not solely or necessarily a cost to the promisor. In some cases, the promisor may, of course, value the promisee's enhanced power. In the case of duress, the ability to offer a promise in exigent circumstances may permit the promisor to forge some sort of solution or craft an exit from the circumstances of duress. That opportunity may not only allow the promisor a better outcome than either submission to the force threatened by the coercer or submission to the coercer's stated demands, but it may also permit the promisor to exert creative agency (albeit in compromised circumstances). For it to represent a true opportunity, though, it must be somewhat plausible to the promisee. If promisors in such circumstances operated under a (public) rule of permission whereby they could promise insincerely or regard themselves as under no obligation, then the promise could not serve, plausibly, as a reliable lever of exit. So, a moral rule that would void or invalidate such promises or would authorize their insincere proffers might not wrong the promisee, but would, I think, wrong potential promisors generally by depriving them of an important moral resource.

This may seem like a strange way of putting it, for one might think that the issue turns instead on the following prudential calculation.[23] Promisors under duress may value the ability to make sincere promises with moral force, because that ability allows them to manage and escape nasty threats made by parties engaging in duress. On the other hand, if potential threateners are aware of this power, that power may represent an opportunity for them to exploit; it may make threats more likely and demands more expensive, if only to inspire more remunerative creative alternatives initiated by the coerced.

So, one might think that this line of reasoning suggests a prudential calculation for all of us: are the opportunities created by the ability to make a believable promise under duress overshadowed by the vulnerabilities those opportunities in turn create, as well as by the likelihood those vulnerabilities will be exploited? A power to promise whose value is that it allows one to escape from a threat that the power itself makes more likely may seem like a dubious resource at best. Further, the information we would need to argue that the opportunity is one that, prudentially, we should protect seems both variable and elusive.

[23] *See, e.g.,* Claire Finkelstein, *Contracts Under Coercion: Should You Keep an Agreement with a Robber,* (April, 2012) (unpublished manuscript); *see also* RICHARD A. POSNER, ECONOMIC ANALYSIS OF LAW 143 (8th ed. 2010); Chwang, *supra* note 1, at 163.

But this purely prudential perspective on the matter is importantly narrow. When I previously referred to the power to make a promise and to convey it believably, I characterized this power as a "moral resource" advisedly. The ability to initiate a promise under duress does not merely represent an opportunity for the promisor to escape whatever is threatened, but represents an opportunity for forging some form of settlement and resolution of conflict.

Even though what is at stake is predominately one's safety and egress from danger, achieving these goals well is a moral and not merely a prudential endeavor. We regularly have moral duties under nonideal circumstances that are not of our making, circumstances for which we are not otherwise responsible. Much of our moral lives have this quality. But though we are not responsible for the situation in which we find ourselves, we inherit responsibilities for managing the situation and facing the challenges it presents, including burdens that, in ideal circumstances, we would not bear. We have reasons to attempt to comport ourselves well in nonideal circumstances, so as not to trample on others or misuse or hoard the arbitrary advantages we happen to have. Beyond that, we also have reasons to aspire to moral progress and to attempt to lift ourselves and others out of our nonideal circumstances.[24]

Although the fundamental moral principles will not differ from those operating in ideal conditions, their instantiation in distinct nonideal circumstances will not always submit to easy application or familiar forms, recognizable from frequent repetition.[25] Moving from a unique, nonideal situation toward circumstances that approach appropriate moral relations may therefore require significant forms of moral ingenuity and innovation, even while these efforts are shaped by familiar moral constraints. Extracting oneself from a situation of duress through a promise (or a series of representations) might be considered a writ-small version, albeit gradual and halting, of the more general but locally crafted transformation from nonideal circumstances toward the regulative ideal that we are all bound to aspire to and support.

This effort is a moral one and not merely a prudential one because one's activity does not merely promote one's interests. It also aims to end or neutralize a wrong—the duress. Thereby, it moves both parties closer toward the regulative ideal through an imperfect, fledgling form of per-

---

[24] See Barbara Herman's related work on the moral meaning (and not merely the prudential significance) of the improvisation involved in creating the South African Truth and Reconciliation Commissions in HERMAN, MORAL LITERACY, *supra* note 6, at 319–30.
[25] *Id.* at 306–07.

suasion and directness, rather than through brute force. The implementation of the idea that such representations have no moral significance (and so permissibly may be falsely offered), or the maxim that they will be offered but not respected would, if universalized, deprive us of a significant moral tool. Except for exhortations unlikely to meet with immediate success, it would leave us little possibility of reasoned resolution and, so, little role for our significant powers of innovation. When one initiates a promise to escape and bring an episode of duress to a close, one therefore invokes an important moral resource that enables moral progress. In so doing, one is obliged to other, future victims and to the moral community generally, to act to protect its renewability rather than risking that this resource will be depleted.

Three Questions

This perspective on promises initiated under duress immediately raises three questions:

1. Why do I characterize promises initiated (and in some respect honored) by the coerced party under duress as a form of moral progress rather than a move from one nonideal position to another?

2. If there is an asymmetry between promises made under duress that are demanded by the coercer and those initiated by the coerced, what accounts for it and how is it related to moral progress?

3. Does this position suggest that promises initiated by the coerced party under duress are *fully* binding?

I will now attempt some answers.

I have so far been suggesting that the ability to initiate binding promises while under duress (and the related obligation that one's initiated representations be veridical, even under duress) represents an opportunity to generate obligations or constraints that in turn generate opportunities and occasions for moral progress. The foundational importance of preserving this opportunity grounds the moral obligation to honor the promise initiated under duress. Against this suggestion it may be observed that the promises that are extracted will, in many instances, effect a transfer of resources from a party who has a right to them to a party who does not. Furthermore, the catalyst of that transfer involves the levying of illegitimate force. So, often, duress will produce illegitimate outcomes, effected by illegitimate means; the fact that a promise served as a way station or conduit passed through before arriving at the illegitimate outcome does not wash it clean. Keeping a promise made under duress just shifts the pieces around but does not represent a step forward.

My answer to this challenge will also supply the answer to the second question, namely, given that duress is the catalyst of the promise, why does it make such a difference in my view whether its cessation happens on terms solely dictated by the party exerting duress or on terms introduced by the victim?

Start with the case of the robber who declares "your money or your life." Meekly or angrily, as the case may be, you hand over your money. In some cases, although you have a self-regarding obligation to resist the duress, you may assume that here there is no chance of disarming or evading the threat. Compare this case of pure capitulation with the case where you instead reply, "Look—I really need this money to get home. But this ring is worth more than the cash I have on me . . . if you take it instead and let me keep the money, I promise not to block its subsequent sale or file a report," or in more intimate cases, ". . . I promise not to tell your sister." Are these situations distinguishable? Should one really keep the promise?

Neither case is any good, but there is something to be said for the latter as distinguished from the former. In the former case, what happens is entirely dictated by the robber using illegitimate means and incentives. In the latter case, three things of moral import occur.

First, the victim exerts some creative agency in the situation and it has an effect on what happens. Although the robber retains most of the power in the situation, and that power is illegitimately wrought and illegitimately deployed, still—the terms of what happens and the method by which it is effected involve both parties acting as agents. Under the first scenario, the robber is the only person articulating terms that are effective. In the second scenario, both agents play a role in determining the outcome.

Of course, promises are not the only moral mechanism that may empower the victim. For example, the victim may show kindness or convey understanding to the mugger in a way that establishes a human connection that defuses the situation. But, in ways not captured by demonstrations of kindness, promises serve other moral and dignitary functions, as the following further two features bring out.

Second, although the robber's interests are predominantly served by the resolution in either case, the negotiated case involves both the advancing of a truncated agenda of the coerced party's morally legitimate interests, *as she sees them*, and their effective acceptance by the party exerting coercion. Notice that it isn't merely that the coerced party gets more that she wants in this dreadful situation. For, the negotiated solution importantly differs from a third case in which the robber spies the ring and says "I want that too" and then, in the rush to run away, drops one's wallet so that the victim loses the ring but retains the money to get home. By contrast with the wallet dropping case, when these results come about because of the proffering and acceptance of a promise, the victim's legitimate interests are (in a defective sense to be sure) recognized and permitted to operate by both parties as a sort of reason for the outcome. The promise, therefore, achieves something that the forging of a human connection through the expression of kindness or understanding may not, namely the mugger's partial acceptance of the victim's *own articulation* of her interests as having weight.

Both of these moments—the introduction of shared agency, albeit hampered, lopsided, and hierarchical, *and* the effective acceptance by the coercing party of the coerced party's articulated interests as relevant to the scenario's resolution—represent substantial *moral* advances over the simple case of effectively exerted duress. To be sure, even in the promise case, the coercing agent's private perspective and his immoral methods still drive the scenario in highly objectionable ways. Still, the negotiated version is more morally complex in salutary ways. The negotiated process introduces elements of what appropriate moral relations would look like into a situation where they are lacking. In some cases, the progress is not merely symbolic but also involves quite substantial achievements, as with negotiated surrenders. It is not a fully satisfactory picture, to be sure, but once a party resorts to duress, we have already exited the realm of the satisfactory.

Finally, when the promisor substantially honors the promise after the fact, the promisor establishes a (thin) foundation for building trust between the promisor (and other moral agents) and the promisee. The promisor demonstrates that despite the promisee's morally criminal behavior, the promisee has not been utterly banished from the circle of potential beneficiaries and objects of fidelity and honor, even if the promisee lacks standing to demand conforming actions as a matter of right. The promisee's criminal behavior may have altered her moral status in some respects, but it has not left her merely a target of repercussions and efforts to contain her bad will. Of course, other measures we take toward criminals (e.g., to afford them rights of due process or to protect them against abusive forms of punishment) also convey this significant stance.[26] What a commitment to abstain from untruthful, nondefensive misrepresentations and to treat an initiated promise made under duress as binding adds is the production of an obligation whose content is not predetermined (as it is in the prohibition against cruel and unusual punishment or the right to counsel). Instead, the content emanates from the details of the interaction with the particular moral criminal. That fact establishes the basis for some trust in what emerges from other interactions and not just trust in adherence to a prespecified, institutionalized list of substantive rights.

This final feature highlights one of the unique moral functions of the promise in nonideal circumstances. Consider the contrast with persuasion, perhaps the most important mechanism of resolving conflict. Persuasion also involves the profound exertion of the agency of the victim and forges an intellectual connection between the parties that *may* result in the absorption of the victim's own position into the mugger's practical agenda. Elizabeth Anscombe once neutralized a mugger's threat in Chicago by reproaching him that this was "no way to treat a visitor" and, then, either shamed him or charmed him (or both) into escorting her through the neighborhood.[27] Obviously, persuasion is more ideal in many ways than resorting to negotiation. On the other hand, persuasion is not always available: it is foolhardy to expect criminals to alter their perspective and their aims so thoroughly on a dime. We need additional moral tools to address nonideal circumstances. Unlike persuasion, negotiation and the offering of a promise does not depend upon effecting a conversion, but only on accepting more modest concessions. Moreover, a promise connects the promisor and promisee over time in ways that persuasion does not. As the third feature of the promise highlights, this connection can facilitate important moral work both by forging bonds of trust and by signaling the impact of criminal behavior on future relationships.

Having argued that initiated promises serve morally important purposes, even when initiated under duress, I hasten to clarify that to regard the promise initiated under duress as having *some* moral force is not tantamount to allowing duress to manufacture rewards. Here, I begin to

---

[26] Jeffrey Helmreich offers an illuminating account of stances as dispositions to treat others in accord with an undertaken normative commitment in Jeffrey Helmreich, "More than Words: Stances as an Alternative Model for Apology, Forgiveness and Similar Speech Acts" (2013) (unpublished Ph.D. dissertation, UCLA).

[27] *See* Jane O'Grady, *Elizabeth Anscombe: Obituary*, THE GUARDIAN (January 10, 2001) (http://www.theguardian.com/news/2001/jan/11/guardianobituaries.highereducation). Liam Murphy alerted me to this story.

ss the third question I posed. For the promise to do its moral work,
uer has to regard it and treat it as having some moral significance.
This idea is perfectly consistent with the concomitant idea that the deployment of duress should be responded to and punished or remedied, as the case may be. Further, third parties, I think, need not come to the aid of the promisee when the promisor either deliberately reneges or for some other sort of reason, breaches (as when execution of her promise is stymied for reasons out of her control). I have only argued that initiated promises induced under duress (that do not themselves involve the promotion of evil) may exert some moral weight. I agree they do not have the same significance, e.g., for third parties, as promises made under appropriate conditions. So, to think these promises have some significance is not to endorse duress or to roll over in its wake.

Why do I say "some" moral significance or "some" moral weight? Why the qualifier? As we have noted, the standard rationale for promissory fidelity is not present: this is not a normal case in which a discretionary right has been shifted from the promisor to the promisee. For the negotiation between the coercer and the coerced to proceed on a public, reasoned basis and not through mere reactions to private predictions of the other's behavior, the promise must not be a farce. Thus, there is reason for the promisor to honor it in some way after the duress and its threat have subsided. At a minimum, I think this means that the promisor cannot pretend the promise was never made. She cannot treat the decision about whether to do what was promised fresh and anew, now that she is out from under the pressure of the duress. This promise shares the fundamental feature of all promises: that it disrupts the normal operation of an agent's discretionary permissions later to reconsider one's announced intentions afresh.

Still, because the promise is made under duress, substantially framed by the coercer's will and terms, there would seem to be legitimate moral room after the fact for the promisor to inject her perspective to a greater degree than under more legitimate promissory circumstances. She may ask, once she is not under duress, what would be reasonable to honor in light of the fact that honoring the commitment in some way is necessary to render possible a rational acceptance of these sorts of resolutions and, thereby, to render possible moral progress without complete conversion. The relevant question cannot be, "What agreement would I have made with the promisee under free and fair conditions of choice?" That question would indulge the fantasy that the nonideal conditions never transpired or never would transpire again. What may be more appropriate is the question, "What aspect of these terms would I accede to that manifest good faith toward our relation and still offer a reasonable incentive to the agent exerting duress, given his limited agenda of interests, to abandon coercion?" This question may permit a less than full execution of the original promise and allow for excising excessive (relative to context) terms that may be the mere products of force and fear.

I have suggested that promises made under duress may have some binding force but do not work in the same way as promises made under voluntary conditions. Under standard conditions, a promise to *phi* at time *t* divests the promisor of her right to reconsider whether to *phi*, that is, her right to entertain any and all considerations that bear on whether to *phi* at *t*. That right is transferred to the promisee who may demand or waive performance by the promisor. Under duress, the promisor divests her standard power fully to reconsider whether to *phi* at the time of performance. But, what is unusual is that this divestment is decoupled from a right to demand performance of the promisor by the promisee. Hence, the promise has some moral force, but of a different sort than the moral force of standard promises, both because the promisee is not directly empowered by the promise initiated under duress and because third parties need not enforce the initiated promise on the promisee's behalf. Further, the substandard conditions of formation (that block the transfer of a right to demand performance of the promise) may also affect how complete the divestiture of the normative power to reconsider is; they may explain why the promise has moral force but may not strictly bind the promisor to the full terms of its original content.

WAIVER

It may be objected, though, that this picture cannot explain the intuitive sense that the promisor is not *at all* bound by a promise made under duress if the promisee (say from remorse for his coercion) waives the promise. If the promisee has no right to performance, how can his waiver be effective? Waiver only makes sense as part of the full panoply of promissory powers, including the right to demand performance, but the idea that a promise under duress has full force seems absurd.

So, how can I explain the apparent phenomenon of waiver given that the promisee lacks the right to demand performance? I contend that "waiver" operates differently in the case of a coerced promise than in the case of straightforward promise. Strictly speaking, in cases of promises initiated under duress, the promisee has no power to waive performance, because the promisee has no right to demand performance. But, when the promisee signals a lack of interest in the promise being kept or makes an effort to "waive" the promise, it may exert a moral effect akin to that of standard waivers for different reasons. Broadly speaking, when the promisee attempts to waive, that waiver satisfies the moral purposes driving my position that the coerced promise has some moral force; given the waiver, there no longer is much point to performance. Specifically: through responsive performance, namely by ending the coercion on the terms of the initiated promise, the promisee has recognized the agency and interests of the promisor. Through the subsequent "waiver," the promisee acknowledges that some sort of performance by the promisor is expected to occur which, thereby, demonstrates that some foundation of trust has been built and internalized. Given the achievement of these purposes, there is no further reason to regard the promise as demanding performance in order to show that the promisor regards the promise as having force.[28]

A COMPETING EXPLANATION

One might object that the combination of the promisee's inability to demand performance, coupled with the promisor's evident permission to modify, unilaterally, the content of the commitment, shows that whatever obligation is here is not really promissory in nature. Perhaps there are nonpromissory reasons at work that are directed at bridging the divide between the parties and forging a human connection; those reasons might misleadingly feed my sense that there is a promissory obligation. In some cases, a level-headed, compassionate victim may look past the threat and perceive the terrible straits that the criminal must be in for him to resort to duress; a sympathetic response may then seem warranted, one that may often bear some relation to what was promised, but is really driven by kindness.[29] That suggestion may seem bolstered by the following example, which I will call *Holton's case*.[30] Suppose a mugger allows a vic-

---

[28] This represents an alternative to the solution of the problem offered by Jorah Dannenberg in his intriguing paper. Jorah Dannenberg, *Promising Ourselves, Promising Others* (June, 2014) (unpublished manuscript). Dannenberg argues that promises involve committing to the value of "giving a say" to the promisee over one's conduct; this may both explain the binding power of promises made under duress and the power of waiver. *Id.* at 19–25. Although we concur about many cases, the idea that one should value "giving a say" to the coercer seems overly strong. The underlying idea may be better captured in the notion of showing some ongoing concern for the coercer's moral standing and moral future, without committing to the idea of actually valuing the agenda and power of the coercer.

[29] Judith Jarvis Thomson and Richard Holton both pursued this objection in conversation and correspondence.

[30] Richard Holton offered the case over e-mail. My version involves a minor modification.

tim to go free after the victim promises to buy the mugger alcohol at an adjacent liquor store that has declined to serve the mugger given a prior unpleasant episode. On gaining her freedom, the victim might go ahead and buy the mugger something, but might reasonably substitute food for alcohol. This example suggests that the underlying motive is sympathy, not some semblance of promissory commitment.

For two reasons, I am unconvinced that kindness or sympathy do the dominant work here, although they may operate as reinforcing motives. First, that one *volunteered* a promise seems to matter, even in *Holton's case*. I have already argued that it matters whether the promise is scripted or initiated. Here is an additional consideration: if mid-threat, the mugger saw a police car go by, startled, and abandoned the crime, one would not be obliged to buy the mugger food, alcohol, or blankets even if fifteen minutes later the mugger and victim happened both to be in the parking lot of the nearest convenience store. Sometimes it might be the right thing to do and other times not. In any case, the gesture here feels more optional than it does when the victim initiates a promise to buy sundries. Yet, considerations of kindness or sympathy should be roughly on a par whether the crime was abandoned midway, whether the mugger demanded a promise to buy alcohol, or whether the promise was initiated by the victim as an alternate resolution to their confrontation. Perhaps, though, one has reason to be more kind or sympathetic to a troubled person who responds to an initiated promise because it shows that person is open to a different sort of relationship than one entirely dominated by force. On this reading, the mugger's responsiveness to the initiated promise does not make one bound by the promise, but the responsiveness may give the victim a stronger connection to, or hope for, the mugger's humanity, which in turn may justify greater kindness or sympathy than in the two contrasting cases.

I remain unconvinced in part because, although I have argued that the content of the commitment is somewhat revisable, it seems as though *what* one has promised also matters. I do not share the intuition that one may substitute food for alcohol in the prior example. Although I agree that, in many cases, the promisor may revise the content of the commitment to account for his compromised bargaining position in the encounter, good faith requires attending to the impetus for agreement. In the prior case, the promise to purchase alcohol motivated the resolution because that good was unavailable to the mugger; whereas, presumably, the mugger faced no obstacle to obtaining food. To substitute food for the promised alcohol might be the kind thing to do, but it seems unduly dismissive of the agreement the parties forged and the (highly imperfect) respect for each other's agency this agreement showed.

Still, whether kindness or sympathy are the explanatory motives or not, there is a larger theoretical concern here. Is it is appropriate to call this agreement a *promise* given its unusual features, namely the promisee's inability to demand performance and the promisor's (limited) unilateral ability to modify the content of the commitment? I agree that this is a peripheral and hobbled form of promise, but because it does involve the promisor's relinquishment of her discretionary right to decide what to do at the time of performance and because what was agreed to and why plays a crucial role in determining what she should do at the time of performance, I think it is not too strained to call this a form of promise. Nevertheless, the label of "promise" does not matter so much for my purposes. Those who would prefer to restrict the use of "promise" to its central case of the full-fledged transfer of a right from promisor to promisee, where the promisee has the right to demand or waive performance and modifications require joint consent, certainly have a case. My main points would not be compromised if we were instead to call these commitments initiated under duress mere "agreements."

THIRD PARTIES AND CONTRACTS

A related issue concerns third parties: I have remarked that because the coercing party does not inherit or gain the discretionary right that the promisor has yielded in some way through the promise, therefore third parties need not come to the assistance of the coercing party if the coerced party reneges or otherwise breaches. Although the promisor may act wrongly by disregarding the promise, the coerced party does not gain a right of performance in contrast to the rights promisees gain from promises made under standard conditions. But, even if third parties need not assist the coerced party, must they respect the performance of the coerced party? If, in response to duress, a coerced party offers her ring rather than her wallet or promises not to testify against the thief, should the thief allow her to retain her cell phone, or if a hostage negotiator promises the hostage-taker that he will be allowed to see his family before being taken into custody, must third parties respect these pledges where the promisor attempts to carry them out, or may they permissibly attempt to obstruct the promisors' performance?[31]

---

[31] The plight of the former hostages in the American Embassy in Iran presents a related example of this problem, but one involving second parties whose legal powers were constrained by an agreement to which they were not parties. In the Algiers Accords that led to

I am not sure that they *must* (and it may depend on the externalities of performance), but where the promisor's performance is in the service of satisfying the terms of conflict resolution, third parties inherit some reasons to respect this performance as contributing to the end of coauthored moral progress.

Why not go further and argue that initiated promises made under duress should be legally enforced? If it is wrong not to honor them in some way, why shouldn't third parties, including the community in its judicial guise, play a role in reinforcing that moral norm by establishing a legal expectation of performance? Or, in other words, if the argument for qualified promissory fidelity for initiated promises under duress succeeds, doesn't it suggest that the legal doctrine of duress should be reformed to

---

the release of the hostages, the U.S. agreed, among other things, to deny legal relief in U.S. courts to the hostages against the Iranian government and hostage takers. Settlement of the Hostage Crisis, Iran-U.S., cl. 11, Jan. 18, 1981, 20 I.L.M. 223. The U.S. government has consistently stood by the Accords as involving regrettable elements, fealty to which, however, is essential for preserving the power to engage in effective diplomacy. *See, e.g.,* Memorandum in Support of United States' Motion to Intervene at 4, Roeder v. Islamic Republic of Iran, 742 F. Supp. 2d 1 (D.D.C. 2010) (No. 08–0487) (arguing that abrogating the Accords would be a foreign policy embarrassment and "imperil the government's '[e]ffectiveness in handling the delicate problems of foreign relations.'") (citing U.S. v. Pink, 315 U.S. 203, 229 (1942); *see also* Brief for the United States in Opposition at 11–12, Roeder v. Islamic Republic of Iran, 132 S. Ct. 2680 (2012) (No. 11–730), ("a repudiation affects the Executive Branch's ability to negotiate future agreements involving similarly grave interests."). Many of the former hostages, however, have lobbied Congress to renege on this agreement and have repeatedly filed suit against the Iranian government to attempt to persuade the courts to disregard the Accords. Their legal efforts have consistently failed. *See e.g.,* Roeder v. Islamic Republic of Iran, 646 F. 3d 56 (2011), *cert. denied,* 132 S. Ct. 2680 (2012); Matthew Wald, *3 Decades Later, Ex-Hostages Press on for Damages from Iran,* N.Y. Times, Apr. 12, 2012, at A15. Although there are further complexities involving agreements between states that I have not directly explored, the arguments I have given provide support for the government's position. It is entirely understandable and morally reasonable, however, for the former hostages to resist the agreement and, through their advocacy, attempt to stymie its enforcement. Their understandable resistance to the agreement provides an additional ground for Congress's decision to provide some direct compensation to the hostages, although the amount ($50/day) seems insultingly paltry. Victims of Terrorism Compensation Act, 5 U.S.C. § 5569 (2006); *see also* Pub. L. No. 99–399, 100 Stat. 853, § 802 (1986). Congress has recently renewed efforts to increase the victims' compensation to as much as $10,000 per day of captivity, i.e., $4.4 million for each victim. Both the Senate and House versions of the bill aim to ratify the Accords' preclusion of direct legal action against Iran, but the Senate bill would compensate only from fines paid by companies that violate the trade embargo with Iran, whereas the House version shows less fidelity to the Accords and would attempt to tap "any funds or property in which Iran has an interest" over which the U.S. has access. *Compare* Justice for Former American Hostages in Iran Act of 2013, S. 559, 113th Cong. (2013), *with* Justice for the American Diplomats Held Hostage in Tehran Act, H.R. 904, 113th Cong. (2013). My arguments suggest we should favor the Senate's approach.

parallel this distinction between initiated and scripted promises, rather than permitting all promises made under duress to be voided at the discretion of the promisor?

My answer draws on a conception of the larger mission and broader meaning of contract law, to which I can only gesture here. Contract law is the primary social institution dedicated to both the facilitation of promises as well as their enforcement, while simultaneously operating as one component of our joint project of creating social resources and distributing them in a fair manner. This is an ideal description. I acknowledge that the actual institutions within this joint project fall substantially short of achieving this joint aim. (Still, contract law itself is not the major offender here in failing to instantiate distributive justice. That finger should be pointed in the general direction of property law and our tax system.)

One way to consider what promises we should legally enforce is to pose the broader questions: First, to what sorts of promises do we wish to lend our collective efforts to facilitate and to enforce? Second, to what sorts of parties do we wish to lend our collective assistance to aid in their efforts to form and execute promises? Third, what sorts of circumstances do we judge as appropriate situations for commitment and exchange?

Of course, contract law should accommodate the ability of citizens to fulfill their duties and live moral lives. Hence, as with the current law on duress, it should not prohibit or interfere with performance by willing promisors. But, were the legal institution of contract to enforce promises made under duress in private suits between coercers and the coerced, it would throw the weight of the community behind the aims of the coercer, even though the moral argument for fidelity does not establish any moral right or claim of the promisee to performance. Without such a claim, the community's joining forces with the coercer seems (highly) inappropriate, given the injustice of the coercing agent's behavior and the injustice of the circumstances the coercing agent created that elicited an agreement. Or, in other words, given the larger portfolio of contract law, the enforcement of promises made under duress would not merely affirm the moral maxim of fidelity for initiated promises, but would also endorse the creation, as well as the resolution, of the flawed circumstances of formation. Because there is reason unequivocally to condemn the circumstances the mugger generates that inspire initiated promises, we have strong reason to refuse to lend any assistance to the mugger in enforcing the promise. Although it is sometimes good for victims to initiate meaningful promises when under duress, the community's refusal to enforce such promises operates as a decisive statement to the mugger that he may not treat another's unjust vulnerability as a valid opportunity for extracting (or inspiring) commitments, particularly when he generated that vulnerability.

Promising vs. More Active Engagement
Another Version of the Dilemma

At this point, it may appear there is a danger that another version of the dilemma may emerge, one that resembles the prudential dilemma I put aside earlier, but in a more complex form that incorporates the moral resources that promising affords. Recognizing initiated promises as binding not only offers victims opportunities to negotiate an exit from duress, but also to play an active role in ending conflict in a manner that involves the partly successful exertion and recognition of their agency. That active role already constitutes a form of moral progress. It also offers a unique sort of opportunity to initiate a process of moral change in a compromised moral agent, one that may occur absent the fairly remote contingencies of capture or complete persuasion. But, protecting and deploying these moral resources may make coercion more likely to occur—a moral disaster in its own right. Muggers and other criminals may be more likely to resort to coercion if they believe that they may be able, thereby, to extract a binding promise that is in their interest.[32]

I am not persuaded that this is a true dilemma. First, this problem does not arrive at what we might call the level of *semi-ideal* theory, that is the level at which the rules of moral behavior are public, although some members of the community remain morally challenged and are not fully

---

[32] Analogous, weighty concerns bear on the contemporary practice of slave redemption, especially in the Sudan. Human rights advocates worry that paying slaveholders to free slaves will generate a market that encourages greater levels of kidnapping and enslavement by people who wish to take advantage of redemption programs. *See* Kwame Anthony Appiah & Martin Bunzl, *Introduction, in* BUYING FREEDOM: THE ETHICS AND ECONOMICS OF SLAVE REDEMPTION 1, 1–5 (Kwame Anthony Appiah & Martin Bunzl eds., 2007) [hereafter BUYING FREEDOM]; Dean S. Karlan & Alan B. Krueger, *Some Simple Analytics of Slave Redemption, in* BUYING FREEDOM, *supra*, at 9; Carol Ann Rogers & Kenneth A. Swinnerton, *Slave Redemption: When It Takes Time to Redeem Slaves, in* BUYING FREEDOM, *supra*, at 20; Arnab K. Basu & Nancy H. Chau, *An Exploration of the Worst Forms of Child Labor: Is Redemption a Viable Option, in* BUYING FREEDOM, *supra*, at 37, 54–61. One uncontestable point that emerges from these discussions is that freeing people, whether from slavery or more temporary forms of duress, should not be approached solely as an episodic event, but rather must be coupled with larger social efforts to ameliorate the social conditions that give rise to the resort to duress.

compliant. As I argued earlier, my position offers no refuge to those who exert duress in the hopes of extracting a promise. Those promises would be "scripted," in my sense, and would not bind. So a rule that judged only initiated promises to be binding would not, rationally, provide an incentive for someone to initiate coercion in the hopes of extracting a binding promise.

But, understandably, this answer may feel unsatisfying. Stepping outside of semi-ideal theory, if victims of duress honor their initiated promises, one may worry that the misleading, external appearance will be that coercion pays. Even if the coercion inspired by this appearance will not generate binding promises, more coercion may nevertheless be inspired by the appearance of a reward. Further, we may not, in the moment or soon thereafter, be able to discern whether any particular bout of coercion was independently prompted or inspired by the misleading appearance that coercion might yield a remunerative offer. That is to say, we may not be able to tell whether an elicited promise is scripted or initiated. So, the concern is that a rule of honoring initiated promises may provoke more coercion and may result in more unjust payouts than would occur absent such a rule.

It is difficult to assess how great of a concern this is. Evaluating the probabilities here requires a great deal of situational knowledge and therefore defies general assessment. As with the prudential dilemma, it seems difficult, if not misguided, to try to evaluate the probabilities in any general way, given the rather complex synergistic variables, including the particular rate of frequency of duress and promising, other situational variables that influence crime, the mitigating effects of any moral progress made through establishing channels of trust and communication, as well as how necessary work on other fronts to eliminate the more significant causes of violence interacts with efforts to establish relationships of trust.

Still, the epistemic elusiveness of the degree of the risk does not offer much solace. One may reasonably find it difficult to shake the concern entirely. Yet, for my purposes, it is slightly off-topic. Because this version of the objection gains traction from the prediction that an observed activity will give rise to a mistaken inference, the objection really attaches more to the question of *whether* and *when* to initiate promises under duress, not whether to breach initiated promises under duress once they are made. That is, this objection does not challenge my core contention that to preserve the moral opportunities that initiated promises represent, it is important to honor them. Even if a concern about providing incentives to crime counsels against frequent initiations, nonetheless that reticence is entirely consistent with the conviction that one should honor initiated promises in order to retain the possibility of a reasoned resolution of conflict and to promote the forging of connections, even in strained circumstances. Otherwise, resigning ourselves to capitulation or brute force are the only options to terminate conflict once it has begun. Not all circumstances may be propitious for the option's regular use, but the option should be preserved for those situations where it may be used without triggering an aggravated cycle of violence.

Should One Ever Initiate a Promise Under Duress?

The rationale behind this argument for honoring whatever initiated promises happen to be made, however, suggests that the protected opportunity to advance credible initiated promises should be used, at least on some occasions; some initiated promises should be made. That is, it is not the sort of option that one preserves as viable but hopes never to use, as with the example of nuclear threat. This is the kind of option one preserves as viable in the hope that circumstances will sometimes permit its deployment. Against this idea, further objections might be advanced questioning whether victims should ever use this option.

Despite the possible collateral moral rewards, initiating a promise that carries moral force, when under duress, may seem to conflict with vindicating one's duties to self. In *Murder and Mayhem*, Barbara Herman offers a Kantian argument for self-defense and contends: "[A] maxim of aggression or violence involves . . . the discounting of my agency. The aggressor would use me (take my life) for his purposes. . . . This gives more than permission for an act of self-defense when that is necessary to resist the aggression. It imposes a requirement that aggression be resisted. Though I may not be able to prevent the aggressor's success, I may not be passive in the face of aggression. Passivity here is like complicity."[33]

One way to understand my argument is in the spirit of Herman's position. My suggestion is that such resistance to disrespect for rational agency may come not merely through the mechanism of physical self-defense, but also through victim-initiated negotiation and engagement as a kind of constructive resistance to the initial disrespect shown by the aggressor.[34]

[33] HERMAN, MORAL JUDGMENT, *supra* note 6, at 129.

[34] Herman gives no indication that physical self-defense is the only appropriate mode of resistance, and in other contexts she stresses the value of innovative remedies. See, for ex-

But, for some, her demand we not be passive and complicit might be thought to raise some objections to my claims. Wouldn't it be preferable, from the perspective of standing up for rational agency, not to recognize the coercer as a negotiating partner, not to give his bargaining position the respect of recognition (given its provenance), and, instead, to try to evade or reduce the success of the duress?[35] Negotiation involves some measure of acknowledgment of the other party as an eligible negotiation partner; this may seem inappropriate, whereas more active forms of resistance and even capitulation do not involve such misplaced forms of recognition. Further, a norm of honoring such promises may permit wrongdoers to profit from illegitimate methods, while subjecting victims to (further) humiliation.[36]

In response, we might distinguish endorsement of or acquiescence in the coercer's maxim from recognition of the coercer's power to wreak destruction. Negotiation involves the latter but need not amount to the former. The relevant resistance comes through the assertion of an independent point of view and the effort to gain recognition of it by one's oppressor. The idea that we might achieve moral progress without some of the undeserving profiting along the way seems unhelpfully utopian, and not merely because their profit is predictable. So too it seems overly fastidious to think that moral progress is not worth it at that price.

If one instead thought that illegitimate starting points precluded all negotiations or that transacting with bad agents was morally excluded on the grounds that it amounted to accepting the legitimacy of their position, then our only methods of effecting moral transformation would be through pure speech and efforts at persuasion; our only methods of self-protection in the interim would be withdrawal or forceful confrontation. Although I am a believer in the power of argument, alongside, I suspect, most readers who have bothered to persist to this point, I don't kid my-

---

ample, her discussion of the South African Truth and Reconciliation Process in HERMAN, MORAL LITERACY, *supra* note 6, at 319–30.

[35] Prior to the Civil War, a fierce and fascinating debate raged among abolitionists over the morality of paying slaveholders to release slaves from slavery. Moral repugnance to compensating slaveholders or giving the appearance of recognizing the legitimacy of the slaveholder's bargaining position fueled some of the resistance to the practice, although many prominent opponents showed greater ambivalence when faced with the ability to engineer the release of a particular person. *See* Margaret M.R. Kellow, *Conflicting Imperatives: Black and White American Abolitionists Debate Slave Redemption, in* BUYING FREEDOM, *supra* note 32, at 200; John Stauffer, *Frederick Douglass and the Politics of Slave Redemptions, in* BUYING FREEDOM, *supra* note 32, at 213.

[36] This objection was pressed by Judith Jarvis Thomson in conversation and correspondence.

self that moral transformation happens merely and completely by thumbing through *Ethics, Philosophy and Public Affairs*, the *Boston Review*, and the *Philosophical Review*. I simultaneously think every public library should subscribe to these journals and that even if that pipe dream were realized, the crime rate wouldn't plummet any time soon.

Moral growth, insight, and transformation often depend upon complex, mediated discoveries arising in the context of relationships with others and the navigation of both similarity and difference.[37] Neither fully principled revolutions nor, on the individual side, epiphanic conversions are commonplace. Sometimes those engaged in wrongdoing are engaged in the sort of momentary weakness of the will from which they could be prodded to emerge on the spot; more often, I fear, the orientation toward wrongdoing is more deeply rooted in character—in rationalizations and wrong-headed orientations toward circumstances that in turn infuse and inform the underlying architecture of desire and perceptions of others, social relationships, and therefore what actions that affect others are choice-worthy. This sort of bunker does not yield readily to reasoned pleading. Moral conversion often takes time. It typically isn't the sort of learning that involves adding new data to a growing archive with a prefabricated, highly structured catalog and prelabeled shelves waiting to be filled. It involves adding and altering perspectives and reasons in ways that require revisions of the entire internal infrastructure.

If so, in the short and medium term, while we protest and wait for pure forms of moral persuasion to latch on and take full root, the alternatives are: stagnation, in which we are subject to unjust force and either capitulate to it or manage to escape; segregation and evasion of unreliable moral agents; or, confrontation through violence. The latter two options may leave wrongdoers shorn of wrongful profits but will also exclude them from joint participation in the moral perspective. These options do not seem notably preferable, in principle or in fact, to negotiated solutions that may *risk* allowing coercers to benefit from malfeasance, but that also involve them with us in joint action that has imperfect, but rudimentary, moral elements and that also marks the beginning of a relationship of trust. The hope would be for that beginning, at least on some occasions, to mature into something more lasting and complete.

Of course, on other occasions, the opportunity would not be well used. Acting in a trustworthy way toward the untrustworthy involves

---

[37] *See, e.g.,* HERMAN, MORAL LITERACY, *supra* note 6, at 130–53; *see also* Seana Valentine Shiffrin, *What Is Really Wrong with Compelled Association?*, 99 Nw. U. L. REV 839, 842 (2004).

risks that may be exploited and frequently should not be taken. I am not arguing that we should always expose our flank to those on a coercive spree, in the naïve hope that a show of moral imagination will spark cooperation and compromise. Interactions with the wicked often require more straightforward methods of protection, defense, and resistance. Sometimes, it is foolhardy to hope that a true opportunity for gradual change presents itself. We may be in a "reiterating game" in which our offered compromise will only contribute to a structural pattern of ongoing domination. That's wrong.[38]

What of the objection that having to honor the promise is cruel and humiliating to the victim by, in effect, prolonging her victimization and her subjection to a coercive force? Having to continue a relationship with the mugger and to serve his interests cannot be fair to the victim. Consideration of the burden that promissory fulfillment would represent for the victim thus casts doubt upon my contention that the promise exerts moral force.

I agree that the emotional burden the victim may experience upon fulfillment (or its contemplation) is a relevant factor in considering whether to initiate a promise at all. It is also relevant to the later questions of whether the promise has moral force and/or whether, even if it does, nonperformance may be excused. I am inclined to think that the impact on the victim speaks to excuse rather than justification for breach, partly because some victims, including many institutional organizations and representatives subject to coercion, may not experience an emotional burden. Further, some victims may reasonably regard the initiated promise and the negotiated solution as an important exercise of their agency under demanding conditions and regard the fulfillment of the promise as a vindication of their honor. The reasonableness of both reactions strikes me as evidence for the view that a strongly felt emotional burden may constitute a complete excuse for nonperformance but not a reason to think the promise itself lacks moral force.

To pick up a related strand: does my argument suggest that I condemn capitulation to duress or that I regard evasion of duress or unobtrusive efforts to mitigate its effectiveness as poor substitutes for negotiation? No, and a qualified yes. Obviously, in many situations, resistance to duress in any form may not be a reasonable, viable option because it is ei-

---

[38] I wrote this paragraph during the first bout of prolonged shenanigans in 2011 over the question of whether to raise the debt ceiling. These circumstances seemed to exemplify the sort of situation in which one (President Obama) should stop attempting to offer more to the ransomers and instead take a harder line.

ther unsafe or simply psychologically unavailable to the threatened agent. Moreover, some cases of capitulation involve courage: whether through enduring a painful loss because resistance would hurt oneself or others to an intolerable extent, or because capitulation may falsely *appear* to others to compromise one's principles or one's dignity. I have in mind here what I take to be the courageous decision of the *New York Times* and the *Washington Post* to publish Ted Kaczynski's manifesto in response to his threat, in the alternative, to continue killing.[39]

Still, where either is possible, is there a reason to prefer evasion and mitigation to negotiation? Take this case: the robber says, "Your wallet or I do you harm." I happen to be a magician. My wallet has a hidden slit that allows me to extract some money surreptitiously. As I hand it over, I could palm $100 without the robber noticing; thereby I would exert my own will without conditioning it on the permission of someone who illegitimately asserts authority over me, frustrate some of the robber's illicit aim, and mitigate the effect of the duress. Or, I could explain my need for the $100 to the robber and get him to agree that I will retain it, perhaps by promising something else of interest to him. Is there a clearly superior alternative? In the first case, the bad will's authority is refused and (partially) frustrated; in the second, the bad will is partly recognized and partly altered. There is a certain pride to be had in the moment of surreptitious subversion when contrasted with that of meek capitulation. Still, what is absent from the subversion as compared to the negotiation scenario, is the forging of a connection through honest and publicly transparent mechanisms of transaction.

I doubt there is a straightforward, uniformly applicable answer to the question of which strategy is morally preferable. Either involves moral sacrifice. I am certainly not claiming that it is morally untoward for individuals to take precautions at night and avoid dark alleys. On the other hand, even were a general social practice and policy of containment and avoidance of those with criminal intent feasible and we could, thereby, achieve perfect frustration of criminal aims, there is something morally inadequate about that approach to moral imperfection, even coupled with a side-project of preaching to trigger conversion. That stance may satisfy an imperative to frustrate the bad will, but it runs a substantial risk that it will not do much to contribute to our joint moral evolution.

---

[39] *See* Howard Kurtz, *Unabomber Manuscript Is Published*, WASH. POST, Sept. 19, 1995, at A01.

Our responsiveness to reasons is often mediated and happens indirectly through the construction of character. The development, maintenance, and evolution of moral character among well-functioning agents generally depend upon a richly textured social atmosphere of supportive relationships and well-structured institutions. If so, why think access to those variegated resources any less important for those with actively compromised moral agency? We have reason to think that moral progress by individuals and by communities depends upon the gradual building of relationships and the slow accretion of trust, rather than the maintenance of distance. It depends on what is at risk and what might be achieved, but in some circumstances, more contact and engagement may be required even at the cost of taking the initiative to give up some of what one would otherwise be entitled to keep.

CHAPTER THREE

A Thinker-Based Approach to Freedom of Speech

Chapter One argued that because of its potential for precision and directness, discursive communication plays a special role in our moral lives. Its reliability renders possible, for example, commitments of trust under fraught circumstances of the kind that I have just discussed in Chapter Two. The need to safeguard its ability to play that role undergirds the wrong of lying in particular. Although it has not been my focus, deception also threatens the full achievement of these interests. Both the prohibition on lying and the prohibition on wrongful deception work, in different ways, to protect the ability of listeners to rely on speech to develop understandings of one another and of the world. These understandings are essential for our mutual flourishing, for the apprehension and discharge of our moral obligations to one another as individuals, and to enable us to act well, in concert, and pursue our collective moral ends.

In this chapter, I draw some connections between these values and freedom of speech. In the chapters that follow, I explore the ramifications of these connections to questions raised by the legal regulation of lies on the one hand, and the use of the lies by social and legal institutions on the other. In this chapter, I argue that, roughly speaking, the same interests that undergird the major ethical prohibitions relating to communication (the strict prohibition on lying and the more variegated prohibitions on deception) also play a role in undergirding freedom of thought and freedom of communication, two related and mutually dependent freedoms that I conjoin under the label "freedom of speech."

As I argued in Chapter One, the prohibition on lying protects the meaningfulness and effectiveness of sincere testimony as a source of knowledge about the beliefs of the speaker. The prohibition on (wrongful) deception protects the ability of listeners to make and rely upon reasonable inferences from the content of such sincere testimony (and from other forms of communicative behavior), while also protecting the ability of speakers to convey information, broadly speaking, effectively. Both prohibitions facilitate the exercise of our abilities to engage in cooperative epistemic relations with one another, relations that have tremendous moral significance.

But, these prohibitions, on their own, would do little to fulfill these functions. They must serve as background complements within an environment that permits and encourages freedom of thought and communication. Unless the social and political environment *allows* (and encourages) sincere communication, the moral prohibitions that prevent its corruption would achieve little. Equally fundamental is our having something to say in the first place. This demands that we ensure an environment in which we are able to develop and exercise our capacities for cultivating and conveying our thoughts, beliefs, and other mental states. My claim is that freedom of speech is a crucial component of such an environment.

I will draw these connections by arguing that the foundation of free speech protection is that freedom of speech is necessary for the development and maintenance of the self *qua* thinker, for freedom of thought, and for discharging other aspects of our moral relations. My argument has two strands. First, sincere and free expression plays a special, though not exclusive, role in the development of the mind and personality of each agent *qua* thinker. Second, the opportunity to engage in free-ranging, sincere communication is an essential condition for the revelation of the information necessary to fully execute our duties to one another (including supporting the full development of one another as thinkers) and to enable us to govern in concert as equals.

My interest in making this argument extends beyond noting the continuity between the prohibitions on lying and wrongful deception and freedom of speech. Taking a thinker-oriented approach to freedom of speech offers a stronger foundation for freedom of speech protections than competing theoretical approaches and affords free speech theory a more natural way to represent the unity between freedom of thought and freedom of communication.

Before proceeding, three caveats are in order. First, in stressing that freedom of speech is an important social and political condition of our realizing, exercising, and fulfilling our moral agency, I do not mean to suggest that the connection between freedom of speech and moral agency exhausts the significance of freedom of speech. As will become clear from the ensuing discussion, agents have reasons to value freedom of speech that bear only an indirect connection to their realization or exercise of their moral agency. Freedom of speech plays a wide variety of roles in our individual lives and in our social lives together. Indeed, because we have obligations to ensure that each person has the opportunity to develop her capacities for thought and to live an autonomous life, perforce we are obliged to support freedom of speech.

Nevertheless, one reason to call specific attention to the connections between freedom of communication, freedom of thought, and moral agency is to bypass a common concern about individual-centered autonomy theories of freedom of speech. Some worry that emphasizing the tight connection between freedom of speech and the conditions facilitating an autonomous life represents an inappropriate foundation for a liberal theory, because it is not the role of the liberal state to favor or promote a particular form of life or conception of the good. I am not persuaded that protecting *the opportunity* to live an autonomous life transgresses any plausible version of this concern, but I emphasize the connection between freedom of speech and moral agency to underscore that this issue need not be confronted. In addition to respecting the human right to develop and function as free thinkers, governments have independent reasons to respect freedom of speech. Freedom of speech is a precondition of fostering moral agency, which in turn is a presupposition of a functioning government of equals—a commitment even the sparest liberal theories affirm.

Second, although my argument about lying has paid special attention to discursive communication between agents, my claims about freedom of speech are not so limited. I do not mean to confine the argument to highly articulate, discursive, interpersonal communication. My arguments extend to a variety of forms of nondiscursive communication, including art, music, and dance, and other avenues of emotional expression. The mental contents that figure in the thinker's well-functioning as such include not only implicit and explicit theoretical and practical reasoning but also the emotions, nondiscursive thoughts, images, sounds, and other perceptions and sensations, as well as the workings of the imagination. My claims also extend to representations of mental content that are not necessarily directed at or shared with others. Although it is a little semantically awkward, I group freedom of thought and freedom of communication together under "freedom of speech," both for convenience and because, under the U.S. Constitution, that label covers both the mental freedom to "speak" to oneself and the freedom to "speak" to others.

Finally, to exemplify how the thinker-based approach may both illuminate a specific legal system of protection and serve as a critical lever for
its reform, I make repeated reference to, and arguments about, the First
Amendment, the free speech protection contained in the U.S. Constitution and enforced within a constitutional scheme that features strong judicial review. Nonetheless, the philosophical core of my argument is not
restricted to the U.S. context, and my emphasis is on the theoretical foundations for any free speech protection in any jurisdiction.

Motivating a Thinker-Based Approach

When it appeals to individual autonomy, contemporary free speech theory tends to ground the free speech protection in the fundamental interests of the listener *or* the fundamental interests of the speaker. Listener-
based approaches stress the interest listeners have in access to information
and the opinions of their fellow citizens so as to make up their own minds
about matters of the day; they stress the illegitimacy of government prohibitions that seek to restrict such access on grounds of distrust, such as
the suspicion that listeners will make poor judgments or be persuaded of
disfavored views.[1] Speaker-based approaches stress the interest speakers
have, as autonomous agents, in expressing themselves and their ideas.
While speakers' expressions will often benefit listeners, speaker-based approaches stress that the speaker's interest does not depend upon her enhancing the understanding of any listeners or conveying an original opinion or idea; each speaker has a fundamental interest in her own articulation
of her ideas—in having the opportunity to be the one who expresses them,
as an aspect of self-governance, whether or not those ideas are already in
the public domain, have been better crafted by others, or are destined
never to reach an audience.[2] When it takes a more social approach, contemporary free speech theory looks either to the conditions of a functioning, often deliberative, democracy[3] or the optimal conditions that would

[1] *See* Thomas Scanlon, *A Theory of Freedom of Expression*, 1 PHIL. & PUB. AFF. 204
(1972), reprinted in T.M. SCANLON, THE DIFFICULTY OF TOLERANCE 6, 14–15 (2003);
David A. Strauss, *Persuasion, Autonomy, and Freedom of Expression*, 91 COLUM. L. REV.
334, 335–60 (1991). Scanlon's position on freedom of speech evolved to become more
complex and to accommodate a greater range of values. *See* T.M. Scanlon, Jr., *Freedom of
Expression and Categories of Expression*, 40 U. PITT. L. REV. 519 (1979), *reprinted in*
SCANLON, *supra*, at 84.

[2] *See, e.g.*, C. EDWIN BAKER, HUMAN LIBERTY AND FREEDOM OF SPEECH 47–69 (1989);
C. Edwin Baker, *Autonomy and Free Speech*, 27 CONST. COMMENT. 251 (2011).

[3] The classic modern articulation of the democracy theory was Alexander Meiklejohn's.

facilitate our, together, exposing and ascertaining the truth or important truths.[4] The literature explores the contest between these approaches, tallying their theoretical virtues as well as their varying abilities to capture fundamental intuitions as to which speech must be protected.[5]

Although the discussion of that contest yields interesting insights into the strengths and limitations of each approach on its own, the pitched battle between them has long puzzled me, even granting the impulse to identify a dominant unifying theory. Any one of these approaches seems objectionably partial and mysteriously so. First, those theories that focus on access to or eliciting potentially useful content, i.e., all but speaker-based theories, struggle to explain why speakers with redundant or repetitive messages to which listeners have plentiful access nevertheless should garner fundamental protection, irrespective of whether the government motive for regulation is itself defective. The same difficulty besets explaining protection for speakers who do not communicate with listeners, but speak to themselves in fora like private diaries. Likewise, some listener-oriented theories struggle to explain why speakers with ill-formed or incoherent messages, e.g., some of the speech of young children or the mentally disabled, should be afforded fundamental protections. Second, by focusing on access to and restrictions on external, public speech, rather than on the processes behind its production, both speaker-based and listener-based theories struggle to explain why efforts at mind-

---

See ALEXANDER MEIKLEJOHN, FREE SPEECH AND RELATION TO SELF-GOVERNMENT 11–27 (1948). For more contemporary and sophisticated articulations, see Joshua Cohen, *Freedom of Expression*, 22 PHIL. & PUB. AFF. 207 (1993), *reprinted in* JOSHUA COHEN, PHILOSOPHY, POLITICS, DEMOCRACY 98 (2009); Joshua Cohen, *Democracy and Liberty, in* DELIBERATIVE DEMOCRACY 185 (Jon Elster ed., 1998), *reprinted in* PHILOSOPHY, POLITICS, DEMOCRACY, *supra*, at 223; Joshua Cohen, *Deliberation and Democratic Legitimacy, in* DELIBERATIVE DEMOCRACY 67 (James Bohman & William Rehg eds., 1997), *reprinted in* PHILOSOPHY, POLITICS, AND DEMOCRACY, *supra*, at 16; Robert Post, *Participatory Democracy and Free Speech*, 97 VA. L. REV. 477 (2011); James Weinstein, *Participatory Democracy as the Central Value of American Free Speech Doctrine*, 97 VA. L. REV. 491 (2011).

[4] Mill is often interpreted as a truth-theorist, although his complex theory also has affiliations with speaker, listener, and thinker-based theories. *See generally* JOHN STUART MILL, *On Liberty, in* ON LIBERTY AND OTHER ESSAYS 20 (John Gray ed., 1988) (1859).

[5] More negatively tinged theories defend freedom of speech protections in terms of the precautions we should adopt to handcuff governments from engaging in abusive practices. Such cautionary theories do not presuppose a community of free thinkers, as I proceed to allege the other theories do. Although they constitute a significant line of reasoning about freedom of speech, because they are purely pragmatic, on their own, they fail to capture why freedom of speech is a foundational protection and they tend to ground slighter protection than seems requisite. They may play a supplementary role, however, in explaining why state violations of free speech rights may present a particular hazard that merits discrete protections.

control and brainwashing violate freedom of speech unless they implicitly advert to an approach more focused on the thinker behind the speaker or listener. Third, theories that stress the integral role of free speech in contributing to the discovery of important truths or facilitating or legitimating democratic deliberation struggle ineffectually to offer a direct defense for interpersonal discourse about personal matters, whether significant or picayune, as well as nondiscursive artistic expression, especially abstract artistic expression.[6]

One obvious way to patch the holes is to combine the insights of these theories by adverting to different theories for different needs. To be sure, there is much to be said for the amalgamated or eclectic approach.[7] From the outset, there is no reason to assume that there is a single best theory of freedom of speech that does it all. But, eclectic, piecemeal theories confront familiar problems of asking how the pieces fit together and which jagged edge is to be filed down when conflicts between the theoretical impulses arise.

The other attractive approach is to ask whether these are really discrete approaches or whether, instead, a deeper connection unifies them. Speaker-oriented theories, listener-oriented theories, truth-eliciting theories, and democracy theories all presuppose, in one way or another, that there is a developed thinker behind the scenes—one who speaks, listens, or contributes to government, and whose self-expression, reactions to

---

[6] See, for example, Robert Post's startling judgment that it is a "close case [] . . . whether family conversations about presidential politics should be protected as public discourse . . . ." Robert Post, *Participatory Democracy as a Theory of Free Speech: A Reply*, 97 VA. L. REV. 617, 623 (2011); see also Weinstein, *supra* note 3, at 496 n. 45. By contrast, Joshua Cohen offers a broader democratic account of free expression, one grounded in his deliberative democratic approach. His approach shows sensitivity to the interests of the citizen *qua* thinker and provides a more plausible grounding than do many other democratic theories for art, religious speech, erotic speech, and other forms of speech that are not explicitly or even indirectly political. *See e.g.*, Joshua Cohen, *Deliberation and Democratic Legitimacy, supra* note 3, *reprinted in* PHILOSOPHY, POLITICS, AND DEMOCRACY, 16, 32–34 (2009). Although our approaches are fairly congenial, Cohen's case for rights of personal, nonpolitical expression stresses what the citizen "reasonably takes to be compelling considerations" or "substantial reasons" for expression. *See e.g.*, Joshua Cohen, *Freedom of Expression, supra* note 3, *reprinted in* PHILOSOPHY, POLITICS, DEMOCRACY 98, 114–20 (2009); Joshua Cohen, *Democracy and Liberty, supra* note 3, *reprinted in* PHILOSOPHY, POLITICS, DEMOCRACY, *supra*, at 223, 248–54. I worry that this emphasis suggests too high a standard to meet for grounding protection for quotidian everyday speech. Many citizens' reasons for their speech, including their interpersonal speech, are not propelled by an intense need, yet in my view do not present any weaker a case for protection.

[7] *See, e.g.*, STEVEN H. SHIFFRIN, THE FIRST AMENDMENT, DEMOCRACY AND ROMANCE 132–39 (1990).

information and others' expression, and contributions to government are, at least potentially, of sufficient moment that they merit fundamental protection. Each contestant theory only makes sense if the individual mind and its free operation (a notion I will say more about below) is valued and treated with respect. If we did not regard the autonomy of the individual *mind* as important, it is hard to see why we would value its expression, its inputs, or its outputs in the way that each of these theories do.[8] Still, although speaker, listener, and democracy theories share the presupposition that the autonomous thinker fundamentally matters, each starts from an intermediate point and hones in on one activity of the thinker, rather than on the thinker herself. Reasoning from the standpoint of the thinker and her interests can yield a more comprehensive, unified foundation for freedom of speech protection than may be achieved by starting from a partial intermediate point.

My claim is that the interests and needs of the underlying thinker presupposed by all of these theories underwrite a freedom of speech protection that unites these only seemingly disparate approaches and yields a fairly broad justificatory foundation for the freedom of speech protection.[9] I don't claim that a thinker-based theory can do it all. Some degree

---

[8] Some purely instrumental theories of freedom of speech that focus on the importance of controlling the excesses of state authority may differ on this point.

[9] Other authors have explored aspects of thinker-based approaches as well, although from different angles and with different emphases. *See, e.g.,* CHARLES FRIED, MODERN LIBERTY 95–123 (2007); Charles Fried, *The New First Amendment Jurisprudence: A Threat to Liberty,* 59 U. CHI. L. REV. 225 (1992); Dana Remus Irwin, *Freedom of Thought: The First Amendment and the Scientific Method,* 2005 WIS. L. REV. 1479; Christina E. Wells, *Reinvigorating Autonomy: Freedom and Responsibility in the Supreme Court's First Amendment Jurisprudence,* 32 HARV. C.R.-C.L. L. REV. 159 (1997); Neil M. Richards, *Informational Privacy,* 87 TEX. L. REV. 387 (2008); TIMOTHY MACKLEM, INDEPENDENCE OF MIND 1–32 (2006); SUSAN WILLIAMS, TRUTH, AUTONOMY, AND SPEECH 130–229 (2004). Martin Redish's stress on individual self-realization does not mention free thought in particular, but he sounds some themes about the relationship between free speech, deliberation, and self-development. *See* Martin H. Redish & Abby Marie Mollen, *Understanding Post's and Meiklejohn's Mistakes: The Central Role of Adversary Democracy in the Theory of Free Expression,* 103 NW. U. L. REV. 1303, 1363–64 (2009); Martin H. Redish, *The Value of Free Speech,* 130 U. PA. L. REV. 591 (1982). In earlier work, I explored the ramifications of a thinker-based approach for compelled speech with Vincent Blasi, in Vincent Blasi & Seana V. Shiffrin, *The Story of* West Virginia State Board of Education v. Barnette: *The Pledge of Allegiance and Freedom of Thought, in* CONSTITUTIONAL LAW STORIES 409 (Michael Dorf ed., 2d ed. 2009) and its ramifications for compelled association in Seana Valentine Shiffrin, *What is Really Wrong with Compelled Association?* 99 NW. U. L. REV. 839 (2005). An earlier version of this material as well as replies by critics, including Vincent Blasi, appear in *Symposium: Individual Autonomy and Free Speech,* 27 CONST. COMMENT. 249 (2011).

of eclecticism is inevitable, and other values will bear on how particular cases or areas of free speech doctrine should be resolved. But, a thinker-based approach can establish some fundamental priorities and offer some structure that provides a framework for the incorporation of these other values. It also reveals how the ethical foundations of freedom of communication are connected to their ethical limits.

Suppose we begin with the following ideas about our valuable status as distinctively individual thinkers. First, we are individual human agents with significant (though importantly imperfect) rational capacities, emotional capacities, moral capacities, perceptual capacities, and capacities of sentience that overlap and exert influence upon one another. Second, our possession and exercise of these capacities correctly constitute the core of what we value about ourselves. Finally, our particular mix, development, and exercise of these capacities, in conjunction with our physical attributes, correctly constitute what makes us the distinctive individuals that we are within our shared historical and social milieu. Asking what social and legal conditions are necessary to respect these capacities and their value, I claim, yields a powerful theory of freedom of speech that encompasses both freedom of thought and freedom of communication, with oneself and with others.

To investigate what conditions are necessary to support these capacities and their meaningful exercise, it may help to delineate some of the core interests of the thinker as such. I posit that in light of the value of these capacities and the interest those possessing them have in exercising them, every individual, rational, *human* agent *qua* thinker in community with other thinkers has specific interests in:

a. *A developed capacity for practical and theoretical thought.* Each thinker has a fundamental interest in developing her mental capacities to be receptive of, appreciative of, and responsive to reasons and facts in practical and theoretical thought, i.e., to be aware of and appropriately responsive to the true, the false, and the unknown.

b. *Apprehending the truth.* Each thinker has a fundamental interest in believing and understanding true things about herself, including the contents of her mind, and the features and forces of the environment from which she emerges and in which she interacts.

c. *Exercising the imagination.* In addition, each thinker has a fundamental interest in understanding and intellectually exploring nonexistent possible and impossible environments. Such mental activities allow agents the ability to conceive of the future and what could be as well as what could have been. Further, the ability to explore the nonexistent and impossible provides an opportunity for the exercise of the philosophical capacities and the other parts of the imagination.[10]

d. *Moral agency.* Each thinker has a fundamental interest in acquiring the relevant knowledge base and character traits as well as forming the relevant thoughts and intentions to comply with the requirements of morality. (This interest, of course, may already be contained in the previously articulated interests in developing the capacity for practical and theoretical thought, apprehending the truth, and exercising the imagination [a–c].)

e. *Becoming a distinctive individual.* Each thinker has a fundamental interest in developing a personality and engaging more broadly in a mental life that, while responsive to reasons and facts, is distinguished from others' personalities by individuating features, emotions, reactions, traits, thoughts, and experiences that contribute to a distinctive perspective that embodies and represents each individual's separateness as a person.

f. *Responding authentically.* Each thinker has a fundamental interest in pursuing (a–e) through processes that represent free and authentic forms of internal creation and recognition. By this, I mean roughly that agents have an interest in forming thoughts, beliefs, practical judgments, intentions, and other mental contents on the basis of reasons, perceptions, and reactions through processes that, in the main and over the long term, are independent of distortive influences. In saying these processes are independent of distortive influences, I mean that the choices of what to think about and the contents of one's thoughts do not follow a trajectory fully or largely scripted by forces external to the person that are distinct from the reasons and other features of the world to which she is responding *qua* thinker.[11]

---

[10] *See* Jed Rubenfeld, *The Freedom of the Imagination*, 112 YALE L. J. 1, 38–39 (2002).

[11] In saying that distortive influences involve *external* forces, I do not mean to exclude the possibility of mental illness or dysfunction as a sort of distortive influence where that mental illness is not part of the relevant agent's identity. If the government were, through controlling environmental conditions or through medication, to induce a condition that provoked hallucinations, I would take that as an interference with the thinker's interest in responding authentically. What matters here is whether the relevant force influencing judg-

So, too, thinkers have an interest in revealing, sharing, and considering these mental contents largely at their discretion, at the time at which those contents seem to them correct, apt, or representative of themselves, as well to those to whom (and at that time) such revelations and the relationship they forge seem appropriate or desirable. These are the intellectual aspects of being an autonomous agent.

g. *Living among others.* Each thinker has a fundamental interest in living among other social, autonomous agents who have the opportunities to develop their capacities in like ways. Satisfaction of this interest does not merely serve natural desires for companionship but also crucially enables other interests *qua* thinker to be achieved, including the development of self and character, the acquisition and confirmation of knowledge, and the development and exercise of moral agency.

h. *Appropriate recognition and treatment.* Each thinker has a fundamental interest in being recognized by other agents for the person she is and having others treat her morally well.

This list may not be exhaustive, but I believe it identifies some of the more foundational and central interests that agents have, independent of their specific projects, interests, and desires, simply in virtue of their capacities for thought, broadly understood to include their capacities for autonomous deliberation and reaction, practical judgment, and moral relations. Briefly summarized, these are interests in self-development, self-knowledge, knowledge of others, others' knowledge of and respect for oneself, knowledge of the environments in which one interacts with others, opportunities for the exercise of one's intellectual capacities, including the imagination, and the intellectual prerequisites of moral relations.

Why Thinkers' Interests Support Freedom of Speech

Speech and protected opportunities to speak and think freely are necessary conditions for the realization of these interests. First, given that our minds are not directly accessible to one another, speech and expression are the only precise avenues by which one can be known *as the individual*

---

ment is external to the *person.* Such forces need not necessarily be external to her mental arena. *See also infra* note 42 with respect to the mentally ill.

one is by others. If what makes one a distinctive individual *qua person* is *largely* a matter of the contents of one's mind,[12] to be known by others requires the ability to transmit the contents of one's mind to others. Although some information about one's thoughts and beliefs may be gleaned from observation, such inferences are typically coarse-grained at best and cannot track the detail and nuance of the inner life of the observed. Communication of the contents of one's mind, primarily through linguistic means, but also through pictorial or even musical representation, uniquely furthers the interest in being known by others. It thereby makes possible complex forms of social life that demand specialization and epistemic cooperation.[13] Furthermore, it helps to develop some of the capacities prerequisite to moral agency, because successful communication demands having a sense of what others are in a position to know and understand. Practicing communication initiates the process of taking others' perspective to understand what others know and are in a position to grasp.

It is important in itself that one be known as the distinctive individual one is. It is also essential for one to be fully respected by others and therefore able to engage in full moral relations with others. Likewise, having access to the contents of others' minds (at their discretion) is essential for being able to respect them, at least insofar as some forms of respect and other moral duties involve understanding and respecting individuals as separate persons and in light of features of their individuality, including their beliefs, reasons, aims, feelings, and needs. Moreover, other forms of moral activity, as well as appreciation of the moral activity of others, require some recognition of agents' motives.

I suspect, moreover, that one cannot fully develop a complex mental world, identify its contents, evaluate them, and distinguish between those that are merely given and those one endorses, unless one has the ability to externalize bits of one's mind, formally distance those bits from one's mind, identify them as particulars, and then evaluate them to either endorse, reject, or modify them. For many people, some thoughts may only be fully identified and known to themselves if made linguistically or rep-

---

[12] I do not mean what individuates one as a creature. In that respect, physical features, including one's genetic composition and perhaps other physical, nonmental facts may be important.

[13] As discussed in Chapter One, this consideration figured large among the motivations behind Kant's views about truthfulness and lying. *See* IMMANUEL KANT, *Of Ethical Duties Towards Others, and Especially Truthfulness, in* LECTURES ON ETHICS (Peter Heath & J.B. Schneewind eds., Peter Heath trans., 1997) (27:444–55).

resentationally explicit. Many find that difficult to do using merely mental language, especially when it comes to sufficiently complex ideas; one has to externalize his or her thoughts through oral or written speech or through other forms of symbolic representation to form or identify them completely. Only then is it possible to evaluate their contents. Other thoughts and methods of tracking one's environment over time require some form of external representation because of the frailties of the human memory; to form the complex thought, one needs the device of external representation to keep track of portions of it over time.[14] The ability and opportunity to generate external representations may both make public what's already fully formed in the mind and may render possible the formation of new sorts of thoughts that cannot take full form in our limited mental space.[15]

Of course, it isn't merely the development and identification of one's thoughts that requires the use of representation and external articulation. To pursue our interest in forming true beliefs about ourselves and our environment, we need the help of others' insights and beliefs, as well as their reactions and evaluative responses to our beliefs. Others can only have the basis for responding, and the means to respond with the sort of precision that is helpful, if they are able to use speech.

My argument that rational human thinkers need access to other thinkers under conditions in which their mental contents may be known with some degree of precision, explicitly recognized as such, and reacted to, is partially but poignantly confirmed by evidence of the disastrous effects of involuntary solitary confinement. Prisoners in solitary confinement deteriorate mentally and emotionally.[16] They progressively lose their grip on reality, suffering hallucinations and paranoia; many become psychotic.[17] "Human beings rely on social contact with others to test and validate their perceptions of the environment. . . . A complete lack of social con-

---

[14] Tyler Burge, *Computer Proof, Apriori Knowledge, and Other Minds: The Sixth Philosophical Perspectives Lecture*, 32 Noûs Suppl. 1, 10–13, 19–22, 27–28 (1998); Tyler Burge, *Memory and Persons*, 112 Phil. Rev. 289, 300–03, 314–21 (2003).

[15] *See also* Macklem, *supra* note 9, at 1–32.

[16] *See, e.g.*, Woodburn Heron, *The Pathology of Boredom*, 196 Sci. Am. 52–56 (1957) (describing the rapid deterioration of cognitive and critical abilities, the inability to focus, the hallucinations, the emotional vacillations, and the distress of subjects placed in sensory and solitary isolation).

[17] *See, e.g.*, Bruce A. Arrigo & Jennifer Leslie Bullock, *The Psychological Effects of Solitary Confinement on Prisoners in Supermax Units: Reviewing What We Know and Recommending What Should Change*, 52 Int'l. J. Offender Therapy & Comp. Criminology 622, 627 (2008); Craig Haney, *Mental Health Issues in Long-Term Solitary and "Supermax" Confinement*, 49 Crime & Delinq. 124, 130–32 (2003).

tact makes it difficult to distinguish between what is real from what is not or what is external from what is internal."[18] Prisoners subject to solitary confinement suffer terrible depression, despair, and anxiety; moreover, their emotional control and stability wanes and their abilities to interact with others atrophies.[19]

Of course, prisoners in solitary confinement endure more than just the lack of conversation and the absence of interlocutors; they lack fundamental forms of control over their lives, other sorts of interactions with persons, and other forms of perceptual access to reality. But, most other prisoners lack this sort of control and lack broader forms of access to the world and yet do not suffer the same degree of mental debility, as do prisoners in solitary confinement.[20] "Whether in Walpole, or Beirut, or Hanoi, all human beings experience *isolation* as torture."[21] What seems to push them over the edge is the absence of regular, bilateral communication. My thought is that to forbid or substantially restrict free expression is not tantamount to solitary incarceration but lies on a spectrum with it: it is to institute a sort of solitary confinement outside of prison but within one's mind.

So, in short, it is essential to the appropriate development and regulation of the self, and of one's relation to others, that one have wide-ranging access to the opportunity to externalize one's mental contents, whatever they are, and therefore to the opportunity to make one's mental contents known to others in an unscripted and authentic way. It is equally essential to be able to receive others' representations, and to enjoy protection from unchosen interference with one's mental contents from processes that would disrupt or disable the operation of these processes. That is to say, free speech is essential to the development, functioning, and operation of thinkers. Further, because moral agency involves the ability to take the perspective of other people and to respond to their distinctive features as individuals, including some of their mental contents, then free speech also plays a foundational and necessary (though not sufficient) role in ensuring that citizens develop the capacity for moral agency and

[18] Arrigo & Bullock, *supra* note 17 (citing the work of Haney, *supra* note 17). Similar evidence presents itself about the effects of uncorrected hearing loss. *See* Stig Arlinger, *Negative Consequences of Uncorrected Hearing Loss—A Review*, 42 INT'L J. AUDIOLOGY 2S17–2S20 (2003) (reporting that hearing loss may reduce intellectual and cultural stimulation, "give rise to changes in the central nervous system, and may affect the development of dementia.").

[19] *See* Haney, *supra* note 17.

[20] *See id.* at 125.

[21] Atul Gawande, *Hellhole*, NEW YORKER, Mar. 30, 2009, at 36 (emphasis added).

have the opportunities and information necessary to discharge their moral duties.

Politically, these arguments should resonate with us, yielding an argument for constitutional protection for freedom of speech, both out of respect for the fundamental moral rights of the person and because a well-functioning system of social cooperation and justice presupposes that the citizenry, by and large, have active, well-developed moral personalities.[22] The successful operation of a democratic polity, as well as its meaningfulness, would also seem to depend upon citizens' generally having strong and independent capacities for thought and judgment. The development, maintenance, and operation of these capacities require open, unrestricted channels of communication.

These considerations support a free speech regime marked by three sorts of process and outcome-based constraints. A government that respected the interests of the thinker as such would refrain, whether through its activity or its declared laws and regulations, from attempting, risking, or having the effect of impeding the meaningful realization of these interests. Hence, it would refrain from: (1) banning or attempting to ban the free development and operation of a person's mind or those activities or materials necessary for its free development and operation; (2) promulgating legal materials or otherwise acting in ways that by intention or effect objectionably interfere with the free development and operation of a person's mind; and (3) acting on any rationales that are inconsistent with valuing this protection. That is, the government cannot be committed to protecting these interests but offer or rely upon reasons that are inconsistent with this commitment, e.g., by adopting a restrictive litter policy on the grounds that it may have the effect of discouraging protests.[23]

This view makes no important distinction, at the foundations, between speech about aesthetics, one's medical condition and treatment,[24] one's

---

[22] *See, e.g.,* JOHN STUART MILL, CONSIDERATIONS ON REPRESENTATIVE GOVERNMENT 24–25 (Currin Shields ed., 1958) (1861); JOHN RAWLS, A THEORY OF JUSTICE 395–587 (1971).

[23] *See also* Seana Valentine Shiffrin, *Speech, Death and Double Effect*, 78 N.Y.U. L. REV. 1135, 1164–71 (2003).

[24] Respect for this right is far from a given. For example, in 2009 Prita Mulyasari was incarcerated in Indonesia for three weeks of pre-trial detention on charges of Internet defamation after she sent an email to friends complaining about a wrongful diagnosis at a local hospital. After an international campaign in her defense, she was initially acquitted, but the Supreme Court of Indonesia overturned her acquittal and upheld a six-month suspended prison sentence. *Indonesia Court Overturns Facebook Woman's Acquittal*, THE TELEGRAPH (Jul. 11, 2011), http://www.telegraph.co.uk/technology/facebook/8630662/Indonesia-court

regard for another, one's sensory perceptions, the sense or lack thereof of the existence of a God, or one's political beliefs. All of these communications serve the fundamental function of allowing an agent to transmit (or attempt to transmit so far as possible) the contents of her mind to others or to externalize her mental contents in order to attempt to identify, evaluate, and endorse or react to given contents as being authentically her own. Further, they allow others to be granted access, on the thinker's voluntary terms, to the information necessary to appreciate the thinker as a distinct individual and to forge a fuller human relation with her. One's thoughts about political affairs are intrinsically and *ex ante* no more and no less central to the human self than thoughts about one's mortality or one's friends; in so far as a central function of free speech is to allow for the development, exercise, and recognition of the self, there is no reason to relegate the representation of thoughts about personal relations or self-reflection to a lesser or secondary category, as democratic and truth theories are prone to do. Pictorial representations and music (and not merely discourse about them) would also gain foundational protection, because they also represent the externalization of mental contents, contents that may not be accurately or effectively captured through linguistic means; after all, not all thoughts are discursive or capable of being fully captured through discursive description.[25]

So, these arguments would support a freedom of speech regime that offered a principled and strong form of protection for political speech and, in particular, for incendiary speech and other forms of dissent, for religious speech, for fiction, for art—whether abstract or representational—and music, for diaries and other forms of discourse meant primarily for self-consumption, and for that private speech and discourse,

---

-overturns-Facebook-womans-acquittal.html; Norimitsu Onishi, *Trapped Inside a Broken Legal System after Pressing Send*, N.Y. TIMES, Dec. 5, 2009, at A6; HUMAN RIGHTS WATCH, TURNING CRITICS INTO CRIMINALS 5, 26–28 (May 2010) *available at* http://www.hrw.org/en/reports/2010/05/04/turning-critics-criminals-0 (also discussing other criminal defamation cases for other consumer complaints).

Indonesia imposes criminal penalties for defamation, enhancing them if the communication is sent over the Internet. Truth, on its own, is not a standard defense. Whether the defense of truth is permitted at all seems to be a matter of the judge's discretion. Further, defendants seeking to use the truth defense in cases not involving public officials must bear the burden of proof and must show that the defamatory statement was offered from necessity or "in the general interest." Pursuing an unsuccessful truth defense may subject the defendant to an even harsher sentence of up to four years in prison. HUMAN RIGHTS WATCH, *supra* at 16–17.

[25] *See* Frank Jackson, *Epiphenomenal Qualia*, 32 PHIL. Q. 127, 128–30, 133–36 (1982); Frank Jackson, *What Mary Didn't Know*, 83 J. PHIL. 291 (1986). *See also* Alan K. Chen, *Free Speech and Instrumental Music*, 66 HASTINGS L. J. (forthcoming 2015).

e.g., personal conversations and letters that, however trivial the subject, are crucial to developing, pursuing, and maintaining personal relationships. These reasons recommend that we provide foundational protection to these forms of communication, by which I mean that there should not be a lexical hierarchy of value between them. Nor should the protections for some depend dominantly on their playing an instrumental role in securing the conditions for the flourishing practice of another. This approach includes, at the foundation of the free speech protection, condemnation of efforts to engage in thought control and other measures that disrupt the free operation of the mind, whether or not such efforts are directly targeted at constraining interpersonal communication.

Compelled Speech and Freedom of Association

A thinker-based approach also yields strong protections against compelled speech and for freedom of association. For example, focusing on freedom of thought, as such, may yield a more straightforward account than many other theories provide of the protection recognized in *West Virginia State Board of Education v. Barnette*[26] against the compelled recitation of the Pledge of Allegiance.[27] So long as its compelled origins are transparent, it is not clear that the compelled pledge restricts listener opportunities, because informed listeners will not mistake the pledge's sentiments as reflecting the considered convictions of the speaker, and the compelled pledge alone does not restrict listeners' access to other points of view. Further, although it seems clear that the compelled pledge violates the free speech rights of the party who must speak the pledge, it is less clear that the compelled pledge squarely engages the standard themes that have occupied speaker-oriented theories. If it is clear that the pledge is compelled and if the speaker may disavow the pledge before and after its recital, the speaker's ability to express herself faithfully is arguably not seriously abridged.[28] The speaker will not be misunderstood by reason-

---

[26] 319 U.S. 624 (1943).

[27] This argument and the history behind the litigation in *Barnette* is further developed in Blasi & Shiffrin, *supra* note 9.

[28] Of course, the necessity for correcting a false impression conveyed to an audience that does not understand the significance of the speech's being compelled may impinge upon the speaker's interest in remaining silent with respect to the pledge and the sentiments and commitments expressed therein; the interests in self-expression must include the ability to gather one's thoughts and engage in self-creation at one's own pace. There is something to this point, but I am not sure that it carries enough significance to bear the full weight of the *Barnette* protection. Correcting a misimpression only requires explaining the significance or

able observers. Reciting others' speech may not be a part of one's project of self-creation, but so long as others' uptake of the speaker's meaning is not disrupted and the compelled speech is not especially time consuming, appealing to speakers' interests, as such, seems a strained line of criticism of the compelled pledge. A more straightforward explanation of the illegitimacy of the compelled pledge would not focus predominantly on either side of the speaker-audience relationship, but rather on the thinker's interests as such.

What seems most troubling about the compelled pledge is that the motive behind the regulation, and its possible effect, is to interfere with the autonomous thought processes of the compelled speaker. Significantly, the compelled speaker is also a compelled listener and is compelled to adopt postures that typically connote identification with her message.[29]

---

fact of compulsion; it does not require the speaker to make up her mind or reveal anything substantive about the pledge. This point, however, may be less persuasive in contexts in which any sort of correction or explanation may implicitly reveal some reservations about the pledge and such revelations would be socially or politically dangerous. Still, I assume the *Barnette* protection holds even for compelled speech that is less fraught (e.g., the speech in Wooley v. Maynard, 430 U.S. 705 (1977)) or that is compelled in less charged contexts.

In any case, it is unclear how much of the substance, whether the positive protection or the negative limits, of the First Amendment protection should revolve around how unreasonable people might interpret the significance of a speech performance. For example, the fact that unreasonable people might take my friend's speech to represent my own views and that their misunderstanding might prompt me to speak on a topic about which I would prefer to remain silent does not begin to ground an argument that I have a right that my friend not speak in a way that may mislead unreasonable interpreters. Because it does not have a clear exception for cases in which a speaker refutes the content of what she reports as she reports it, the republishing libel doctrine also wanders a little too close for my comfort to the view that the limits of the First Amendment may be dictated by the unreasonable reactions of readers. *See* RESTATEMENT (SECOND) OF TORTS § 578 (1977).

[29] These features compound an independent objection to the compelled pledge, namely that the government wrongly commandeers another person to carry its message and thereby treats the person as a means. *See, e.g.*, Laurence Tribe, *Disentangling Symmetries: Speech, Association, Parenthood*, 28 PEPP. L. REV. 641 (2001). At first blush, this complaint seems more relevant to substantive due process than to free speech, because similar complaints may be made when the government forces individuals to perform non–speech related acts that fall within the government's purview and should be performed by government. But this complaint closely interacts with free speech concerns. It seems degrading to the status of the independent, autonomous thinker that she be forced to serve as a puppet for the government and to mouth its concerns rather than reserving her speech for her own; forcing an independent thinker to be a mouthpiece seems inconsistent with the full absorption of respect for independent, autonomous thinkers as such. One advantage of the thinker-based theory is that it supplies principled limits to the commandeering complaint, helping to explain why commandeering *individuals* to carry the government's message may be objectionable, whereas requirements to pay money to subsidize a message may be permissible and why requiring companies to carry others' or the government's messages may be permissible.

The aim, and I believe the potential effect, is to try to influence the speaker to associate herself with the message and implicitly to accept it, but through means that bypass the speaker's deliberative faculties.[30] Compelled speech of this kind threatens (or at least aims) to interfere with the free thinking processes of the compelled speaker (who is also, here, a listener) and to influence mental content in ways and through methods that are illicit, in that they are nontransparent, employ repetition, and operate through coercive manipulation of a character virtue, namely that of sincerity, which itself is closely connected to the values of freedom of speech.

A further advantage of a thinker-centered approach is that it yields a distinctive approach to freedom of association that both explains its centrality and depicts the relation between "intimate" and "expressive" associations as continuous. Again, the approach is not antithetical to other theories of freedom of speech, e.g., speaker-based or listener-based theories. But, occupying a thinker-based perspective orients one more immediately to the centrality of association than do other theories that seem to value association through a more circuitous route. For example, even once one adopts a capacious view of the content covered by a free speech norm, speaker-oriented theories have tended to think of associations as bundles of speakers who come together to amplify their speech—to ren-

---

See, e.g., Turner Broad. Sys. v. F.C.C., 520 U.S. 180 (1997); Johanns v. Livestock Mktg. Assoc., 544 U.S. 550 (2005).

[30] See Blasi & Shiffrin, *supra* note 9, at 433–40. Some results in cognitive psychological research may lend support to the worry that compelled speech may illicitly influence the speaker's thoughts. See, e.g., Robert W. Levenson et al., *Voluntary Facial Action Generates Emotion-Specific Autonomic Nervous System Activity*, 27 PSYCHOPHYSIOLOGY 363, 364, 368, 376, 382 (1990) (exercises directing actors and non-actors to configure their faces as though they were experiencing emotion as well as those directing subjects to relive a past emotional experience significantly influenced subjects' current mental and emotional states); Paul Ekman & Richard J. Davidson, *Voluntary Smiling Changes Regional Brain Activity*, 4 PSYCHOL. SCI. 342, 345 (1993) (distinguishing between the presentation of voluntary and involuntary smiles but finding that deliberately produced smiles generate some of the brain activity associated with positive emotions); Robin Damrad-Frye & James D. Laird, *The Experience of Boredom: The Role of the Self-Perception of Attention*, 57 J. PERSONALITY & SOC. PSYCHOL. 315, 315 (1989) (reporting "[m]uch research" that "people . . . induced to act as if they held particular emotions, attitudes, motives, or beliefs" report later having these mental states). The studies tend to confirm the view that actions can influence feelings and beliefs, not just reflect them. Some of these studies conflate more behaviorist views (that the relevant mental states are identical to a set of activities) and epistemological views (that one's mental states are known by observing one's behavior) with the causal thesis we are interested in (that the relevant mental states may be caused by and not only causes of the relevant activities). See, e.g., *id.* One might (as I do) believe the causal thesis without endorsing the tenets of self-perception theory about its underlying mechanism, namely that agents infer their mental states from their activities and that these inferences either constitute their mental states or cause these mental states to happen.

der it louder or to garner more attention for their messages. The model
has been to think of speakers as having a prior message that brings them
together. Their associations, on this model, have the primary function of
facilitating more effective, clearer communication of these ideas, formed
prior to association. The association serves a conduit or a "pass through":
it enhances the effectiveness of the message's transmission, much as a
bullhorn or a microphone would. This is roughly the picture presupposed
in the line of freedom of association cases that culminated in *Boy Scouts
v. Dale*, which held that the First Amendment invalidated the application
of an antidiscrimination statute that would have required the Boy Scouts
to retain a gay scoutmaster on the grounds that the forced inclusion of
the scoutmaster would alter or distort the Boy Scouts' message disapproving of homosexuality.[31] The difficulty with this model is that it pays
little attention to associations' formative role with respect to the content
and topics of speakers' messages. This model renders associational freedom contingent on an association's ability to show that it has a clear
message and that regulations would alter that message or disrupt its
distribution.

By contrast, a thinker-based view, through its emphasis on the thinker's need to interact with others to develop capacities and particular
thoughts, immediately identifies the foundational role of voluntary associations in a free speech theory. If, as a general matter, our intellectual
development and, indeed, our basic sanity depends upon our communicative interaction with others, and, if we conceive of the function of
speech as critical to this development, we are more likely to be attuned to
the ways in which associations serve as sites of idea formation and development, and to recognize the ways in which the development (and not
merely the broadcasting) of content occurs through mutual collaboration
and mutual influence in explicit and implicit ways. Such an approach
would not focus predominantly on whether regulations affect the ability
to maintain a static *message* of an association, but on whether regulations interfere with the ability of associations to function as sites for free
mutual cognitive influence. Such an approach would protect voluntary
associations' ability to include or exclude members, irrespective of
whether the association aims to develop a message, has yet to form a message, is open to changing their message, or has any opinion or proof
about whether a potential or current member would affect their message.
This seems to be the preferable way to defend the Boy Scouts' freedom to

[31] Boy Scouts of Am. v. Dale, 530 U.S. 640 (2007).

include or exclude members at will, without attributing to the organization a particular critical message about homosexuality and thus hinging their associational freedom on their remaining inflexible with respect to that message, or interpreting the meaning of the inclusion of a person on the strength or effectiveness of that message.

Individual Speech v. Business Corporate and Commercial Speech

On the other hand, this approach can render sensible the notion that nonpress, business corporate, and commercial speech may differ from individual speech and that noncommercial associations may differ from business associations. In particular, the protection of business corporate and commercial speech, as well as that of commercial associations, may assume a weaker form and may rest upon separate, more context-dependent and instrumental foundations. First, business corporate speech does not involve in any direct or straightforward fashion the revelation or development of individuals' mental contents.[32] Both corporate-to-corporate and corporate-to-individual speech often bears only an indirect relation to the revelation and development of the thinker or the intellectual, emotional, or moral relations between thinkers. Of course, thinkers may have an interest to access corporate speech because corporate and commercial speech may report information about one's given environment; but, in other circumstances, the point of corporate speech, as well as other commercial speech, is to *alter* the environment, e.g., to manufacture desire, not to report information.

To be sure, however, altering the environment is also an aim of advocacy speech by individuals. That aim in no way diminishes the protection that should be afforded to it. Advocacy speech represents a form of exercise of thinkers' interests in developing their moral agency and in treating one another well by attempting to discern and to persuade others of what each of us, or what we together, should think and do. By contrast, non-

---

[32] *See, e.g.*, Steven H. Shiffrin, *The First Amendment and Economic Regulation: Away from a General Theory of the First Amendment*, 78 Nw. U. L. Rev. 1212, 1246 (1983) (discussing the structure of the corporation and the distance between its speech and the views of its shareholders); C. Edwin Baker, *The First Amendment and Commercial Speech*, 84 Ind. L. J. 981, 987–89 (2009) (stressing that commercial corporations are limited forms of entities created for instrumental reasons and that the people who operate within them do not act fully autonomously); Citizens United v. FEC, 558 U.S. 310, 465 (2010) (Stevens, J., dissenting) (discussing the differences between corporations and human beings and the distance between corporate speech and any individual points of view).

press, business corporate and commercial speech, by design, issues from an environment whose structure does not facilitate and, indeed, tends to discourage the authentic expression of individuals' judgment.

To be sure, many workers within the corporate environment exercise skills of judgment and creativity within the constraints of the business enterprise, and many may endorse those constraints as reflecting their own independent judgments. But, as Ed Baker has argued, the competitive structure of the economic market and the narrowly defined aims of the corporate or commercial entity place substantial pressures on the content of corporate and commercial speech that are not directly responsive to the convictions of its members. So too may the internal structural design of the corporation.[33] In Baker's view, corporate business speech content has a "forced profit orientation," and does not represent a "manifestation of individual freedom or choice."[34] Baker's starkly-put position may involve a degree of over-generalization given market imperfections, market actors who are true believers, and market actors using the market and speech within it to further external and sincere moral goals.[35] I might put the point more weakly, observing that external environmental pressures render more tenuous any charitable presupposition that such speech is sincere, authentic, or the product of autonomous processes. Nonetheless, I concur with him that the market's structure tends "very strongly [to] determine [corporate and commercial] speech content."[36] These distortive influences render more precarious claims that strong presumptions against speech regulation in this domain reliably serve the interests of the thinker *qua* speaker or the thinker *qua* listener as the recipient of such communications.

Moreover, because corporate entities' primary purpose is participation in the commercial milieu, where they substantially control access to material resources, powers, and opportunities, the fair distribution of which is requisite to just relations, we have a joint social interest in their operation, including their communications. It is not merely that these entities do not share the interest of individual thinkers and that their autonomy is not intrinsically valuable, but also that they are mere parts, although

---

[33] *See* Shiffrin, *supra* note 32.

[34] *See* BAKER, *supra* note 2, at 196, 204; C. Edwin Baker, *Paternalism, Politics, and Citizen Freedom: The Commercial Speech Quandary in Nike*, 54 CASE W. RES. L. REV. 1161, 1163 (2004); Baker, *supra* note 32, at 985–87.

[35] *See* Seana Valentine Shiffrin, *Compelled Association, Morality, and Market Dynamics*, 41 LOY. L.A. L. REV. 317, 320–21 (2007).

[36] *Id.*

highly powerful ones, of a joint social enterprise whose proper operation is crucial to the fair terms of social cooperation. Together, these considerations provide reason to treat nonpress, business corporate, and commercial speech as nonstandard within a free speech theory. Depending on context and content, their nonstandard nature will *often* justify treating such speech as the permissible target of a more comprehensive scheme of economic regulation, including antidiscrimination regulations that might not reasonably apply to voluntary, noncommercial associations.[37] I say *often* because although a limited commercial agenda and the competitive market climate tend to dominate the factors that drive corporate speech, our free speech doctrine in this domain should be open to and supportive of efforts by moral agents to expand the agenda of business enterprises beyond commercial profit into more morally responsive enterprises and, perhaps, to recognize exceptions to commercial speech regulation when its application would hamper morally motivated, responsive speech within the commercial domain.[38]

But why, it may be asked, think that structural conditions render corporate speech more determined and less authentic than, say, speech by members of a religious group whose dissent may earn them expulsion? The members may regard their expulsion from this voluntary association as analogous to the market death that Crest (to take a purely hypothetical case) would suffer were it gamely to admit in its advertising that its product was worse than its rivals, just higher-priced.[39] I do not deny that sincerity and unpopular speech may often come with great costs to the person, but I regard the differences between the cases as follows. The market and legal pressures for Crest to say what it needs to say to promote its business, despite strong doubts about its speech or activity, are tighter and greater than the pressures for a religious thinker not to change her mind in light of her sincere doubts. Moreover, Crest is a simpler entity with a less complex set of interests. When a believer changes her mind in

---

[37] *See also* Baker, *supra* note 32, at 994; Shiffrin, *supra* note 35. For criticism of this stance, see Eugene Volokh, *Speech Restrictions That Don't Much Affect the Autonomy of Speakers*, 27 CONST. COMMENT. 347 (2011). I assume here that the government's motives in regulating commercial or business corporate speech would be permissible ones, that is to say that they would not be driven by a rationale that is inconsistent with valuing the autonomous operation of the mind. The requirement that the government's rationale must be a permissible one, as I specify above, is not suspended in this domain (or any other).

[38] *See* Shiffrin, *supra* note 35.

[39] For a version of this concern, see Susan Williams, *Free Speech and Autonomy: Thinkers, Storytellers, and a Systemic Approach to Speech*, 27 CONST. COMMENT. 399, 407–08 (2011).

light of her sincere doubts, she serves her own interests as a thinker directly by responding to what she takes to be the truth. Her continued affirmation of religious tenets furthers her interests as a thinker only if that affirmation is actually sincere. Further, although her expulsion from a religious community may involve tremendous costs to her, it does not (typically) involve her complete eradication as a thinker and as a complex person with a variety of aims and potential sources of social connection. Whereas, Crest's interests to maximize profit and to survive in a competitive market are not furthered by its sincere admission that its products are inferior (except and only insofar as it has instrumental reasons to admit this when it believes others already perceive or suspect their inferiority). The actual sincerity or accuracy of its communications are irrelevant to its interests, except to the extent that sincere, accurate messages play an instrumental role in gaining or retaining market position, either because of others' perceptions or because of the sort of regulations I am arguing are constitutionally palatable.

Much more would need to be said in a full treatment of this topic, including something about the more complex cases of nonprofit corporations that operate in a market environment; the press, which operates in a market environment but whose interests are more closely aligned with accuracy and sincerity; and other market actors who pursue morally infused agendas. With respect to the latter, I have in mind enterprises like individual businesses whose moral raison d'etre structurally constrains and dominates any effort to generate profits. For example, a business may be designed to demonstrate that it is possible to function effectively while paying fair wages or farming organically. Its moral agenda may be compromised by speech regulations that lump them together, e.g. in mandatory advertising schemes, with businesses that are doggedly morally indifferent to wage equity or environmental stewardship.[40] But, in brief, as a general matter (subject to exceptions based on contextual details), I take for-profit, nonpress commercial speech, and the speech of commercial associations to differ from individual noncommercial speech (and the speech of voluntary associations) because of the fiercely competitive and fairly inflexible environment in which the former operate, because (generally) the commercial entity's interests are so narrowly defined that the accuracy and sincerity of its speech are valuable to it only instrumentally, if and when outside pressures make those virtues indirectly valuable, and because these entities, via a competitive framework, play a large part in

---

[40] *See* Shiffrin, *supra* note 35.

our system of distributing resources and opportunities. Finally, with respect to freedom of association, forced inclusion of an unwanted member into a voluntary association threatens its identity as a free site of mutual cognitive influence and thereby impinges on the free speech interests of its members, whereas regulating commercial speech or regulated membership in a commercial association (through, e.g., employment discrimination rules) does not threaten its interests or identity as a business. The narrowness of the commercial entity's agenda is no surprise: the nonpress commercial entity is not a really a person and for the most part, with some important exceptions, the quality of its speech and its products do not intrinsically enhance or detract from the satisfaction of its interests or aims depending upon whether its speech is sincere, accurate, morally sensitive, or wildly reckless. These features do not hold to as great a degree when it comes to individuals, nor are they structurally true of them. Thus, regulations on commercial entities' speech and associational activity should be subject to different, more permissive standards of review.

Children and the Mentally Disabled

The discussion thus far has taken the central figure of free speech to be a thinker with a fairly robust capacity for thought, broadly construed. In some of us, these capacities are especially fledgling, partial, or compromised. Nonetheless, agents with lesser or less-developed capacities still have an interest in their development, operation, and externalization. Although the degree of development and future potential may make some difference in some cases and contexts, at its core, a free speech theory should not deliver fundamentally different results depending upon whether we are discussing children, the mentally disabled, those suffering dementia, or fully formed adults. All such thinkers have interests in developing the capacities they possess, in having opportunities to externalize their mental content both to determine what they endorse and affiliate with and to allow themselves to be understood by others, and in having access to the thoughts of others. The urgency of these interests does not dissipate because capacities are underdeveloped or stunted. Indeed, for children, their interests have a special urgency because childhood is the most significant time to develop these capacities. Furthermore, the thinker's interests in externalizing his mental content to gain possible distance from it, to affirm some of it as his own, and to convey it to others so that he may be known as the distinctive individual he is, do not depend on those mental contents being well organized, highly articulate, or discursive. Those interests also pertain to emotional states, incomplete thoughts, and nondiscursive mental content, which are themselves distinctive features of the individual (and often serve as the preliminary, potential components for more organized and discursive thoughts).[41]

In this way, a thinker-based approach may offer different and more straightforward arguments for protecting the freedom of speech of children and the mentally disabled than other prominent theories.[42] Those theories that protect freedom of speech because of the potential quality of what speakers may have to offer to the public debate may struggle to explain why freedom of speech rights should extend to young children or significantly mentally disabled adults. Further, their justifications for protecting older children's speech largely hinge upon nurturing children's future potential to contribute as adults and not on their contemporary interests. A thinker-based approach more naturally and directly covers this wide range of citizens.

This position is, of course, compatible with the contention that the shape and content of one's free speech rights may differ depending upon the degree of one's development of the relevant capacities. I do not dispute that contention, but the relevance of a limited degree of development of rational capacities often seems misunderstood. One approach seems to be that the full development of these capacities is an eligibility criterion for participation in a free-speech regime. As with age-based eligibility for driving, one must pass a certain threshold before one qualifies

---

[41] This clarification responds to welcome pressure from Vincent Blasi, *Seana Shiffrin's Thinker-Based Freedom of Speech: A Response*, 27 Const. Comment. 309, 310–12 (2011).

[42] It also offers resources to think about the free speech rights of the mentally ill, although the issues here are knotty because mental illness may be a transitory state for some and a permanent condition for others. Although it is easy to conclude that inducing mental dysfunction or mental illness violates freedom of speech, other questions pertinent to whether compulsory treatment violates freedom of speech for the mentally ill are harder both because, for some patients, their mental illness may not represent an external force but may comprise a key part of their personality or felt identity, and because many of the pharmaceutical treatments for mental illness interfere with other aspects of mental functioning. These factors, as well as the question *who* should have the ability to decide whether the illness is an external force or a component of the person, render the free speech analysis of the right to refuse treatment for the mentally ill sufficiently complex that they cannot be tackled here. Some helpful treatments of the issues include Jennifer Colangelo, *The Right to Refuse Treatment for Mental Illness*, 5 Rutgers J.L. & Pub. Pol'y 492, 506–10 (2008); Bruce J. Winick, *The Right to Refuse Mental Health Treatment: A First Amendment Perspective*, 44 U. Miami L. Rev. 1 (1989); Lawrence O. Gostin, *Freedom of Expression and the Mentally Disordered: Philosophical and Constitutional Perspectives*, 50 Notre Dame Law. 419 (1975).

for full free speech protection. Until one is a full-fledged, able adult, one is ineligible to speak freely and, until that point, the government has some latitude to regulate one's speech on grounds that the *content* is offensive, unseemly, inappropriate, immature, or may induce poor decisions— grounds that would be impermissible if applied to adults. Principles of this kind seemed to drive the early decisions in *Bethel School District v. Fraser*,[43] which upheld the discipline of a student speaker for making a student-campaign speech with some lewd content and *Hazelwood School District v. Kuhlmeier*,[44] which upheld the censorship of student-written articles about pregnancy and divorce in a student newspaper, partly on grounds of the inappropriateness of the subject matter for minors. This approach was recently reaffirmed in *Morse v. Frederick*,[45] which upheld the discipline of a student for off-campus speech at an optional school-sanctioned event. (Mr. Frederick had unfurled and refused to take down a banner proclaiming "BONG HiTS 4 JESUS," which, while difficult to decipher, perhaps connoted a pro-drug message.)

The rationale behind all of these cases, that minors are *per se* ineligible to listen to or generate certain messages because of their content, would be antithetical to a thinker-based approach.[46] The thinker-based approach's emphasis on externalizing mental content and interacting with other thinkers as a method of *developing* one's mental capacities renders eligibility criteria invalid. Foundationally, freedom of speech is as crucial to children as it is to adults. True, their inexperience may make them more vulnerable to the risks and burdens associated with authoring or hearing inappropriate, offensive, and dangerous speech. But those challenges should be met through the supervised practice, instruction, and guidance that we can offer through counter-speech, social support, and other interactive modeling in the classroom (and in other social contexts), rather than by paralyzing or penalizing the developmental activity that needs to progress in order for children to refine and convey the thoughts

[43] 478 U.S. 675 (1986).

[44] 484 U.S. 260 (1988). Two distinct rationales played a role in the *Hazelwood* decision regarding the privacy of the subjects and the failure to meet other journalistic standards in the context of a journalism course. These rationales seem independent of the eligibility criterion rationale and, depending on the facts, might be compatible with a thinker-based approach.

[45] 551 U.S. 393 (2007).

[46] For other discussions of children and the First Amendment, see Blasi & Shiffrin, *supra* note 9, at 440–42; Colin M. Macleod, *A Liberal Theory of Freedom of Expression for Children*, 79 CHI.-KENT L. REV. 55 (2004). *See generally, Symposium: Do Children Have the Same First Amendment Rights as Adults?*, 79 CHI.-KENT L. REV. 3 (2004).

they have now and for them to go on to achieve greater intellectual independence and reflexive resilience. A more developmental model of freedom of speech would view "mistakes," such as ill-considered speech or ill-considered views, as steps within the learning process, rather than as episodes to be prevented through strict eligibility criteria for permissible speech.

On this more developmental approach, two features of children's early development may make a difference to the shape and form of their freedom of speech rights. First, their early developmental stage may justify their subjection to rather comprehensive forms of compelled education, which include structured speech activities involving prolonged bouts of compelled listening and solicited speech.[47] I say "solicited speech" rather than "compelled speech" because, largely, although schools may be reasonably empowered to require students to speak about particular topics and even to represent accurately what others think about those topics, free speech principles still foreclose demanding that students represent particular content or viewpoints as their own, in their own voice. That latter form of compulsion would seem to jeopardize the authenticity of students' own judgment, by attempting to influence their thoughts through repetition and sanctions, rather than through understanding and persuasion through reasoning. When this compulsion is coupled with restrictions on students' own expression, it jeopardizes their ability to represent themselves and to have their own beliefs known, appreciated, and evaluated by others. Such compulsion also forces students to practice and habituate themselves to gratuitous insincerity.

Second, where there is evidence that some forms of speech might substantially hinder the development of this potential or cause unusual sorts of psychological harm to which the fully developed adult is not susceptible and that cannot be reasonably mitigated through counter-speech or other forms of assistance, those vulnerabilities may give rise to grounds for the targeted regulation of speech directed at children, whether by adults or by children. Technically speaking, this has been the approach of the recent Court, but its implementation of this idea seems perverse. Without citing explicit evidence, it has found psychic harm from rather pedestrian sexual innuendo and from isolated nonliteral expletives on broadcast media, but has deemed there to be no risk of psychic harm

---

[47] To deliver those forms of compelled education may require some time, place, and manner restrictions on *when* students can speak freely in order to ensure that educational activities are not interrupted.

from exposure to very graphic depictions of and virtual participation in extremely violent behaviors in video games.[48]

Is Speech or Freedom of Speech Special, and If So, in What Way(s)?

I have been arguing that reasoning from the needs of the free thinker helps to undergird a strong, broad, and unified account of freedom of speech. One might ask why and whether a thinker-based approach singles out speech, and freedom of speech in particular and whether such an approach has the resources to explain and justify the specially protected status of freedom of speech, with its particular contours, in our constitutional and political firmament.

These questions might be formulated along three dimensions. First, how would a thinker-based view explain why the freedom of speech protection encapsulated in the First Amendment is predominantly negative, prohibiting regulation and interference with authentic expression and its reception? Why doesn't it also generate positive requirements, such as the provision of education or treatments for mental illness, enterprises that are surely *as* connected to the development and functioning of the thinker as are protecting opportunities and pathways of expression?[49] Second, how would a thinker-based view explain why the First Amendment protection encompasses only state action and does not, itself, extend to pro-

---

[48] On the one hand, consider *FCC v. Fox*, 556 U.S. 502 (2009), in which the Court upheld an FCC policy change penalizing isolated, nonliteral expletives on broadcast media because the FCC judged, without supporting evidence, that fleeting profanity harms children. Relying apparently on *modus tollens*, Justice Scalia's majority opinion demurred that "[i]f enforcement had to be supported by empirical data, the ban would effectively be a nullity" and "it suffices to know that children mimic the behavior they observe." *Id.* at 519. This approach harkens back to *FCC v. Pacifica*, 438 U.S. 726, 748–49 (1978), in which the potential harm to children justified restrictions on "indecent" words on broadcast media, and to *Bethel School District No. 403 v. Fraser*, 478 U.S. 675, 684 (1976), in which the Court asserted that schools have an interest in protecting children from mildly lewd speech. In both cases, virtually no evidence was presented of harm to children from the speech. Yet, in *Brown v. Entertainment Merchants Ass'n*, 131 S.Ct. 2729, 2738–39 (2011), the Court struck down a California law imposing restrictions and labeling requirements on the sale and rental of violent, participatory video games to minors, in large part for lack of sufficient evidence of a direct causal relationship between exposure to the games and violence by minors. Although these fluctuations may reflect the standard of review applied in the different cases and thus, technically, may not mark an inconsistency, the standard of review is itself partly driven by assessments of the values and dangers of the speech.

[49] *See, e.g.,* Thomas Scanlon, *Comment on Shiffrin's Thinker-Based Approach to Freedom of Speech*, 27 CONST. COMMENT. 327, 332 (2011).

hibit private censorship and other private forms of interference with freedom of speech?[50] Third, how would a thinker-based view explain the special and distinct protection of *speech* in the constitutional universe by contrast with other significant autonomous activities, such as the formation and pursuit of intimate relationships or one's employment, activities that are also closely connected to the development of the mind and the self?[51] Although one could understand these questions as challenges to the account, one might also take them as opportunities to understand how the values that underlie freedom of speech relate to a particular institutional expression of those values.

I resist the idea that a persuasive theory of freedom of speech must fully account for the contours of a particular form of institutional protection and, on its own, make sense of its limits and bounds. We might instead regard it as a virtue that the theory makes sense of the continuities we feel between our freedom of speech protection, the obligation to educate children and their moral right to an education, the moral injunction against private censorship, and the substantive due process protections safeguarding intimate associations and rights over one's body. Rather than asking that a theory of the moral values underpinning freedom of speech make sense of the boundaries of the institutional protection on its own, the more sensible requirement would ask that the theory of the underlying importance of freedom of speech be compatible with the institutional forms and limits we think sensible. This also permits the recognition that, within limits, other institutional forms of expression and protection are compatible with the same theoretical foundations.

A thinker-based theory does suggest that we have a political duty to educate our children as well as to refrain from censoring their thoughts and communications and from interfering with their access to others' contributions. Certainly, a constitutional system that acknowledged the connection between education and guarantees of freedom of speech and treated them as on a constitutional par, recognizing a right to both, could find support in a thinker-based theory. Yet, a thinker-based theory is also compatible with allowing certain sorts of institutional concerns to gain a

---

[50] *See, e.g.*, James Weinstein, *Seana Shiffrin's Thinker-Based Theory of Free Speech: Elegant and Insightful, but Will It Work in Practice?* 27 CONST. COMMENT. 385, 388–89 (2011).

[51] *See, e.g.*, Frederick Schauer, *Must Speech Be Special?* 78 NW. U. L. REV. 1284, 1289–92 (1984). Some of Post's criticisms of autonomy theories of freedom of speech appear to be versions of the complaint that such theories cannot explain why speech is special. *See* Post, *supra* note 3, at 479–81, 484, 487.

foothold and to recommend that a special, distinctive status be accorded the freedom of speech guarantee. We *might* take the position that education and freedom of speech equally engage with our duties to support the development and expression of the autonomous thinker. At the same time, we might think that institutionally, constitutional guarantees operate most successfully when they are, largely, judicially enforceable and where the judiciary is competent and independently enabled to guarantee their protection. Further, at the constitutional level, we *might* take the view that the judiciary is more competent to articulate, develop, and enforce negative rights, whereas, often, positive programs demand greater legislative structuring and involvement and the sort of flexibility to evolve over time that requires a judicial posture different from the posture that well serves the protection of negative guarantees. Moreover, in some social contexts, standard political pressures might suffice to ensure adequate levels of education, whereas dissidents and other casualties of intolerance may, as a more regular matter, require special forms of protection insulated from political processes. Institutional arguments of these kinds may explain why the provision of a certain level of education is both essential to the values underpinning a freedom of speech culture and is a moral right, and also why it might be regarded as a mandatory legislative priority but might not be afforded the status of a fully judicially enforceable constitutional right.[52] This possible basis for an institutional separation, however, should not be taken to suggest that a robust system of education is unnecessary for a functioning free speech culture or for achieving the significant values that freedom of speech promotes. Consequently, distinctive constitutional free speech concerns may arise when structuring or regulating educational bodies.[53]

Similar points may be made about the state action doctrine, that is, the doctrine that the First Amendment protection against abridging freedom of speech only regulates state, but not private, actors. As with the moral right to education, a thinker-based theory supports the moral right against private censorship as well as public censorship. A constitutional

[52] Of course, that would not vindicate *San Antonio Independent School District v. Rodriguez*, 411 U.S. 1 (1973), the case in which the Court held the Texas school-financing system based on local property taxation constitutional, despite the claim by poor families that the system disproportionately favored those with higher property taxes, i.e., the wealthy. Where a significant government service, one essential to constitutional values even if not constitutionally mandated, is offered or funded on an unequal basis, that inequality constitutes strong grounds to recognize an equal protection violation.

[53] I attempt to illustrate this point with respect to academic freedom and the university in Chapter Six.

system that enshrined protections against both forms of censorship might better protect the underlying moral rights than our current system, which protects one at the constitutional level and the other, more contingently, at the legislative level. On the other hand, there may be reasons to render the protection against public censorship discrete. Given the size, power, and ubiquity of the state, the state may represent a more daunting threat to freedom of speech than the disparate threats that arise from various and varied private sources. The immensity of the state and the power it may quickly muster may require a staunch, foundational, targeted, and highly visible counterpoint for balance. (Of course, the strength of this distinction wanes in contexts where private entities control vast amounts of resources and have a ubiquitous presence, i.e., where the term "corporate dictatorship" resonates in practice.)

Moreover, what counts as private censorship may differ and present more complex challenges than what counts as public censorship. There are easy cases of parallelism, to be sure, such as when strangers threaten to harm advocates if they continue to voice their political views. Employer sanctions against employees for disfavored, off-duty speech irrelevant to bona fide job requirements also represent, in my (more controversial) view, a straightforward parallel. But, there are hard cases as well. For example, while the government may not permissibly exclude a citizen from citizenship or from elective office on account of his or her political views, a voluntary private association must be able to exclude members on the basis of their thoughts and speech. Rather than constituting an offensive violation of freedom of speech, associational exclusion may be a crucial mechanism by which associations function as collective fora for free communicative activity and mutual influence. Although that judgment seems easy, more difficult calls arise in deciding when private employment discrimination on the basis of a citizen's private expression represents a case of illegitimate private censorship and when, by contrast, it represents reasonable policing of associational boundaries or a bona fide occupational demand. Some part of the answer to that question may depend on the role private employers play in the economy and in the provision of basic employee needs, and on whether or when they function, importantly, as private expressive associations. These factors may differ in different social contexts. Hence, it would be compatible with the thinker-based theory for a political system to decide that what counts as private censorship is sufficiently fluid that the moral right is better protected through legislation than a judicially enforceable constitutional right.

Is state censorship any different? Mightn't its boundaries also be sufficiently fluid to justify a system of mere, contingent legislative protection? It is hard to get at this question without addressing a number of related issues about institutional structure that are too large to tackle here, including whether constitutional protections generally should be linked to judicial enforceability or might be adequately, or even optimally, protected through a constitutional designation of priority, but one administered by legislative action.[54] These issues are important, but I want to bypass them here and work within the structure of the U.S. system, which, largely, associates matters of constitutional importance, and particularly matters of individual rights, with judicial enforceability.

Assuming that structure, there is a further distinctive reason to object to state censorship and ensure protection against it specifically and discretely. The state, unlike private agents, is supposed to be especially dedicated to the welfare of each of its members and so has a special duty to promote the conditions of its members' development and flourishing. Moreover, in a democratic state, the state's speech and action are meant to represent the collective action and collective expression of an inclusive association of independent minds. Of course, complex issues surround the question of how to understand and defend the idea of the collective action and expression when the relevant collective is not unanimously supportive, directly or by compromise, of the collective's substantive output. Although I cannot tackle those issues here, I do not think they are insuperable. The structure of an answer would, I think, amount to the claim that each of us as individuals has duties to participate in the fair, inclusive political collective in our relevant context, given our duties to support justice and given that, assuming its decision procedures are fair and followed, the relevant collective's decisions are politically attributable to its members, even when its decisions do not match the judgment of an individual member. On a theory of this kind or on most other theories of democracy that do not reduce democracy merely to crass politics, the fair functioning, the value, and the legitimacy of public democratic action presuppose that community members have (and regularly exercise) the ability to develop as full thinkers and then contribute their sincere and independently formed perspectives to the process of collective decision-making. State abrogation of freedom of speech, then, is self-undermining in a distinctive way. For that reason, and to underline that

<hr/>

[54] *See, e.g.,* Stephen Gardbaum, The New Commonwealth Model of Constitutionalism: Theory and Practice 47–76 (2013); Jeremy Waldron, *The Core of the Case Against Judicial Review,* 115 Yale L. J. 1346, 1369–95 (2006).

reason publicly, protection against state censorship may merit a discrete and special mechanism of protection.[55]

Finally, let me turn to other forms of autonomous, individual expression and their connection to freedom of speech. It seems a strength of this theory of freedom of speech that it can account for the sense that there are free speech values implicated within so-called intimate associations as well as expressive associations, and in related, highly personal decisions, such as those that pertain to reproduction and sexuality as well as decisions relating to the boundaries of life. One way to put this point is that the thinker-based approach renders entirely sensible the sometimes-maligned "penumbra" theory of *Griswold*[56] and *Roe*,[57] in which decisions over whether to contracept and whether to abort were portrayed as falling within the protective shadow cast by other provisions of the Bill of Rights.

First, certain substantive due process protections provide the preconditions for a meaningful free speech protection. If we accept the First Amendment and its justifications and we accept that our form of rational agency requires that social connections develop and flourish, then we must provide safe havens for thought, communication, and mutual influence. The relevant forms of safety come both in numbers, i.e., in having associates with whom we may share thoughts and who may witness what happens to us, and in our ability to select with whom and in what ways we will share fundamental forms of intimacy. If the state could prevent intimate associations, it would obstruct individuals' ability to forge the sort of authentic social connections that are essential for the development and maintenance of the personality and the free intellect. So too, if it could require certain individuals to have intimate associations, it would render their connection forced and inauthentic, rather than free and mutually supportive. Contraception and abortion rights may be seen as applications of the freedom not to be forced into an unwanted intimate association with an embryo, fetus, or future child.

Second, the central substantive due process protections are extensions of the values protected by freedom of speech. Sexual intimacy, for example, expresses and may reveal any of a variety of mental states towards another: in the good cases, feelings of love, affection, or at least lusty attraction. To take another example, the recognized constitutional right to

---

[55] Still, I hasten to add that by articulating an account of the distinctiveness of state censorship and the theoretical significance of state action, I do not mean to endorse the Court's indefensibly underinclusive interpretation of the scope of state action.

[56] Griswold v. Connecticut, 381 U.S. 479 (1965).

[57] Roe v. Wade, 410 U.S. 113 (1973).

refuse medical care, even when one's intention is thereby to hasten death, bears a close connection to one's ability to control not merely the bodily experiences one endures, but also whether one remains in control of one's mental functioning, whether one's thoughts remain continuous and one's own, and whether one may continue to present one's self to others in an authentic way, on the one hand, or to maintain the privacy of one's thoughts, on the other. A commitment to the autonomy of the thinker as such may partly undergird not only the right to refuse treatment but also more positive rights to terminate one's life, at least when disease jeopardizes the thinker's standard mechanisms for exercising and maintaining control over her mental capacities.[58]

But although (free) sexual intimacy, control over the physical boundaries of one's existence, and speech are all exercises of autonomy that, in some circumstances, relate to the core interests of the agent *qua* thinker, they are not all equally standard forms of communication or transmission of mental content; hence my remark that many substantive due process protections are *extensions* of the values protected by a free speech principle, rather than instantiations of it. A kiss typically expresses a happy reaction, attraction, or a warm attitude, by which I mean to invoke the sense of "express" that is not synonymous with "communicate," but instead means "to display and to manifest" an attitude.[59] Although a men-

---

[58] *See, e.g.*, Cruzan v. Missouri, 497 U.S. 261 (1990) (recognizing a constitutional right to refuse treatment but permitting strong evidentiary requirements for its exercise); *but see* Washington v. Glucksberg, 521 U.S. 702 (1997) (upholding a state ban on assisted suicide and indicating skepticism about a constitutional right to commit suicide directly). Although more general rights of autonomous control over one's life or one's body may justify more sweeping rights to commit suicide, the penumbral argument I appeal to here may shed some light on why many arguments for the right to die focus on the special cases of subjection to significant pain, mental deterioration, or terminal disease. When physical conditions threaten patients' ability to maintain mental integrity and deliberative control over the content and course of their thoughts and their expression, there may be special free speech-related arguments for the right to die. Restraints on suicide in these cases threaten to imprison patients in mental conditions where they have little capacity to think freely and to control the presentation of their thoughts.

[59] Philosophers of language often use "expressives" (and its cognate verb) to refer to speech acts that in addition to conveying content also manifest it in a more active, direct way. *See, e.g.*, John R. Searle, *A Taxonomy of Illocutionary Acts, in* 7 LANGUAGE, MIND, AND KNOWLEDGE, MINNESOTA STUDIES IN THE PHILOSOPHY OF SCIENCE 344 (Keith Gunderson ed., 1975), reprinted in JOHN R. SEARLE, EXPRESSION AND MEANING 1, 15 (1979); John R. Searle, *What is Language? Some Preliminary Remarks*, 11 ETHICS & POL. 173, 181 (2009). Other speech acts may do even more, as with commissives, performatives, and declarations. *See* KENT GREENAWALT, SPEECH, CRIME, AND THE USES OF LANGUAGE 57–63 (1989) and J.L. AUSTIN, HOW TO DO THINGS WITH WORDS 32–33, 151–57 (1965). By "communicate" and its cognates, I mean to capture both the transmission of content as

tal attitude may be inferred from it, a kiss is not standardly deployed merely to externalize that attitude and convey the fact of its existence. A kiss can be used that way, but its communicative use is parasitic upon the connotations of its expressive function.

This, of course, is a fraught distinction,[60] but it is one that I think has a point, for it connects to two of the reasons why speech is special. I have argued that speech facilitates some of the core interests of autonomous agents by rendering their mental contents available to others and vice versa, thereby enabling them to know one another, to cooperate with one another, to investigate the world, and to enhance their understanding of our environment and our circumstances, which in turn enables (though it does not ensure) moral agency.

A major reason the external representation of mental content and its communication plays a foundational role in furthering these ends is because, in general, it is so much more precise and informative than many of its nonessentially communicative, expressive counterparts. I mean something here as mundane as that an explanation of the reasons why one disapproves of another's conduct and a description of the emotional reactions that conduct gives rise to conveys more content than a wordless punch in the nose. Some content conveyed by communication cannot reliably and accurately be conveyed through other means. When it comes to the interest in being recognized and known as the person one is and having an outlet from the isolation of one's mind, curtailments on speech represent a severe incursion, because speech provides unique modes of access to the contents of other minds. I do not mean to include only discursive communication here: a melody or painting of the image in my mind (that is, an external representation of my internal visual imagery), may convey more

---

well as the transmission of one's (presumed and often implicit) agreement or belief in that content. Still, despite the familiarity of this use of "express" in the philosophical literature, I couldn't be more aware that my use of "express" is not a salutary term in a context in which "freedom of expression" is right at hand and sometimes is used interchangeably with "freedom of speech." No better term has occurred to me.

[60] I will not here go into detail about the various fault lines and strengths of different accounts of this distinction. Rubenfeld's general discussion of the distinction is basically sensible. *See* Rubenfeld, *supra* note 10, at 42–44. Articulating the distinction from the perspective of sorting regulations sensitive and insensitive to it, he asks whether the relevant harm that a regulation targets is caused by the communicative aspect of the expressive act or by some other element of it. I defend something like this approach in Shiffrin, *supra* note 23. I disagree with Rubenfeld in thinking however that governmental intent to punish or restrict communication as such is a necessary condition of running afoul of First Amendment protections; we agree that it may be a sufficient condition. *See* Jed Rubenfeld, *The First Amendment's Purpose*, 53 STAN. L. REV. 767, 775–78, 793–94 (2001).

of my mental contents, including but not limited to my mood, than approving or disapproving behavior. It necessarily conveys more about my private mental contents than silence and its visual analog.

Generally, regulations on the nonessentially communicative expression, manifestation, or implementation of mental contents *as such* do not preclude the communication or transmission of the mental contents they express. Restrictions on my ability to express my anger through violence do not preclude my transmitting my anger through communicative means: by saying I'm angry, detailing my complaints, or depicting the emotional maelstrom through words, images, or sounds. A restriction on the emotion's nonessentially communicative expression does not threaten to isolate me in my mind. A restriction on communication does.

This observation is perfectly compatible with the recognition that some forms of expression convey more than words, images, or sounds can on certain occasions. It may well be that, on some occasions, the depth of my anger can only be conveyed through violent aggression. Perhaps it is at this point that we reach the moral limits of whether we can be fully known by others. I am neither arguing that agents have absolute rights to ensure that (any and all) others fully understand their mental contents on all occasions, nor that externalized representations of thoughts always convey more than behavior that acts upon those thoughts in ways that differ from merely externalizing a representation. But, by and large, speech is special because it is a uniquely specific mechanism for the transmission of mental contents and their discussion, evaluation, development, and refinement, independent from and prior to their implementation in action.

Certainly, the transmission of mental contents sometimes immediately effects or implements them: directed at the relevant person, the desire to insult or, in certain contexts, to humiliate or to subordinate, can be implemented merely by being communicated. But as a general matter, communicative methods of transmitting mental contents generate the possibility of an intermediate workshop-like space in which one may experiment with, advance tentatively, try on, revise, or reject a potential aspect or element of the self or of one's potential history before directly affirming it through endorsement or implementation.[61] One cannot preface, even implicitly, one's thrown punch with "maybe," "consider the possibility," or, "for now, this is my tentative judgment," and thereby mitigate the seri-

[61] Nevertheless, on occasion, it may be inappropriate to convey to some people even purely exploratory thoughts and ideas that may have moral significance, however explicitly inchoate they are in form.

ousness of the assault or somehow soften the impact of one's fist. Yet, prefatory remarks or implicit tempering cues *will* qualify a proposition subsequently articulated so that it becomes less than a full-blown assertion. Furthermore, we find both intelligible and significant our abilities effectively to revise, clarify, or even retract what we've begun to say, simply by using further words. Although sometimes the further speech will have to follow immediately if it is to be effective as a retraction as opposed to a later rethinking, our linguistic practice allows us to use speech to formulate and even generate our thoughts without the first stab at articulation rigidly gelling immediately into a final draft: we can try on an idea by articulating it without it immediately sticking to us or representing us. Such tentativeness is less available with most actions. I cannot *revise* or *retract* my intentional punch by following it immediately with more violence, cringing, or even with regretful words. A further stream of punches may *clarify that* my assault was intentional, but beyond that rudimentary clarification, further light on why I threw the punch will typically require words (or images).

The capacity for speech to be tentative and exploratory—to allow us in a noncommittal way to try on an idea, whether to formulate it at all or to assess its plausibility or fit with oneself—is closely related to and helps to underpin a more familiar idea about the specialness of speech, namely that we must protect the ability to discuss and conceive of even those actions we may reasonably outlaw, because protecting our speech and our conception of such actions permits us to revisit and justify our regulation. Thereby, we may retain the ability to reassess the aptness and legitimacy of our regulation and to change course if we conclude that we are mistaken. As Thomas Emerson observed, "Thought and communication are the fountainhead of all expression of the individual personality. To cut off the flow at the source is to dry up the whole stream. . . . Hence, society must withhold its right of suppression until the stage of action is reached."[62]

I acknowledge that not all speech stops short of action. Further, where there is a divide between speech and action, the line is not always clear. Nonetheless, there are some special features of speech that render it distinct from other forms of autonomous action that go beyond the development and revelation of mental content. These distinctive features, I submit, play some role in explaining why speech is special and why autonomy accounts may reasonably place a particular premium on preserving and protecting speech as such.

---

[62] Thomas I. Emerson, The System of Freedom of Expression 9 (1970).

CHAPTER FOUR

Lying and Freedom of Speech

In Chapter One, I argued that a lie is an assertion that the speaker knows she does not believe, but nevertheless deliberately asserts, in a context that, objectively interpreted, represents that assertion as to be taken by the listener as true and as believed by the speaker. Given that understanding, I argued that the primary, distinctive wrong of lies as such does not inhere in their deceptive effect, if any, on listeners, but instead in their abuse of the mechanism by which we provide reliable testimonial warrants, a mechanism we must safeguard if we are to understand and cooperate with one another and to achieve our mandatory moral ends. Of course, many lies also cause or attempt wrongful deception, by violating the speaker's duty of care toward the listener not to cause or risk the formation (or confirmation) in her of a false belief. On many occasions, when lies are deceptive, the deceptive components may reasonably represent the most salient part of the wrong done to their victims. But, what I call "pure lies" need not involve deception or the intent to deceive. They need not even be false; a speaker may lie by asserting what she believes to be false yet, unbeknownst to her, happens to be true.[1] Yet pure lies, like deceptive lies, abuse the mechanism of direct communication and threaten the basis of our testimonial trust with one another.

In Chapter Three, I argued that similar considerations about the significance of speech to our personal intellectual development and to our moral agency undergird the view that legal regimes must offer strong protections for individual freedom of speech. Freedom of speech is an essential social condition for the development, maintenance, and full value of freedom of thought, and for the full and proper exercise of our

---

[1] For instance, Betsy lies when she fabricates and solemnly asserts, for her private amusement, that it snowed yesterday in Phoenix even if, against her belief to the contrary and unbeknownst to her, Phoenix had a fluke flurry. She lies even if no one comes to believe it snowed in Phoenix and even if no one believes that Betsy believes it.

moral faculties. For these reasons, I argued that freedom of speech is a fundamental human right and an indispensable precondition of a just social and political scheme.

Together, these two positions—the strong condemnation of lies as such and the derivation of freedom of speech from similar argumentative foundations—prompt questions about the legal regulation of lies. Does a strong commitment to freedom of speech preclude regulation of lies *as such*, as many have thought? *Prima facie*, the philosophical case I have sketched for freedom of speech suggests, to the contrary, that freedom of speech may not extend to deliberate misrepresentations of the speakers' beliefs. That case stresses the significance of opportunities to speak and hear *sincere* speech (as well as speech transparently used to pursue our other nontestimonial uses of communication). Deliberately insincere speech should not garner the same sort of respect because it does not participate, even at the fringe, in the same values as sincere or transparent speech. Moreover, if deliberate misrepresentations undercut the warrants we have to accept each other's testimonial speech, then we have reason to think that deliberate misrepresentations interfere with the aims of free speech culture.[2] They not only demonstrate a culpable indifference to the validity of the warrants offered to the particular listener, but they damage the rational basis supporting our testimonial practices, which are crucial elements of a thriving free speech culture and fundamental components of a social environment that supports the moral agency of thinkers. If the wrong of the lie is as insidious as I have argued, that wrong supports a strong *prima facie* case for identifying and marking that wrong through the signal of legal regulation and for using some of the powers of legal regulation to rebuke (and perhaps deter) its occurrence.[3]

Many commentators, as well as a majority of the Justices of the Supreme Court, however, judge that freedom of speech may pose a general

[2] Although my topic is speakers' deliberate misrepresentation of their beliefs and not false positions as such, related considerations lead me to endorse Frederick Schauer's dismay at the prevalence of factual falsity in the culture, but I resist his skepticism that autonomy theories of freedom of speech have "little to say" about the problem or our legal options. Frederick Schauer, *Facts and the First Amendment*, 57 UCLA L. REV. 897, 916–19 (2010).

[3] *See also* Mark Tushnet, *"Telling Me Lies": The Constitutionality of Regulating False Statements of Fact* 24–25 (Harv. L. Sch. Pub. L. & Legal Theory, Working Paper Series, Paper No. 11–02), *available at* http://ssrn.com/abstract=1737930 (arguing that "[p]ublic regulation can be understood as expressing a distinctively *public* judgment that certain lies are quite bad, supplementing . . . private condemnation . . . .").

and fundamental obstacle to the legal regulation of lies as such. This position, I will argue, is mistaken.

In identifying that mistake, however, my aim is not to advocate for the comprehensive legal regulation of lies. Rather, my more modest objective is to show that, theoretically, legal regulation of lies need not offend the important values protected by freedom of speech and, in particular, by the free speech traditions articulated within First Amendment jurisprudence. The theoretical point seems worth making both because of the seriousness of the wrong of lying and because our discussion of the moral complexities of its regulation seems stunted by a preoccupation with free speech worries.

Still, I stop short of direct advocacy of general legal regulation of lies for two reasons. First, although I am unconvinced that there is any *intrinsic* free speech problem with the legal regulation of lying, there are important pragmatic concerns about the potential for governmental abuse that might, in some circumstances, be unleashed by such regulation. These concerns are serious ones, although, as I will suggest, they may have been overstated. Nonetheless, that assessment is better made on a case-by-case basis and not on the basis of sweeping legal or philosophical arguments. Second, as I will argue in Chapter Five, I have strong reservations about the legal regulation of the pure lie with respect to personal, autobiographical speech. These reservations emanate from considerations about equality, fraternity, and toleration, however, and not from freedom of speech. Attention to these sorts of considerations has been missing from cultural and legal discussions, I suggest, because misplaced free speech concerns have dominated the conversation. Thus, showing the compatibility of free speech values with legal regulation of lies may not, on its own, make a comprehensive case for its constitutionality or desirability.

Clarifying the scope and limitations of free speech arguments would not only counsel greater attention to other values, but also has specific practical implications. It would suggest that our constitutional scrutiny of legal regulations of lies should be far more focused on the specifics of their design, namely whether the particular factual circumstances of their application raise credible concerns about government abuse. In addition, the argument I offer also suggests that the evidentiary standard for regulating lies, whether pure or deceptive, may permissibly be lowered. As I will argue, free speech concerns do not require, as a condition of regulation, any showing of actual deception, the risk of a deception of the audience, or the intention to deceive; that is, the defendant's lie need not have implanted or reinforced false beliefs in the audience (or risked doing so).

Hence, where legal regulation of lies is apt, it may suffice, without triggering constitutional alarms, to show that the defendant deliberately asserted what the defendant did not believe. This simpler standard could ease the burden of regulating lies by commercial actors and corporate entities, among others.

In what follows, I focus on deliberately advanced misrepresentations of the speakers' beliefs, excluding ambiguous cases such as spontaneous utterances that may be insufficiently considered to count as deliberate. I will also cordon off defensive misrepresentations offered only in response to intrusive or unreasonable inquiries or demands, ones that threaten reasonable privacy interests. I bracket these cases in part because as defensive acts, they may be insufficiently deliberate, but also because they may represent justified cases of misrepresentation. To put it in the terms introduced in Chapter One, intrusive, unreasonable (even if inadvertent) demands for private information may generate a suspended context in which listeners have no objective warrant to take the speaker's assertion to be sincere or true; more weakly, such circumstances may give rise to excuses. In any case, I want to start with clear cases of unprovoked, deliberate statements that a speaker offers to be taken as true and represents as her belief, but that, in fact, she believes are false.

While considering these issues, it may help to have specific examples in mind. Consider these: First, the regulation of the clearly deliberate, nonspontaneous, "autobiographical lie"—e.g., lies about one's personal characteristics or accomplishments in public, in private conversation, or on a website such as match.com or, as in the case of Lance Armstrong, in one's autobiography.[4] Second, the regulation of the expert lie outside the fiduciary context—e.g., a lie by an expert about matters falling within her expertise that may turn into a pure lie that violates no code of conduct when told outside an employment or fiduciary context such as a lie told by a doctor, lawyer, food professional, or plumber about a matter within her expertise in a book, an article, or party conversation. Suppose a chef opines at a dinner party that food safety regulations have become overly rigid and falsely insists that one can safely leave potato salad out all day

---

[4] *See, e.g.*, Amended Class Action Complaint and Demand for Jury Trial, Stutzman v. Armstrong, No. 13–00116 (E.D. Cal. Mar. 7, 2013), 2013 WL 1178749 (class action seeking damages and injunctive relief against Armstrong and his books' publishers for fraud and for negligently misrepresenting Armstrong's two purported autobiographies as fact, not fiction). The District Court judge dismissed the claims against the publishers and some claims against Armstrong, but not the fraud, deceit, and negligent misrepresentation claims against Armstrong. Stutzman v. Armstrong, 2013 WL 4853333 (E.D. Cal 2013). The entire case was voluntarily dismissed with prejudice on October 18, 2013.

or a plumber falsely declares her conviction that organic products work just as well as harsh chemicals at dissolving clogs. Their audiences may not believe what is said and may not believe that their speakers believe them, although the context is not a joking one. If these lies are somberly offered yet not believed, they may serve as examples of pure lies that would not fall under standard regulations of deceptive speech.

Of course, such lies, as well as lies told in professional or commercial contexts, may often deceive listeners. They may also, therefore, be subject to regulation on the grounds that, when deceptive, lies may materially harm particular listeners. I put aside that possibility to focus on the pure lie as such, independent of any deceptive effects. My contention is that well-crafted regulation of such lies need not raise any First Amendment difficulties even absent evidence of deception or its likelihood. The pure lie may be a rare specimen, but establishing the consistency of regulating the pure lie with freedom of speech would thereby show that from a First Amendment perspective, deceptive lies could be regulated *qua* lie, even when evidence of their deceptive impact proves elusive.

Freedom of Speech

Perhaps the best place to begin is with the U.S. Supreme Court's recent decision about free speech and autobiographical lies. *United States* v. *Alvarez* invalidated the Stolen Valor Act, a federal statute that attached criminal liability to falsehoods about one's service and awards in military service,[5] on First Amendment grounds.[6] I have no wish to defend the Stolen Valor Act or its constitutionality, in particular. I focus on the case because it airs some of the most prominent free speech arguments against legal regulation. Also, by offering a concrete case, *Alvarez* helps to highlight which objections to legal regulation are more contingent, attaching to a specific method of regulating lies.

The case arose from the following event. At a water district board meeting in Claremont, California, Xavier Alvarez, a board member, falsely bragged that he was a retired Marine and a recipient of the Con-

[5] Stolen Valor Act of 2005, 18 U.S.C. § 704 (2006).

[6] United States v. Alvarez, 132 S. Ct. 2537, 2542–47 (2012). Prior to the *Alvarez* ruling, lower courts divided over the Act's constitutionality. *Contrast, e.g.,* United States v. Robbins, 759 F. Supp. 2d 815 (W.D. Va. 2011) (upholding, against a First Amendment challenge, the conviction of a defendant who lied about receiving the Vietnam Service Medal when running for political office), *with* United States v. Strandlof, 667 F.3d 1146 (10th Cir. 2012) (overturning the conviction of a defendant charged with falsely representing himself as the recipient of the Purple Heart).

gressional Medal of Honor. These claims were neither approximations of the truth nor understandable spontaneous exaggerations. They were fabrications from whole cloth. Indeed, Mr. Alvarez notoriously misrepresented himself, falsely claiming on other occasions to be a Vietnam veteran, a wounded member of the team that successfully freed [*sic*] the American ambassador during the hostage crisis in Iran, a police officer, and a professional hockey player. He was indicted under the Stolen Valor Act and pled guilty, while reserving his right to mount a constitutional challenge to the Act. His sentence included approximately $5,000 in fines, 400 hours of community service, three years of probation, and routine drug testing.[7] Alvarez challenged his conviction on the grounds that the Stolen Valor Act violated the First Amendment, and he persuaded both the Ninth Circuit Court of Appeals and the Supreme Court.[8]

Although the Act did not specifically require the defendant to have a particular mental state as an element of liability (and some of the plurality opinion of the Supreme Court directed its criticism at legal regulation of falsehoods *per se*),[9] principles of charitable construction and constitutional avoidance would suggest the Act should be interpreted to attach liability only to deliberate falsehoods and not to accidental, unknowing, or good-faith mistakes of fact.[10] So interpreted, what made the Act interesting is that it did not tailor the regulation to contexts in which deception would be likely or the topic especially germane. Although it homed in on lies that were also factually false and bore on the speaker's military distinction, the Act did not restrict its coverage to particular fora of speech, such as representations to government officials, to the public, or within employment or commercial contexts. Thus, factors that might be significant to a duty against deception, such as the locale in which Mr. Alvarez spoke and his status as a board member were, strictly speaking, irrelevant to his liability to prosecution under the Act.

---

[7] Judgment and Probation/Commitment Order, United States v. Alvarez, No. 07–1035 (C.D. Cal. Jul. 21, 2008), 2008 WL 8683050.

[8] United States v. Alvarez, 617 F.3d 1198 (9th Cir. 2010), *denied reh'g*, 638 F.3d 666 (9th Cir. 2011); *Alvarez*, 132 S. Ct. 2537 (2012).

[9] 18 U.S.C. § 704(b). "Whoever falsely represents himself or herself, verbally or in writing, to have been awarded any decoration or medal authorized by Congress for the Armed Forces of the United States, any of the service medals or badges awarded to the members of such forces, the ribbon, button, or rosette of any such badge, decoration, or medal, or any colorable imitation of such item shall be fined under this title, imprisoned not more than six months, or both." *See Alvarez*, 132 S. Ct. at 2539–40.

[10] *See Alvarez*, 132 S. Ct. at 2552–53 (Breyer, J., concurring); *id.* at 2558 (Alito, J., dissenting); *see also Robbins*, 759 F. Supp. 2d at 818–19.

Thus, the Act took seriously what the Court had suggested in passing dicta multiple times over the years; namely, it endorsed the broad position that false (factual) speech as such has no First Amendment value and so may be regulated for a legitimate purpose.[11] Despite the Court's extended flirtation with this broad position, when confronted with a statute predicated on this position, the *Alvarez* Court flatly rejected it as inconsistent with freedom of speech.[12] As I will argue, the Court stumbled here with respect to its analysis of lies.

Contingent Defects

Some of the Court's concerns in *Alvarez* revolved around serious defects in the Stolen Valor Act that, while important, do not represent intrinsic features of the legal regulation of lies. The Stolen Valor Act did not represent the epitome of well-crafted legislation. By attaching criminal penalties to pure lies, authorizing up to a *year* of imprisonment if the lie concerned certain distinguished medals, such as the Purple Heart,[13] the statute offended for its disproportionate remedy.[14] That charge, however,

---

[11] *See, e.g.,* Gertz v. Robert Welch, Inc., 418 U.S. 323, 340 (1974); Bose Corp. v. Consumers Union of U.S., Inc., 466 U.S. 485, 504, n. 22 (1984); BE & K Constr. Co. v. NLRB, 536 U.S. 516, 530–31 (2002); Hustler v. Falwell, 485 U.S. 46, 52 (1988).

[12] *Alvarez,* 132 S. Ct. at 2551.

[13] 18 U.S.C. § 704 (d) (2006).

[14] The prospects for finding disproportionality under current judicial doctrine, however, are grim for two reasons: the Court's general unwillingness to recognize disproportionality in criminal sentencing and its general failure to regard criminal penalties as excessive in the speech domain. *See* Harmelin v. Michigan, 501 U.S. 957 (1991) (endorsing the constitutionality of a life sentence without possibility of parole given to a person without prior felony convictions, found to have possessed 650 grams of cocaine); Lockyer v. Andrade, 538 U.S. 63 (2003) (upholding the constitutionality of two consecutive twenty-five year to life sentences for a previously convicted felon in a three strikes regime who stole $150 worth of videotapes); Vincent Blasi, *Toward a Theory of Prior Restraint: The Central Linkage,* 66 MINN. L. REV. 11, 26–27 (1981) (noting the Court's reluctance to police the severity of criminal sanctions on speech); Margot Kaminski, *Copyright Crime and Punishment: The First Amendment's Proportionality Problem,* 73 MD. L. REV. 587 (2014) (decrying failure to use proportionality analysis in copyright sentencing); Michael Coenen, *Of Speech and Sanctions: Toward a Penalty-Sensitive Approach to the First Amendment,* 112 COLUM. L. REV. 991, 994 (2012) (noting that a "penalty-neutral" approach largely governs First Amendment cases, with some small pockets of penalty-sensitivity). More recent cases have found it unconstitutional to sentence juveniles to life sentences without the possibility of parole. Perhaps they offer reason to hope that meaningful review of disproportionate sentencing has been rekindled, although their heavy emphasis on the juvenile status of the offender suggests a more limited reading. *See* Miller v. Alabama, 132 S. Ct. 2455 (2012) (overturning a mandatory life sentence for juvenile homicide under the cruel and unusual

would not impugn a more carefully drafted statute with moderate civil penalties or other civil remedies for its violation.

Moreover, the use of criminal penalties, even if proportionate, may exacerbate genuine concerns about selective prosecution and the self-censorship associated with regulating the lie.[15] There is no question that it is troubling to enable the police, and the government more broadly, with a legal avenue to prosecute activity that, it is alleged, most of the population has intimate familiarity with.[16] The concern is not, realistically, that mass prosecutions would transpire. Rather, the concern is with enabling government officials to threaten individuals who have garnered the government's disapproval with prosecution, a threat that could intimidate dissidents.[17] This is an important worry, and it suggests the wisdom of designing the legal regulation of lies with the primary motive of conveying a standard of conduct rather than deterring misconduct through powerful threats, regularly prosecuted. Using moderate civil regulations rather than criminal penalties might go some distance to address these concerns.

Of course, it is possible that civil regulations, too, may chill sincere speech. Crafting further safeguards might be required to arrest the potential for government abuse or its perception. This might be achieved by limiting the statute's applicability to repeat offenders, requiring multiple complainants, requiring strong proof that the defendant actively believed her statement was false (rather than showing an inference of what the defendant must have believed in the circumstances or a showing of recklessness),[18] allowing the defense that the misrepresentation was necessary

---

punishment clause of the Eighth Amendment); Graham v. Florida, 560 U.S. 48 (2010) (overturning the life sentence for a juvenile convicted of non-homicidal felony).

[15] *See, e.g.*, Brief of Professor Jonathan D. Varat as Amicus Curiae in Support of Respondent at 21, United States v. Alvarez, 132 S. Ct. 2537 (2012) (No. 11–210), 2012 WL 195302.

[16] The familiarity of all with lying seems unquestionable, but further precision about frequency is hard to come by, as I discuss in Chapter One, note 28.

[17] *See* United States v. Alvarez, 132 S. Ct. 2537, 2547–48 (2012). *See also* Jonathan D. Varat, *Deception and the First Amendment: A Central, Complex, and Somewhat Curious Relationship*, 53 UCLA L. Rev. 1107, 1109 (2007). For strong caution about the casualness with which chilling arguments are deployed absent strong evidence, see Leslie Kendrick, *Speech, Intent, and the Chilling Effect*, 54 Wm. & Mary L. Rev. 1633 (2013). Kendrick's call for greater precision and data about the chilling effect is well taken. Still, sensitivity to the likely impact on concerned citizens should not be stifled (nor does Kendrick so advocate) while we await a stronger evidentiary basis for making finer doctrinal distinctions.

[18] Some speakers may speak or act in ways that strongly suggest they do not believe a prior statement. Although that evidence may indeed be probative, in this domain it is important to rule out the possibility that the speaker harbored a contradiction in her beliefs of which she was unaware. The argument I am advancing for the regulation of lies does not

to protect a reasonable expectation of privacy, allowing proof of government harassment to constitute a complete defense, instituting independent avenues for relief upon showings of illicit governmental motive, and incorporating sanctions for irresponsible accusations by civilians to forestall private harassment.[19] Such protections may be cumbersome, but I am not here exploring the administrability of a permissible regulation of lying. I am just exploring whether regulations could be crafted without violating freedom of speech protections.

Another defect of the Stolen Valor Act was that, as crafted, it was not viewpoint-neutral, because it did not regulate all deliberately false speech or even all deliberately false speech relating to public service or one's wartime activities. The Act penalized misrepresentations about honored military service but, through omission, immunized misrepresentations about dishonorable military service, honorable diplomatic or Peace Corps service, activism protesting the war, or conscientious objection. This narrow focus of concern is in tension with the principle of R.A.V. v. St. Paul that the First Amendment demands that even unprotected speech may not be regulated for an impermissible purpose, namely a governmental determination that some viewpoints as such are privileged over others.[20]

Important as the issues about abusive enforcement practices and clumsy drafting are, I want to put them aside. Largely, they are contingent objections to the particular version of legal regulation of lies embodied in the Stolen Valor Act and to its criminalization. To pursue the intrinsic free speech problems (if any) with the regulation of lies, we should turn our

---

directly extend to include the legal regulation of self-deception, even culpable self-deception, a category that raises further issues about freedom of thought.

[19] Greater creativity with agents of implementation and with the form of remedies might further alleviate anxiety. Regulation of insincere political advertising, for example, might be implemented through nonpartisan review boards, empowered to require that, for a specified period, offenders fund disclosures that their prior advertisements were found deliberately misleading.

[20] In R.A.V., a hate speech statute was overturned on the grounds that although it could be construed to regulate unprotected "fighting words," it discriminated between different viewpoint-based categories of fighting words, penalizing discriminatory fighting words but immunizing antidiscriminatory fighting words. R.A.V. v. City of St. Paul, 505 U.S. 377, 383–84, 388–89, 391 (1992). That interpretation of the statute at issue in R.A.V. was questionable, but the basic principle that a speech-discriminatory motive may not be deployed as the engine of regulation, even if it is targeted at otherwise regulable speech, has merit. See also Chaker v. Crogan, 428 F.3d 1215, 1228 (9th Cir. 2005) (holding a California penal code section unconstitutional because it criminalized deliberate misrepresentations criticizing peace officers but not deliberate misrepresentations supporting peace officers); Varat, supra note 17, at 1118 (2007) (discussing Chaker and the application of R.A.V. to regulations of false speech).

attention to a fair, well-designed civil statute that addresses a viewpoint-neutral range of deliberate misrepresentations offered in contexts that are clearly serious and nonfictional in presentation, and nonintrusive on reasonable domains of privacy. Imagine that this scheme imposed high evidentiary standards, modest remedies, and safeguards to reduce the potential and the fear of government abuse.

Would *that (imagined) statute* be consistent with freedom of speech? Do the Court's opinions in *Alvarez* give us reason to think not? Although the Court's majority divided between two opinions,[21] those two opinions convened on a number of putative free speech defects besetting the regulation of lies: first, regulations of lies are forms of content-discrimination, a First Amendment anathema that provokes skepticism and the highest standard of review; second, there is insufficient evidence that lying causes the sort of harm that could surmount free speech concerns; and, third, even deliberate falsehoods have free speech value. These arguments are all unpersuasive.

Content-discrimination

MUST REGULATION OF LIES BE CONTENT-DISCRIMINATORY?

To many free speech advocates, the prospect of regulating lies has seemed an immediate nonstarter because it is often framed as the regulation of speech on the basis of its content, a posture highly suspect and usually lethal from a freedom of speech perspective.[22] My contention is that this preliminary objection, though ubiquitous, is mistaken. When framed in a general way, the regulation of lies as such is not clearly a content-based regulation in the sense in which that pejorative classification is typically

---

[21] Justice Kennedy wrote a plurality opinion that garnered three additional votes; Justice Breyer wrote a concurring opinion, also signed by Justice Kagan.

[22] *See, e.g., Alvarez*, 132 S. Ct. at 2543–44 ("[T]he Constitution 'demands that content-based restrictions on speech be presumed invalid . . . '" (quoting Ashcroft v. ACLU, 542 U.S. 656, 660 (2004))). For a recent sustained analysis of the constitutional hostility to content regulation, see Leslie Kendrick, *Content Discrimination Revisited*, 98 VA. L. REV. 231 (2012). The proponent of these regulations may object to this discussion on the grounds that the prohibition on content-based regulation generally applies to speech falling *within* the scope of First Amendment protection. Part of the issue here is whether deliberate misrepresentations fall within or outside that umbrella in the first place. I propose to lay that chicken-and-egg issue aside because, however accurate, the contention that they fall outside the First Amendment's protection requires an explanation. That explanation, to be persuasive, will have to engage with the concerns that drive the classification of regulations on deliberate misrepresentations as content-based, even if at the end of the argument one concludes that the prohibition does not strictly apply to this speech.

meant. To regulate the lie is to regulate deliberate misrepresentation by a speaker: that is, it is to prohibit (or otherwise regulate) a speaker from presenting something *she believes to be false* as though she believed it to be true. The predicate of regulation is not that the content of the speech is false. Recall, as I argued earlier, a statement may be true but still be a lie when the speaker disbelieves it. Rather, the predicate of the regulation is the conjunction of the speaker's mental state toward the content, namely that the speaker believes it to be false, and her presentation of that content, nevertheless, as though it were true and believed by her to be true.

One tip-off that this regulation is not really content-based is that if the same speaker or someone else uttered the same statement yet believed it (and that utterance possessed the same meaning), that speech would not fall afoul of the regulation. This suggests we are rather far from the standard stomping grounds of content-regulation.

Moreover, were we to regulate, our reason for regulating need not be content-based. The *prima facie* argument offered above is that the lie interferes with the aims and function of a free speech culture not through its content or through the reactions of the audience to its content, but rather because its serious utterance falsely represents itself as presenting the thoughts of the speaker and thereby misuses the exclusive tools we have to share our sincere beliefs with one another; in so doing, it scrambles and distorts the channels of communication deployed by the sincere. This impetus for regulation does not stem from disagreement with the content of the speech or from a worry about how others react to its content, but rather from the fact that insincere, but seriously presented, representations interfere with our ready, reliable ability to transmit our mental contents, whatever they may be, and have them taken as testimonial warrants of our beliefs.

So, both our motives as well as the target of regulation seem compatible with valuing freedom of speech. Neither seems content-based. Indeed, such regulation may be partly motivated by an interest in protecting the reliability and the perceived reliability of speech; so understood, such regulations advance free speech values in ways analogous to time, place, and manner restrictions that aim to ensure that speakers can be heard and are not drowned out by competitors or hostile audience members. If lies interfere with the successful transmission of recognizable testimonial warrants and therefore with effective communication, regulations on lies may serve the values that underpin freedom of speech. Further, legal regulations of the lie need not have a content-discriminatory impact. As I go on to argue, regulating the lie need not chill, preclude, or burden valuable speech.

That's my general argument. To unpack it a bit, it may help to make some preliminary distinctions between the speaker, the proposition she utters (the meaning of the utterance), its truth-value, her attitudes and beliefs toward the proposition she utters, her motivation for producing the utterance, and the attitudes and beliefs she has toward her utterance. So, for example, Abby, the speaker, declares that "The brown dress no longer fits Sally," and thereby expresses that the brown dress once did but does not now fit Sally, Abby's daughter. Abby utters a true proposition, believes the proposition she utters, is unhappy about its content because its truth means a shopping venture is in her future, says it because a new outfit needs to be purchased, but is unhappy about *uttering* the proposition to Kristin, Sally's other mother, because Abby knows that airing this fact will bring some stressful financial pressures to the forefront of Kristin's consciousness. Without looking at Sally, Kristin insincerely replies, "The dress still fits her perfectly." She utters this insincere statement in order to deflect the social pressure to set a time for a shopping expedition and to repress the bubbling financial stress. Abby is angered by Kristin's utterance, both because of Kristin's insincerity and because Abby understands that Kristin is attempting to weasel out of mall duty.

Abby's anger toward Kristin's insincerity is a personal analog of a legal reaction to insincere speech. Abby is not deceived by Kristin's reply. She neither believes the dress fits nor that Kristin believes the dress fits. Abby reacts to Kristin's misrepresentation of her belief *about* the proposition she has uttered and to the reasons that give rise to the insincerity. Abby is not, however, upset about the content of Kristin's proposition *per se*. Abby would be thrilled were the dress to fit Sally. Further, were Kristin sincere (but incorrect), Abby might be bemused by Kristin's failure to notice the height of the hem or, in a darker mood, annoyed by her sartorial negligence. In these cases, Abby's reaction is to Kristin's motivations for her utterance and Kristin's beliefs about the truth-value of what Kristin utters, not to the uttered proposition's meaning. And, though some of her reaction is to Kristin's motive, it isn't entirely to Kristin's effort to avoid an unpleasant task. Had Kristin been forthcoming and said, "The dress is tight but I don't feel like being part of the solution," they could have had a direct, open conversation about the division and importance of their respective duties. Had Kristin been silent, Abby could have pressed her to engage the subject. But, by addressing the subject insincerely, Kristin engages and represents herself as engaged, but this representation is false. Thereby, Kristin keeps herself and her beliefs at an un-acknowledged distance with which Abby cannot directly engage.

Attending to these distinctions may help to clarify that regulations of lies do not target the meaning of the utterance but rather the speaker and her relation to her utterance. Because regulation triggered by the speaker's belief or disbelief in the uttered proposition's content need not include elements relating to its content, its truth value, or the reactions of an audience to the substance of the proposition, regulating insincere speech need not constitute content-discrimination.[23]

This argument demands some refinement. Sometimes the identity of the speaker bears on the content of the speech. This is obvious, of course, where the first-person pronoun is invoked. "I am hard at work," has a different meaning and refers to different occupations and persons depending on the identity of the speaker. Even where demonstratives are not used, the identity of the speaker (and other contextual features) may make a difference to content, as well as to the sort of speech act that is engaged in. The rabbi who, looking at a sloppily presented plate of food, pronounces, "That is not kosher," conveys that the food does not meet certain religious strictures. The secular supervising chef who says, "That is not kosher," uses "kosher" in a more colloquial sense and conveys that it is unacceptable to serve food in such a slapdash way. The CEO of an automobile company who declares publicly, "The 2015 model meets the highest safety standards," issues a warranty or guarantee. The blog reviewer who writes the same sentence does not issue a warranty but merely reports on the claims of the manufacturer and the National Highway Traffic Safety Administration.

Although who the speaker is may have some bearing on the content of what is expressed because the speaker's identity forms part of the (public) context that determines the utterance's meaning, still, the speaker's private, unexpressed belief, disbelief, and attitudes toward her utterance do

---

[23] Interestingly, regulating deceptive speech as such inches closer toward content-regulation because such regulation is motivated partly by a concern that the audience will be misled by the *false substantive content* of the utterance. Nonetheless, regulation of deceptive speech does not transgress the *values* associated with the aversion to content-regulation because it is primarily justified by the content-neutral grounds that the speaker has (and should have) a particular responsibility to ensure accuracy in this domain and that the listener is not a free, willing participant in the communicative relationship but is wrongly manipulated into accepting the content. *See also* David Strauss, *Persuasion, Autonomy and Freedom of Expression*, 91 COLUM. L. REV. 334, 335, 365–68 (1991) (arguing both that deception involves objectionable manipulation and that "a rational person never wants to act on the basis of false information").

not form part of that context. Whether an utterance is a lie is determined by the speaker's mental stance toward the content, that is, by her conscious disbelief of the utterance's content coupled with her deliberate intention to present that utterance to be taken as true. Those mental stances may be, and typically are, private and opaque at the time of utterance. Given that communication is essentially a public, shared activity, the meaning of an utterance within communicative activity could not sensibly vary from the private contents of the speaker's (or listener's) mind. So, whether an utterance is a lie or not should (generally) be irrelevant to the public meaning of the proposition uttered; hence, regulation of lies is not inherently content-discriminatory.

WHY WE CARE ABOUT CONTENT-DISCRIMINATION

The classic forms of content-discrimination about which we rightfully worry, however, regulate speech because of the meaning of the utterance. Canonical content-discrimination responds to the meaning of an utterance, by, for example, showing hostility to criticism of authority, hostility to an advocacy of Communism, or a sense that certain matters (e.g., sexuality) should not be public topics of discourse. The content-discriminatory regulation thus hinges on the meaning of what is said, but not on the beliefs of the speaker about that meaning. Indeed, where a regulation discriminates based on the content of the speech, whether the speaker mentally endorses or rejects the proposition uttered is irrelevant to the cause of action and to the utterance's regulability or nonregulability.

Sometimes, as with child pornography statutes and hostile audience regulation, the content-discrimination is indirect. The government regulates because it objects to the audience's (perceived) response to the content of the message. In *New York v. Ferber*, a child pornography case, the state objected to the audience's anticipated enjoyment of the materials and the effects that reaction to content had on the market, spurring production of more child pornography.[24] In the hostile audience cases, the government's objection was that the audience's hatred of the speaker's

---

[24] That content-based regulation was upheld because of the compelling interest in protecting children in *New York v. Ferber*, 458 U.S. 747, 756–74 (1982). The Court has since retreated from that content-based rationale and aligned behind a rationale focusing on the use of children in the *actual* production process of the regulated materials and not merely its stimulation of demand for child pornography. *See* Ashcroft v. Free Speech Coal., 535 U.S. 234, 249–51, 253–54 (2002) (striking down a child pornography regulation to the extent that it applied to images that only appeared to be of actual children, even though its circulation and sales may have stimulated the market for the production of actual child pornography).

message generated excited reactions of an unwelcome sort.[25] *Snyder v. Phelps*,[26] the recent case holding that protestors near a military funeral engaging in offensive speech could not be held liable for causing the intentional infliction of emotional distress, involved both sorts of content-discrimination, direct and indirect. Oversimplifying a bit, through the application of the emotional distress cause of action, the government was regulating speech both on the grounds that its message (at a particular venue and time) was outrageously offensive and that the audience of the speech would experience a devastating emotional reaction to the deliberately cruel message and its presentation at that time and place. Although the cause of action requires showing that the protestors intended to cause distress or were reckless with respect to that effect, the protestors' own attitudes toward and beliefs *toward* the messages they carried, i.e., whether they endorsed, reviled, or were skeptical of those messages, would not serve as evidence that the elements of the cause of action were met, nor would they serve as defenses.

These examples reinforce my contention that classic forms of content-discrimination involve regulation in reaction to the substantive content of the proposition uttered and the reception of that substantive content by its audience. They do not single out the speech on the basis of the speaker's belief or attitude toward its content; content-discriminatory statutes are indifferent to these facts.

Nonetheless, although I am arguing that legal regulation of lies need not involve content-discrimination, one might think that the Stolen Valor Act involves content-discrimination, as must any plausible form of legal regulation of lies. The Stolen Valor Act, for instance, focuses on speech with a particular content: misrepresentations *about* extraordinary military service. Even if the arguably viewpoint discriminatory aspect of the Act were remedied, so that it focused more broadly on misrepresentations about one's participation or lack of participation in military service or public service, that revised act's requirements about sincerity would

---

[25] Putting aside the so-called "fighting words" doctrine, the Court, largely, has refused to allow the prospect of hostile audiences' negative reaction to a speaker's message to constitute a reason for regulation. *See, e.g.*, Terminiello v. Chicago, 337 U.S. 1 (1949) (invalidating application of a breach-of-peace ordinance to speakers whose speech created crowd antagonism); Forsyth Cnty. v. Nationalist Movement, 505 U.S. 123, 134 (1992) (invalidating a municipal fee mechanism that varied fees for parades depending on the level of predicted hostile reaction by others). *But see* Feiner v. New York, 340 U.S. 315, 319–21 (1951) (upholding conviction for disorderly conduct against a speaker because his provocative political speech caused restlessness and threats of violence).

[26] 131 S. Ct. 1207 (2011).

still be triggered only by certain sorts of content—those about public service, but not donuts, political parties, or medical care. The dilemma is this: while comprehensive regulation of all lies might not constitute a form of content-discrimination, any tailored statute triggered by subject matter would; but, such tailoring seems essential to avoid granting the government an unthinkably vast amount of power, power that would, in turn, re-ignite valid concerns about government abuse. So, any plausible form of legal regulation of lies would concentrate on lies about certain subject areas. That focus, in turn, would again return us to the realm of content-regulation.

I am less certain that the path to content-discrimination is inexorable in light of the content-independent reasons that should motivate governmental regulation. If the legally relevant objection to lying is that the lie threatens the basis for trust and reliance on others' testimony, this objection renders especially salient those circumstances under which others' testimony concerns especially important matters or those circumstances under which listeners are especially reliant on others' testimony. Although the former category may hone in on content-oriented topics, the latter category need not. Instead, it may be characterized as involving those circumstances in which speakers have special access to (or special authority about) information, rendering listeners reliant on speakers' testimony because they cannot easily or readily verify what is said in another way. Such a focus corresponds to a salient, content-independent method of determining the scope of legal regulation by fixing on the relationship between the speaker (or the conditions of her speech) and the utterance. Perjury laws do this by restricting their scope to the utterances of speakers who testify under oath. The federal False Statements Accountability Act may be understood to do something analogous, to regulate false statements on the basis of a content-neutral identification of the recipient of the transmission: lies *to government officials* are regulable.[27]

A more ambitious, speaker-oriented regulation might regulate lies by experts about the topics of their expertise, whether they are certified as experts on a topic, e.g., board-certified lawyers, accountants, and medical professionals, or, casting more broadly, they have or claim to have expertise about a topic, whether certified or not, such as manufacturers about their products, real estate developers about their plans, and even indi-

---

[27] 18 U.S.C. § 1001 (2006). I say "may" because the language of the federal False Statements Accountability Act is also susceptible of a content-based reading—that lies *about* matters within the jurisdiction of the federal government are regulable.

viduals about themselves.[28] Regulating lies by experts about the contents of their actual, certified, or claimed expertise does not single out content. Rather, it attaches to a feature of the speaker and the relationship between the speaker and the utterance. This relationship is singled out as meriting regulation for content-independent reasons, namely that listeners should be able to rely upon the sincerity of experts because they have or claim special access to information that listeners either do not have, or reasonably should not be expected to cultivate on their own.

This understanding of the purpose of regulating lies might also support a "secondary effects" analysis of topic-specific regulation. Although the Court has sometimes been overly keen to identify secondary effects,[29] the secondary effects doctrine, properly understood, permits topic-specific regulation where the effects of speech merit regulation for reasons independent of its particular content or its reception. Suppose, for example, the reputation and trustworthiness of drug manufacturers fell to a low because of a spate of contaminations at factories, coupled with a lack of transparency about the problems. The government might then decide to regulate lies about pharmaceuticals specifically from a concern that misrepresentations would hobble the trustworthiness of future claims important to assisting people making decisions about their medications. Here, the regulation would be targeted to expert lies about a particular topic, but the grounds for the regulation would be that the strength of testimonial trust in utterances about that topic, whatever their content, was particularly vulnerable for reasons that were content-independent. Hence, regulation of lies and even some topic-specific regulation of lies may be framed and justified in ways that are at some remove from the territory of content-regulation.

---

[28] Singling out the special responsibilities of experts making pronouncements within their area of expertise may offer a different rationale for asymmetrical liability in situations like *Kasky v. Nike*, in which Nike's advertisement touting sound labor conditions in its factories, which turned out to be untrue, was subject to different standards of accuracy than statements by its critics. *See* Kasky v. Nike Inc., 45 P.3d 243 (Cal. 2002), *cert. denied*, 539 U.S. 654 (2003). Although the discussion of this case has focused on Nike's status as a commercial speaker (and a corporate, nonindividual speaker), it may be independently relevant that Nike is an expert on conditions in its own factories, and this fact may subject it to special requirements of accuracy about facts within its expertise. A related argument is that Nike had special access to information about its own factories and the legal ability to exclude others who wished to visit to verify or disconfirm Nike's allegations, giving Nike a special obligation of accuracy.

[29] As I discuss elsewhere in Seana Valentine Shiffrin, *Speech, Death, and Double Effect*, 78 N.Y.U. L. Rev. 1135, 1165–71 (2003).

Compelled Disclosure

Perhaps a better way to categorize regulation of lies is as a form of compelled disclosure intended to facilitate a relationship of transparency, on equal footing between the speaker and listener, and thus to protect our relationships of epistemic cooperation. The case might be so framed as follows. As a default, we should be warranted in taking a person's freely volunteered speech to be sincere.[30] Prudentially, our complex social lives, involving the division of labor at every turn, depend on our ability to rely upon others' conveyed beliefs on a regular basis. Our moral lives likewise depend on our accurate knowledge of others' beliefs, feelings, and situations if we are to respond well to them, and our democratic lives depend upon respectful and, often, responsive engagement with the positions and concerns of others. Indeed, given these normative purposes, we may have some obligation to treat their speech as sincere, absent evidence to the contrary. To adopt a posture of epistemic remove or doubt toward them would involve distrust. That distrust would hinder our ability to engage with and respond to them fully, as equals; and without evidence of untrustworthiness, distrust seems unfair.

Where someone is, or represents herself to be, an expert on a topic, that warrant is heightened and justifiably so. Identifying and epistemically relying on experts in some areas of knowledge, allows us to engage in epistemic divisions of labor that make possible the complex forms of social life that facilitate sophisticated understanding of our environment, richer and healthier lives, lives that may manifest greater independence from the vagaries of the physical environment and from dependence on particular individuals, and the development of diverse sets of opportunities that are tailored to individuals' diverse abilities and interests. Our epistemic reliance on experts only functions well when we are warranted in our default epistemic dependence on their testimony.

Offering insincere speech under the guise of sincerity threatens the rational warrant to engage in these salutary forms of epistemic dependence. Because we have strong reasons to protect these environments of warranted dependence, disclosure rules are justified. Should one wish to volunteer insincere speech, one must disclose this, whether through direct discourse or by taking advantage of culturally well-understood mechanisms of disclosure, such as deploying a sarcastic tone, evidently exag-

[30] See, e.g., Tyler Burge, *Content Preservation*, 102 PHIL. REV. 457, *passim* and especially 466–68 (1993). *See also* C.A.J. COADY, TESTIMONY (1992).

gerating in ways that indicate parody or irony, publishing under the rubric of fiction, performing in a play or other theatrical setting, or otherwise speaking in a context that is culturally understood not to call for somber testimonial speech (e.g., certain contexts in which demands of etiquette are understood to drive content).[31]

So understood, legal regulation would not react to the liar for the content of what she said but for violating rules of compelled disclosure.[32] Such rules of compelled disclosure would be importantly less demanding than most rules of compelled disclosure, because most rules demand disclosure of the identity of the speaker or the articulation of specific messages.[33] This rule would require neither. I suggest we regard legal regulation of lies as a content-independent form of compelled disclosure that is compatible even with anonymous speech. All this form of regulation requires is that the speaker (who may remain anonymous) disclose, whether through explicit or through customary means,[34] that she does not believe her speech if it otherwise is presented in a way that would support an objective interpretation that the speech is presented as somber, testimonial speech. Properly framed, I think the question of the legal regulation of lies is whether freedom of speech is inconsistent with requiring disclosure of the modality of the speech, so understood, or whether other important values counsel against such requirements.

To summarize, because the aim of the regulation is to facilitate the ability of speakers to convey, and listeners to understand, that the speaker transmits her sincere belief, this aim seems far afield from the standard

[31] I am here describing, in a different way, the idea of suspended contexts, discussed in Chapter One. A related form of disclosure is one in which the speaker reveals that she serves as the spokesperson or translator for another party. In such cases, the speaker places herself in a justified, epistemic suspended context with respect to whether her utterances represent her beliefs, *but* the presumption of truthfulness may still hold with respect to whether the spokesperson's utterances accurately represent the person or entity that she represents.

[32] *See, e.g.,* Milavetz, Gallop & Milavetz v. United States, 559 U.S. 229, 236 (2010) (contrasting disclosure requirements to combat otherwise misleading speech and affirmative limitations on speech and holding that, at least for commercial speech, the former calls for a less exacting form of scrutiny than the latter).

[33] *See, e.g.,* Riley v. Nat'l Fed'n of the Blind of N.C. Inc., 487 U.S. 781, 799 & n.11 (1988) (invalidating a requirement that a fundraiser immediately disclose what percentage of donations are passed on to the charity, but indicating that a disclosure requirement that a professional fundraiser merely identify herself as such would pass First Amendment muster).

[34] The "customary" means employed to signal that the content is not intended to be taken as true may be tailored to shared understandings with particular audience members and need not conform to a widespread social custom. Here, we might borrow from what is necessary to fulfill the objective intention test in contracts.

concerns about content-regulation, namely that the government is attempting to control or suppress speech with particular contents. To the contrary, this sort of regulation merely aims to ensure that whatever is being sincerely conveyed can be successfully conveyed and recognized as sincere without distortion. Such distortion is generated when insincere speakers fail to constrain their insincerity to a justified and identifiable context. In this way, regulation of lies closely resembles noise regulation that aims to confine the side effects of noise within one speech domain from seeping into another in ways that obstruct the ability of participants in the latter to hear and understand one another.

Of course, the ultimate issue is not whether legal regulation of lies is content-discriminatory. Whether this regulation constitutes content-discrimination or not, what matters is whether this speech regulation intrudes upon, restricts, or otherwise inhibits valuable forms of speech or whether, in other ways, it manifests an unacceptable hostility or presents unreasonable burdens to speakers and listeners. So, let's turn to the other arguments offered for wariness about the legal regulation of lies.

Harm, Particularized Victims, and Freedom of Speech

A prominent refrain in both Justice Kennedy's and Justice Breyer's opinions in *Alvarez* is that there was an insufficient showing of relevant harm.[35] In Justice Kennedy's opinion, this complaint had a causal flavor: there was insufficient evidence that lying directly and irreparably *caused* the honor of veterans to diminish.[36] Justice Breyer's opinion echoed this concern but emphasized that there was no particularized harm because Mr. Alvarez deceived no one.[37] Their complaints dovetailed with their gen-

---

[35] United States v. Alvarez, 132 S. Ct. 2537, 2545, 2547–49 (2012); *id.* at 2554–56 (Breyer, J., concurring). *See also* United States v. Alvarez, 617 F.3d 1198, 1212 (9th Cir. 2010). *See generally*, Larry Alexander & Emily Sherwin, *Deception in Morality and Law*, 22 LAW & PHIL. 393, 408–09, 433 (discussing the general requirement of harm [or, in contract, induced agreement] as an element in the legal regulation of deception). *See also* David Han, *Autobiographical Lies and the First Amendment*, 87 N.Y.U. L. REV. 70, 117 (2012) (emphasizing that either a particularized effort to gain material advantage over the listener or the infliction of "colorable material harm" should be preconditions of regulation).

[36] *Alvarez*, 132 S. Ct. at 2549 (plurality opinion).

[37] *Id.* at 2554, 2556 (Breyer, J., concurring). *See also* Charles Fried, *The New First Amendment Jurisprudence: A Threat to Liberty*, 59 U. CHI. L. REV. 225, 238 (1992); Varat, *supra* note 17, at 1120–21; State v. 119 Vote No! Comm., 957 P.2d 691, 696–97 (Wash. 1998); Brief of Professor Varat, *supra* note 15, at 2. The related claim—that no specific person was adversely affected—should be disputed. When the transparent or suspected liar presents himself as other than he is, he immediately initiates a relationship with his audience while simultaneously conveying that he resists participation in that relationship in good

eral concern with government overreach: a demand that there be a tight connection to relevant harm would set limits to what might otherwise be a rather broad grant of government power.

Although these concerns complement each other, as I argued above, there are other ways to address the concern about over-enabling the government. Does the purportedly loose connection between lying and legally cognizable harm to specific people raise independent free speech concerns? As a general matter, neither version of the complaint that there is an insufficiently tight connection between lying and legally cognizable harm seems tenable as an independent objection. Justice Kennedy may well be right that the administration failed to demonstrate that the lies of Mr. Alvarez and others like him diminished the esteem in which actual veterans and service-members were held by the public. But, as I have stressed, there are other harms to consider. As I have been arguing, deliberately false speech does damage to our collective testimonial framework by giving us reasons to doubt that a person's word is reliable as such and that somber testimonial speech provides us with warrants to take what is offered as representing what is believed. That is, deliberately insincere speech does collective harm by ambiguating signals that function well only when fairly clear, signals whose preservation and use are crucial for sustaining a functional moral and political culture.

Lies directed at particular individuals also do particularized harm by corroding the foundation of justified testimonial trust between the liar and her audience members. Thus, Justice Breyer shows shocking insensitivity when he blithely suggests that ". . . in family, social, or other private contexts . . . lies will often cause little harm."[38] To the contrary, in relationships that regularly draw upon such trust and may gain some of their special significance by the ongoing vindication and exercise of such trust, betrayals of that trust would seem to wreak special damage on the relationship and its meaning.[39]

Notably, these arguments appeal to the *reasons* for belief that are supported or undermined by people's testimonial practices. The diminishment of the listener's warrant to believe the speaker merely on her say-so is a rational entailment from the speaker's lie. The diminishment of the

---

faith. Being invited or drawn into a bad-faith relationship that one cannot exit is arguably harmful; it is certainly a poor way to be treated.

[38] *Alvarez*, 132 S. Ct. at 2555.

[39] We may shrink from direct regulation of much intimate communication, but surely it is not on the grounds that intimate lies are innocuous.

warrant is not an empirical event to be observed or measured. Consequently, because this is not primarily an empirical argument, the demand for empirical causal proof is inapposite.

To be sure, this nonempirical problem has important empirical counterparts. When people appreciate that their reasons to accept others' testimony have been diminished, the culture of trust will noticeably deteriorate. (Some of us fret we have already reached this point; others, I find, are more sanguine about the current culture.) But, we need not wait for this consequence to appear for the public interest to be adversely affected. I am not merely making the point that a reasonable prediction of the consequence would be enough, just as the government may preemptively adopt noise regulations that preclude the operation of gas compressors in a residential neighborhood rather than having to wait for a cacophony before addressing its predictable cause. My further point is that we are already adversely affected when our reasons to believe others are threatened, whether we realize, acknowledge, and internalize that threat or not. So too we are adversely affected when lies introduce an epistemic need to investigate and confirm the particular reliability of individual speakers or their reliability about specific topics, e.g., when we must garner particular evidence of their truthfulness as individuals or about specific topics before we may take their speech to offer acceptable warrants. Again, we may have this need before we recognize it.

To demand not only empirical evidence of harm but also a showing of particularized harm to specific people as a constitutional prerequisite for governmental regulation is a rather perverse idea, especially in light of "standing" doctrines that preclude private suits to vindicate diffuse collective harms. That is, requirements of particularized harm usually figure in "standing" requirements that identify which parties are eligible to pursue *private* actions on their own behalf.[40] One of the justifications for the standing doctrine is that governmental regulation, rather than private suits, represents the more appropriate way to handle diffuse threats to the collective interest.[41] Hence, it is rather jarring to encounter the undif-

---

[40] *See, e.g.*, Lujan v. Defenders of Wildlife, 504 U.S. 555, 560 (1992) (requiring an actual or imminent, concrete and particularized "injury in fact" for an individual to have constitutional standing to sue).

[41] *See, e.g.*, Warth v. Seldin, 422 U.S. 490, 500 (1975) (arguing that one reason for the prudential standing doctrine is to prevent courts from "decid[ing] questions of wide public significance even [when] other government institutions may be more competent to address the questions . . . ."); United States v. Richardson, 418 U.S. 166, 179–80 (1974) (arguing that generalized grievances are meant to be addressed through the political process); *see*

ferentiated impact of pure lies as a rationale for invalidating governmental regulation. Given our strong standing doctrines, governmental regulation becomes the only mechanism to vindicate diffuse, collective interests. To demand a showing of particularized harm as a condition for government regulation in this domain, then, seems, confusedly, to extend standing requirements to state action, an extension that conflicts with a leading justification of the standing doctrine and the responsibility it assigns to government to vindicate collective interests.

We can lay bare the peculiarity of Justice Breyer's demand that particularized harm must be shown by drawing a limited comparison to regulations on excessive noise, or time, place, and manner restrictions that levy specific ceilings on noise (think of requirements that audiences use whispers rather than megaphones for side-commentary at a lecture). One legitimate aim of noise regulations is to enable others to speak and be heard without distortion, strain, or intermittent interruption. Preserving the ability of all to speak and be heard is a constitutionally legitimate aim, even if no particular parties are singled out or injured by violations of the ordinance (suppose that in the face of such noise, all parties declined to try to speak or listen, so no one's speech in particular was disrupted). The point of demanding a showing of harm is to ensure that speech is not regulated merely because many find it distasteful or to ensure that the regulation pursues a legally appropriate interest and does not regulate immoral behavior as such. These are legitimate aims, but they do not entail a requirement of *particularized* harm. These constraints are satisfied if the motivation for regulation is to preserve the scheme of reliable communication or to adopt a public stance that reliability is a communal good.

I have been arguing that a stress on particularized harm through deceptive impact reflects an overly restrictive understanding of the wrong of the lie. Correcting this myopic view would also impugn the common invocation of "counter-speech" as a preferable response over regulation. The Court, for example, argued that the dangers associated with misrepresentations could be sufficiently addressed through the remedy of counter-speech, a less restrictive alternative than legal regulation.[42]

---

also *Lujan*, 504 U.S. at 576–77 ("Vindicating the *public* interest . . . is the function of Congress and the Chief Executive."); Allen v. Wright, 468 U.S. 737, 751 (1984) (reviewing that the standing doctrine "embraces . . . the rule barring adjudication of generalized grievances more appropriately addressed in the representative branches").

[42] *Alvarez*, 132 S. Ct. at 2549–51.

Counter-speech can be an effective remedy where the putative harm of speech flows from its content and counter-speech can expose the reasons to reject that content. Hence, counter-speech can expose the false content of a deceptive representation and thereby guard against the risk of the audience gaining false beliefs. Of course, where the information is not widely known or is exclusively possessed by the speaker, this option may be unavailable or delayed, rendering it only partially effective.

Counter-speech does not, however, speak to the damage from the lie itself, independent of its likely deceptive impact. The lie itself indicates a willingness on the part of its issuer to use speech to misrepresent while presenting that speech as veridical. This willingness undermines the reliability of that speaker's testimonial warrants. It gives us *reason* to reduce our confidence in testimonial warrants from the speaker. Counter-speech by others cannot restore *those* warrants. Only an apology and a demonstrable commitment to change by the liar could do that, but that is neither something we can rely on nor what the "counter-speech" advocates have in mind.

The demonstration that our fellow citizens are willing to lie may also give us reason to doubt testimonial warrants as such even more generally. Should members of the public come to believe that such willingness may be widespread, socially tolerated, or that our own obligations to truthfulness wane when the conditions of reciprocity are flouted, the consequent reduction may be severe. Although our obligations to truthfulness do not, as I have argued earlier, diminish just because others contravene them, the state may reasonably take an interest in forestalling or responding to currents in the culture that in fact reduce compliance with politically relevant forms of moral behavior, even if those currents represent unjustified reactions to others' malfeasance.

Whether by government or by individuals, counter-speech castigating lying may help dispel the impression that deliberate misrepresentation is acceptable and help keep moral morale and resolve high. But, counter-speech cannot dispel the impression that it is legally discretionary whether to misrepresent (and so acceptable in that way). More importantly, it cannot work against the unreliability of the speaker that the speaker's own misrepresentation introduces. Whereas, if legal regulation were effective in motivating (some) speakers not to misrepresent and in establishing public recognition of a collective interest in truthful speech, in these ways it would be qualitatively more effective than counter-speech.

Distinguishing the Value of False Speech from the Disvalue of Misrepresentation

THE MILLIAN ARGUMENT

A complementary argument, made alongside the appeal to counter-speech, is that even false speech has value, for the Millian reason that entertaining the false provokes exposition and exposure of the truth and sharpens our understanding of it.[43] That venerable idea is misapplied here and does not discredit legal regulation of the *lie*. The Millian argument concerns propositions expressed by an utterance and the value of the expression of those propositions, even if they turn out to be false. It does not purport to justify the *disbelieved utterance* (whether it is true or false).

Notably, in the passage in *On Liberty* where Mill advances his argument for the value of false speech, he is discussing the merits of the suppression of opinions, arguing that people should be allowed to express *their actual opinions*, even if their opinions are false in the sense of being wrongheaded.[44] That is, he stresses the importance of having the opportunity to say what one believes or what one thinks one *might* believe, even if these believed propositions are false. This opportunity connects directly to the needs of the thinker to externalize her (actual) mental content to garner the reactions of others and to assess whether she in fact wishes to continue to endorse it. Once we distinguish between sincere opinions that happen to be false or incorrect and insincerely expressed opinions, Mill's argument makes sense only if we consider the former; it lacks clear application to the latter.[45]

I will elaborate. First, Mill's argument makes little sense in the case of lies on matters about which the speaker has special or exclusive access to relevant information. A false statement can only provoke exposure of the truth when others have timely access to evidence relevant to justifying or challenging the relevant proposition. Where the speaker has special or exclusive access to relevant information and functions epistemically as an expert, the checking function Mill imagines is blocked and this argument falls flat. Hence, it seems difficult to celebrate the value of false speech on Millian grounds if one has in mind expert speech about

---

[43] *See id.* at 2553 (Breyer, J., concurring).

[44] JOHN STUART MILL, *On Liberty, in* ON LIBERTY AND OTHER ESSAYS 20 (John Gray ed., 1988) (1859).

[45] *See also* Schauer, *supra* note 2, at 905 (observing that Mill was discussing opinions and not factual assertions).

factual matters for which there is limited public access (e.g., expert speech about company policy, the contents of a secret formula, or what transpired at a private meeting), and the same is true of many forms of autobiographical speech, the foundations of which the speaker has special access to.[46]

Second, Mill's own discussion imagines sincere opponents, both attempting to express and make progress on discerning what is true. He is not extolling the virtues of false statements *per se*, and certainly not of *deliberate* misrepresentation. Rather, the argument aims to vindicate the rights of sincere minorities to make their case, even when the consensus is against them. The argument imagines a vigorous debate between parties who both have access to what relevant information exists on a topic, such as the existence of God, both advancing their best understandings of how to interpret the evidence. It is difficult to extrapolate from the right of the sincere to attempt to persuade others of what they believe, to a right of the insincere to engage in deliberate misrepresentation.

There are strong reasons to resist that extrapolation. Our respect for others demands that we permit them to lay bare their beliefs and that we grapple with their sincere takes on the world. Moreover, given the fallibility Mill rightly emphasizes, we should be open to the possibility that we are incorrect and others are right. That idea, however, is a far cry from the idea that among the myriad of logically possible positions for us to entertain, we should be indifferent about which propositions we consider, paying equal attention to those actually believed by speakers and those disbelieved by the speakers who forward them as true.

Mill's argument from fallibility, while stressing open-mindedness as a reaction to the possibility of error, is not a component of a larger cynicism or nihilism. Rather, it serves as counsel to assist in the discovery of truth. It assumes that we stand some chance in doing so. In our efforts to advance the project of discovering the truth, we have to focus our inquiries. Our time and attention are limited. If we aim to identify and appreciate the truth, it is beyond foolhardy to devote those limited resources by launching off from random starting points. It makes sense to take seriously the sincere hypotheses (and doubts) of those also seeking to advance the truth who have considered the matter in good faith, and it makes sense not to assess that good faith in terms of our sense of the

---

[46] David Han makes this point about the autobiographical lie as well. *See* Han, *supra* note 35, at 93. Of course, not all autobiographical speech emanates from an expert foundation. Some of one's autobiographical details are better known and more directly known by others, e.g., information about one's early childhood and one's parentage.

validity of the hypotheses themselves. But, none of these considerations suggest that we should be equally open to hypotheses that are actively, though not transparently, rejected as unworthy by those advancing them.

I do not dispute the importance of a vigorous presentation and a careful consideration of *important* counterarguments, even those that are both false and believed by no one, as a method of fully appreciating the case for the correct position and ensuring that it is in fact correct. The issue is whether it is a central aspect of their value that such arguments be presented not just vigorously, but represented as *believed* by the advocate *even when* that representation is false. It may be true that the presentation of a counterargument is less powerful and easier to dismiss when it is presented as merely a counterargument and not backed by the full weight of the speaker's conviction. That surely gives a reason, as Mill himself argued, for hearing contrary opinions "from persons who actually believe them; who defend them in earnest, and do their very utmost for them" rather than from lackluster reporters who immediately discredit the contrary opinion they dutifully recount.[47] The centrality of vigorous advocacy also supports the importance of establishing contexts of argument in which competing advocates advance contrary positions, but where the advocates on all sides are understood to serve as the representatives of positions, while leaving their personal convictions ambiguous and obscured. Thereby, the arguments stand for themselves and do not depend upon the authority of their articulators. This is, I take it, the posture of advocates in the courtroom, who are meant to represent their positions with ferocity but are barred from representing their positions as their personal conclusions.[48] Unbridled advocacy for false views may be important, but its purposes may be achieved without protecting deliberate misrepresentation.

Thus, Mill's real but often mischaracterized point that sincere advocacy is superior to patently insincere advocacy does not vindicate equating the sincere, but misled, advocate's speech with the liar's speech. It gives us no reason to think that we would lose valuable speech if the law required insincere advocates either to divulge their disbelief *or* refrain from unambiguously representing their position as their sincere, personal

---

[47] MILL, *supra* note 44, at 42.

[48] *See, e.g.*, MODEL RULES OF PROF'L CONDUCT R. 3.4(e) (2002). "A lawyer shall not . . . assert personal knowledge of facts in issue except when testifying as a witness, or state a personal opinion as to the justness of a cause, the credibility of a witness, the culpability of a civil litigant or the guilt or innocence of an accused . . . ." Nearly every U.S. state has either adopted this language or some version of its content.

conviction.[49] Mill's argument provides no reason to believe that the insincere speech of the liar will add something essential that the zealous, but ambiguously committed, advocate lacks. Both lack sincere conviction, but the former misrepresents himself and the latter does not.

Deliberate misrepresentation should give us pause, and not merely because the liar devalues his testimony and contributes to a broader culture of unreliability. It also conflicts with our political obligations to compromise. As I remarked earlier, part of the respect we owe to others is to listen and grapple with their good-faith beliefs about the world and how we should live together. Often, politically, we should do more than listen and engage. Healthy political life demands some degree of compromise and adjustment to others' points of view, even when one has the political power to ignore the positions of the out-voted. Put aside controversies about *how much* one should compromise and whether one should ever compromise about matters of justice. On nearly any view of the social foundations of legitimacy, stability, and mutual respect, according some weight to the genuine convictions and preferences of competing political sides is an important aspect of governance.[50] But this posture and the willingness to forgo insistence on what one believes best only makes sense if citizens do not misrepresent those convictions.

Deliberate, unambiguous misrepresentation not only eviscerates the point of compromise, it fuels its cynical opposition. It justifies the suspicion that parties do not negotiate and compromise from genuine positions of conviction, but rather that they advance false positions to gain leverage and advantage. Misrepresentation undermines the crucial sense of reciprocity—of mutual commitment to acting and arguing in good faith—that is essential to sustaining a culture of well-considered compromise.[51] Thus, the proffering of insincere opinions does not sharpen our

[49] To provide a safe cushion for spontaneity and emotional expressions of zealousness, it may be prudent to adopt strict standards about what counts as unambiguous affirmation and, as a default, assume that advocacy may be (implicitly) uncertain, hypothetical, or contingent.

[50] *See* Avishai Margalit, On Compromise and Rotten Compromises (2010). For a Republican's concern that this approach to governance is waning within the Republican party, see David Brooks, *The Mother of All No-Brainers*, N.Y. Times, Jul. 5, 2011 at A21.

[51] See also the related argument of Micah Schwartzman that strategic, insincere political arguments diminish the epistemic value of deliberation in Micah Schwartzman, *The Sincerity of Public Reason*, 19 J. Pol. Phil. 375, 378, 392 (2011). Schwartzman's argument operates within the ideal of public reason in which citizens are expected to support policies and offer political arguments on grounds others could reasonably accept. My argument hinges on a weaker premise about the conditions for achieving reasonable compromise,

political convictions in the way that merely false but sincere opinions do.[52] Instead, their recital either threatens the legitimacy of the content of our compromises or threatens our willingness to engage in them, that is, it jeopardizes our willingness to discharge a political duty.[53]

SELF-DEFINITION

Let me turn to the argument that regulation of lies would interfere with an individual's interest in "self-definition."[54] An individual's privacy interests and her interests in control over the presentation of her persona can be protected by her selective choice of what true things to reveal and whether to reveal information at all. But, it is rather hard, I think, to classify lies as elements of the project of self-definition: saying something false about oneself does not make it true or thereby render the voiced characteristic a true aspect of oneself. Advocates of this position leave it unclear how the protection of the lie contributes to the project of self-definition and, concomitantly, why the ability to present edited and partial (but sincere) accounts of oneself is insufficient to satisfy the interest in self-definition.[55] The ability to decide what to reveal and to what

---

conditions that must be present in both ideal and nonideal conditions. Indeed, protecting the conditions of fair compromise may be especially important if we do not adhere to the requirements of public reason and if citizens advocate positions that rely on comprehensive theories of the good (and/or factual theories) that others may reasonably reject.

[52] In extolling the necessity of truthfulness to furthering legitimate political compromise, I do not mean to diminish the importance of irony, rhetoric, storytelling, humor, or self-discovery through communication within public discourse. *See* Elizabeth Markovits, *The Trouble with Being Earnest: Deliberative Democracy and the Sincerity Norm*, 14 J. POL. PHIL. 249, 250, 260–66 (2006) (worrying that an ethic of sincerity excludes other forms of discourse). My claim is only that the uses of nontruthful discourse should be transparent to interlocutors (although the signal of its invocation need not be so clunky as to interfere with its effectiveness).

[53] For these reasons, I am less convinced than my esteemed colleague that the admittedly powerful instrumental arguments against regulating deliberate dishonesty in political advertising carry the day. *See* Varat, *supra* note 17, at 1108, 1120–22.

[54] *See* Han, *supra* note 35, at 104–08, 127–28; United States v. Alvarez, 638 F.3d 666, 674–75 (9th Cir. 2011) (Kozinski, C.J., concurring).

[55] Han does not confront this question, but rather emphasizes that one's partial revelations about oneself run the risk of deceiving listeners into thinking that the partial story is more representative of the whole than it is. *See* Han, *supra* note 35, at 101–02. He then attempts to leverage this argument to suggest that direct misrepresentations are no more disturbing than the partial, true revelations whose potential for deception we already tolerate. *See id.* This argument fails, I think, for two main reasons: first, there are independent objections to direct misrepresentation apart from the risk of deception and second, listeners exposed to partial revelations are capable of assessing that what they hear is partial and may both adjust their conclusions accordingly and ask further follow-up questions to gauge the extent and content of the absent information.

propositions to commit are indeed fundamental components of auton-omy, components that undergird much of the protection against com-pelled speech. Yet, protection of those abilities does not preclude moral or legal prohibitions on lies. Moreover, if an aspect of one's self-definition consists of one's relations to others, that project is stymied when others misrepresent themselves. The relationships one thereby forms are not based on a mutual and commonly understood foundation and the re-sponses to one's speech that one receives do not help one hone one's self-understanding, because they are not responses to sincere, if tentative, representations of oneself.

By way of rejoinder, it could be insisted that an aspect of self-definition involves making up one's mind and figuring out what one thinks. That process, as I argued in the last chapter, may reasonably require communi-cative interaction with others in which one articulates propositions to see if they ring true, much as one might try on a dress to see if it fits. Testing the proposition for this purpose may involve asserting it in a definitive, rather than a tentative register, much as assessing a true fit demands zip-ping up the back and not merely holding up the garment in front of the mirror. Although, as I maintained when discussing the Millian arguments about the value of false speech, tentative or qualified pronouncements may be sufficient to allow audiences of contested propositions to assess the arguments in and against their favor, for some people and some is-sues, matters may differ when they attempt to identify their core commit-ments. In such cases, determining whether something "fits" oneself may require a more wholehearted assumption of the mantle.

This argument has greater purchase with respect to the articulation of opinions, e.g., about immigration reform and the legitimacy of the death penalty, or about one's intentions, e.g., to seek a new career or to alter one's religious practice, than it does with respect to other sorts of facts, including the kind of historical autobiographical facts uttered by Mr. Al-varez about his actual military service. Still, one might make a credible case that, in some instances, the assertion of autobiographical fact, even about a past event, can play a role in assessing whether that assertion is true; for example, some people in emotional distress may, in reaction to a therapist's hypothesis, assert they were victims of past abuse to see if, once said aloud, it resonates as true.

This version of the self-definition argument speaks more to how regu-lation should be crafted than to the constitutionality of all such regula-tion. The lie encompasses assertions made without qualification that the speaker does not believe but presents to be taken as true and as believed.

Arguably, the sorts of exploratory assertions discussed above need not be presented to be taken as true but may be presented in a more experimental mode (even if unqualified), so they need not involve lies in this sense at all. But, given the likelihood of exuberance and exaggeration in matters of self-presentation, such efforts may not always be carefully constructed and may involve the use of lies so understood.

Even so, the self-definition argument only has strong purchase where the speaker is uncertain. It does not really apply when the speaker makes repeated, confident assertions over time of propositions that she definitively rejects as false. Such utterances are not credibly understood as central to self-discovery, but they do threaten our testimonial relations. These observations suggest a distinction between the moral conception of a lie and the legal conception of the lie. Morally, one may lie when one confidently asserts propositions about which one knows one is agnostic or lacks sufficient evidence to support a belief (and one's assertion happens outside a justified suspended context). But, to ensure breathing room for the process of self-discovery, in autobiographical cases, the legal definition of the lie should be more restricted, applying to the somber, unqualified assertion of propositions that one actively *disbelieves*.[56] Thus crafted, the regulation would ensure that the agnostic struggling to locate her position is not accidentally captured. Adopting this narrower definition of the lie for legal purposes seems appropriately sensitive to the self-definition interest.

Perhaps the threat posed by legal regulation to self-definition is that legal regulation muddies the public expression of one's sincerity. Some worry that if lies are subject to legal penalties, then truthful claims may be interpreted as the product of legal coercion and legal compliance rather than emanating from an individual speaker's moral earnestness.[57] Further, given the backdrop of legal regulation, listeners will be unsure whether a sincere speaker spoke from the motive of legal compliance or from moral earnestness.

This complaint that well-crafted, non-draconian legal regulation will objectionably crowd out sincerity or its perception seems far-fetched. In most cases that would fall under legal regulation, agents need not speak on the matter at all, and their voluntary decision to communicate and

---

[56] I advocate this restriction only for the autobiographical lies of individuals. In my discussion of "puffery" in Chapter Six, I criticize the legal regime for permitting businesses to issue strongly worded opinions about their products when they are insincere or lack reasonable evidence that would support a sincere belief in those opinions.

[57] *Alvarez*, 638 F.3d at 675 (Kozinski, C.J., concurring).

reveal information in the first place would convey their good will, even if the law required that such communications be sincere. A speaker interested in conveying her motivations for speaking sincerely could clarify why she was revealing what she was revealing and could, through her other actions and through other speech, reinforce that her sincerity was not primarily determined by the threat of legal regulation. The insecure listener could ask questions to prompt further revelations about the reasons for the speech and the nature of the relationship. This is, roughly, how we manage the present latent uncertainty about whether truth-tellers are motivated by the value of sincerity or by the prospect of facing extralegal, social sanctions for insincerity.

Moreover, it is unclear why legal regulation would alter the dominant motive for sincerity. Most moral agents will engage in sincere utterances (or remain silent) for the general reason that sincerity is morally and usually prudentially required (whether that be concern for the audience, for the communicative relationship, for the integrity of communication, or for some other reason unrelated to its legal status). We do not worry that legal regulation of assault, theft, or littering undermines the meaning of safe relationships and conscientious environmental behavior. Rather than replacing our moral motivations, a well-designed law regulating pure lies would more likely supplement them. It would provide a public articulation of our collective interest in sincerity and establish a set of background expectations that might serve as a sort of backstop motivation for moral compliance for the good-but-tempted moral agent, and perhaps as the primary motivation for the more compromised moral agent. With respect to the latter, if the law does make the dispositive difference to whether the agent tells the truth or not, the law will not have undermined the meaning of his sincerity, because it will not have converted an instance of well-motivated sincerity into a coerced utterance.

HARD CASES OF INTEGRITY AND CONTESTED CONCEPTS

Before leaving issues of self-definition and identity, let me address some related hard cases, all of which involve contested concepts that in turn propel misrepresentations motivated by sincerity and considerations of personal integrity. Consider these three cases:

> *Transgender resistance*: Kris, a transgender woman who is chromosomally male, somberly and sincerely declares, "I am a woman," but knows that she speaks to an audience who will reasonably understand her to mean her chromosomal sex is female. Kris sincerely

believes that chromosomal and other sex-based criteria of gender are inappropriate, and so she speaks using her own criteria, although she is aware that her audience deploys chromosomal and other sex-based criteria.

Resisting bigotry: A local bigot asks Kim whether a newcomer to the local bar is a "such-and-such," where the actual term deployed is a derogatory label; although Kim knows the newcomer may meet all of the factual criteria embedded within the concept "such-and-such," Kim issues a denial, "No, she's not," because she refuses to acquiesce to the bigotry embedded in the particular term.

Political resistance: In Freedonia, Max's friend Bailey is convicted of the felony of seditious libel for publishing a truthful story that detailed a public official's embezzlements. Max regards the seditious libel law as an offense to democratic principles and a core violation of basic human rights. Consequently, he regards Bailey as a hero, not a criminal. In Max's view, to be a criminal requires the violation of a serious and fundamentally just law. When Max is subsequently interviewed for a position with the government, he is asked a series of yes or no questions, one of which is whether he associates with any criminals. Max knows that according to the government's criteria, which seem to govern the context of an official interview by the state, Bailey qualifies as a criminal in virtue of her conviction. Max believes, however, that these criteria are seriously morally defective and that it would be wrong to acquiesce in them. So, he answers "no."

In all of these cases, the speaker's beliefs and opinions place her sincerity in conflict with the conceptual presuppositions of the context (or at least of the known understandings of the audience).[58] Cases like these raise (at least) two questions: First, are these misrepresentations lies? Second, are they protected by freedom of speech as forms of sincerity and identity formation or identity performance?

[58] I am grateful to Netta Barak-Corren for raising the transgender case, and to Mark Richard for raising questions about the related issue of how to view communications between speakers and listeners who disagree over the standards of precision appropriate to the use of a particular concept in a particular communicative context, e.g., what level of wealth constitutes being "rich." For like examples and a discussion of the relevance of such disagreements to other disputes in epistemology and the philosophy of language, see Mark Richard, *Contextualism and Relativism*, 119 PHIL. STUD. 215 (2004).

It may seem peculiar to say that these speakers lied because they all sincerely applied the standards they endorse and, in light of those standards, said what they believed to be true. Yet, epistemically, the audience would reasonably, or at least predictably, misunderstand the speaker. The speaker would have misrepresented his or her beliefs, assessed under the criteria of the concepts that the speaker is aware are operating in the context, but without revealing that she deploys different criteria.

One fairly straightforward way to resist classifying the first two cases as lies is to regard them as falling into one of the categories of justified suspended contexts. The first speaker resists an invasion of privacy that threatens to transform into a form of bigotry. This misrepresentation, thus, may fall into the categories of the suspended contexts of reasonable privacy protection or reasonable self-protection and defense. So, for my purposes, her statement is not a lie. (Or, as others may see it, it is not a wrongful lie.) So, too, the second case resembles a milder version of the cases discussed in Chapter One, in which misrepresentations offered to avoid directly contributing to a wrongful end were justified. Here, we might understand the request to confirm a bigoted classification, especially one that might have repercussions for the target's safety, as creating a suspended context, so that the listener should not expect answers to be sincere or to convey reliable information.

The details may matter. The suggestion of danger may do some work in how we think about the first two examples. When that suggestion is removed, we may edge closer to regarding these misrepresentations as lies. This seems clearer in the third case, *Political Resistance*, which lacks this feature. Bailey is in no new danger if Max agrees that Bailey is a criminal. Although Max's motives for denying that Bailey is a criminal are admirable and Max speaks sincerely by his own lights, the brevity of his answer is morally troubling. Were he presented with the opportunity to say more than "yes" or "no," something would be morally amiss if he did not elaborate by indicating his disagreement with the presuppositions of the context. Moreover, whether Max can elaborate or not, a spare "no" may risk deception. Additionally, the conscientious but undisclosed, private use of different conceptions of the same concept or different standards of precision frustrates the purposes of communication.

In light of these complexities, what should we say? On the one hand, given his sincerity, it feels awkward to declare that Max lies, because his declaration is driven by his conscientious objection to the presuppositions embedded in the question. On the other hand, liars do not always have venal motives; the fact that Max is morally motivated does not itself seem like a reason to deny that he has lied. We might be tempted by the more refined idea that one does not lie if one speaks sincerely with reference to one's own conception of relevant standards and concepts or perhaps, even more narrowly, if one speaks sincerely with reference to morally correct standards and concepts. Although these suggestions have some plausibility, ultimately, it seems that merely private sincerity is insufficient to insulate one from the charge of lying. Merely private sincerity still subverts the communicative relationship in a nontransparent way. To privilege merely private sincerity risks some of the familiar pitfalls associated with the doctrine and practice of "mental reservation"[59] by confusing the ethics of a bilateral communicative relationship with the ethics of purely personal virtue.

We may better capture our sympathy for Max, on some versions of the story, by focusing on the constrained nature of the colloquy—the demand for an unadorned "yes or no" answer. When the constraints of a colloquy prohibit explanatory clarifications and thereby do not permit the speaker to convey her thoughts with the precision necessary for a modicum of accurate self-presentation, those constraints themselves thereby subvert the purposes of the truth presumption and of non-suspended contexts. It is, therefore, no surprise that we feel that some freedom of speech values are at play, although I suspect the free speech concerns attach not to Max's answer but to the artificially stunted nature of the communicative exchange.

My tentative suggestion, then, is that otherwise reasonable demands for information that take the form of requiring a simple "yes or no" answer, when combined with significant (unjustified) obstacles to clari-

---

[59] The doctrine of mental reservation emerged in Catholic theological circles in the sixteenth century. According to this doctrine, if a speaker voiced a proposition she did not believe but then qualified it mentally and privately such that she did believe the combination of its public and private elements, then she did not lie. For example, if asked whether one took money from the kitty and, in fact, one had but did not wish it known, one could say, "No, I did not take money from the kitty," and then add, mentally, the qualification "in the last two hours." The doctrine is obviously insufficiently sensitive to the social purposes of communication and the interests of hearers. It may have seemed attractive to those focused on whether, in the presence of God, a being purported to have access both to one's mind and to one's public statements, one affirmed propositions one believed to be false and whether one resisted self-deception. More moderate use of it was advocated by some as a way to elude unjust danger or unjust inquiries. *See* PEREZ ZAGORIN, WAYS OF LYING 153–221 (1990); *see also* SISSELA BOK, LYING 35–37 (1978). Interestingly, the federal oath of office executed by all U.S. officials (but the President) explicitly excludes mental reservation. One must swear to ". . . take this obligation freely, without any mental reservation or purpose of evasion . . . ." 5 U.S.C. § 3331 (2006).

fication,[60] generate a justified suspended context with respect to their answers. The obstacles to clarification create a *pro tanto* normative permission for the questioned party to refuse to adhere to those embedded standards and presuppositions within the communicative context when adherence to them would place her sincerity and beliefs in tension; where clarification is significantly constrained, the recipient of the communication has reason to doubt that he has received an accurate account of the contents of the speaker's mind and has no basis for complaint about *that fact*.[61] Where the speaker has an opportunity to expand upon his answer and clarify the disagreement about the applicable criteria, but forgoes that opportunity, then I think it is fair to say that he has (wrongfully) lied. Further, even though the speaker's misrepresentations may be driven by motives of sincerity and personal integrity, they do not seem to be protected by freedom of speech. Freedom of speech would protect the speaker's full explanatory answer, and, often, her right to give a full explanatory answer or a refusal to answer, but not the middle ground occupied by the deliberate misrepresentation.[62]

MISREPRESENTATION TO FURTHER SOCIAL RELATIONS

Finally, some commend insincere speech for its role in lubricating social relations and thereby connect insincere speech with free speech values. It is alleged that misrepresentations play an important role in etiquette, by strengthening relationships that would be made fraught by (too much)

---

[60] Think of those frustrating forms and surveys that offer only inadequate classificatory options and no box for comments.

[61] I bracket the more complicated question of when recipients would have grounds for complaint if they were thereby deceived by the speaker's answer. That question is more complex, in part because with respect to the duties surrounding deception, it may matter whether the recipient is among those responsible for, or beneficiaries of, the constraints placed on the communication; whether the recipient has reason to know of the constraints; and when speakers are responsible, if ever, for preventing unreasonable inferences by listeners.

[62] A further question concerns whether the speaker must herself be the party who elects not to avail herself of the opportunity to give a fuller answer. If that responsibility be vested in another independent party, it may help to explain why leading questions may be posed within a courtroom but yet witnesses under oath may perjure themselves if they privately substitute their own standards and conceptual criteria for the operative ones governing in the courtroom. Within an adversarial system, the reason the witness might be expected to answer truthfully within the confines of the operative standards is that the attorney on the other side has the ability to ask further open-ended questions that permit clarification. Because the point of communicative endeavor within the courtroom is to elicit the truth through fair and adversarial means, we might locate the responsibility for protecting the communicative environment to the judge and the attorneys, rather than to the particular witnesses.

truth, and by saving oneself and others from embarrassment and invasions of privacy.[63] Although this line of argument is driven by some important insights, its strength relies on conflating lies with reticence, mere
deception, and with the use of suspended contexts in which the presumption of sincerity does not operate. The case for the legal regulation of lies
does not depend on the questionable view that we must adopt a practice
of frequent, regular revelations of all painful truths or a practice of correcting all misunderstandings of our audience. There is an important
distinction between directly advancing and affirming a falsehood and
permitting (and even encouraging) another to form or retain a false belief. In some cases, the latter violates a duty of care toward supporting
the accuracy of others' beliefs, but in other cases, especially in domains
of privacy and social relations, there may be no such default duty. Yet
many of the examples offered by way of demonstrating the value of lies
of this kind instead involve failures to disclose painful information or
partial truths that may, predictably, be misunderstood by listeners as denials of painful truths. As I discussed in Chapter One, when the listener
develops or retains a false belief from a sincere communication coupled
with a failure to disclose, this is a case of deception but not of a lie because the false belief is not the result of a direct and explicit misrepresentation of the speaker's thoughts and does not involve the abuse of testimonial warrants.

The deterioration of the reliability of testimonial warrants is especially
worrisome, not merely because reliable warrants backing personal revelations are the foundation of strong social and moral relationships, but
because such warrants may figure among the last resorts to repair other
breaches of trust. When deception or reticence are inappropriately used
or when parties mistreat one another in the myriad ways of which we are
capable, the apology and the truthful, detailed and direct attestation to
correct the misunderstanding promulgated by deception operate as crucial remedies. If those mechanisms are sullied too, digging our way out of
cynicism, distance, and distrust may prove progressively more and more
infeasible.

To be sure, there are some persuasive examples involving the articulation of propositions the speaker privately rejects, such as exclamations of
joy at the prospect of a dreaded reunion. These cases, when persuasive,
seem however to involve standard forms of etiquette (as do many of the

---

[63] *See, e.g.,* United States v. Alvarez, 132 S. Ct. 2537, 2553 (2012) (Breyer, J., concurring); United States v. Alvarez, 638 F.3d 666, 674–75 (9th Cir. 2011) (Kozinski, C.J.,
concurring).

permissible forms of deception discussed above). Social norms of etiquette, as I argued in Chapter One, often operate in the kinds of justified suspended contexts in which we use communication to achieve purposes other than advancing propositions to be taken as true, e.g., cementing minimal commitments to social inclusion. This is publicly understood and the face-saving claims of unknown sincerity that people make within such contexts are not well-characterized as lies because, objectively understood, they are not forwarded to be taken as true. Some false claims, made defensively, to shield one's privacy from invasive and inappropriate (however innocent) inquiries should also be understood to operate in suspended contexts and should be understood as deflections, rather than lies (at least for moral and legal purposes).

There is no gainsaying that lies may have instrumental value and that they may be used as means to further otherwise good ends. But the same might be said of many other wrong actions, of many other regulable actions, and even of other forms of recognizably regulable speech. The proceeds of theft may be directed at poverty relief. Intentional defamatory speech might be used to increase the sales of newspapers whose profits all go to worthy charitable causes; fraudulent speech might be used to generate market activity and consumer confidence when the economy is faltering; incendiary speech might be used to spark violence that in turn creates effective pressure for needed government reform. So while it is undeniable that lies may be motivated by and used to further worthwhile ends, as may a range of other activities legitimately subject to legal regulation, lies are not essential to the achievement of these ends. Yet, they do inflict a unique form of damage on our ability to use communication for our most essential purposes.[64]

What is at issue is not whether lies can be used to further the speaker's ends or whether they may be used to further important and significant social ends, but whether these facts bear on whether lies have significant free speech values. My contention is that because the lie does not directly participate in the values underlying freedom of speech and because its use threatens many of the substantial purposes that motivate a free speech regime, we have reason to doubt that freedom of speech demands that lies be immune from regulation. Merely showing that lies can be put to instrumentally valuable use does not dislodge that conclusion. What would have to be shown is that lies have some overarching, unique value

---

[64] I discuss a subset of those cases in which lies are purportedly essential to uncovering the truth, such as the lies involved in police interrogations and certain forms of academic research in Chapter Six.

that cannot be readily achieved through other, more benign forms of action or sincere speech. The arguments canvassed for the value of the lie fail to meet this measure.

The Level of Review

Before I conclude the discussion of freedom of speech, I want to acknowledge what many legal readers will have noticed long ago: that my analysis did not proceed by identifying and then applying the appropriate standard of review, whether strict scrutiny, intermediate scrutiny, or rational basis. Nor have I suggested what standard of review should apply to regulations of deliberate falsifications. This is not because I endorse the view that lies (or false speech) fall outside the scope of the First Amendment.[65] My rationale is three-fold. First, I find the standard-of-review analysis at best a highly flawed heuristic device that summarizes the conclusions of arguments that first must be made; it rarely serves as a helpful algorithm for addressing new or hard issues. Second, I am fairly skeptical of the idea that regulations on some sorts of speech fall entirely outside the scope of the First Amendment, but rather think that the usual examples are either entirely wrongheaded (e.g., the obscenity and fighting words doctrines) or better explained as cases in which First Amendment concerns are adequately answered. And third, because even were I more sympathetic to the idea that some speech regulations fall outside the scope of First Amendment protection, I am not confident legal regulations on lying would fall among them.

If, for practical purposes, I were pressed to reformulate my conclusions in terms of the appropriate standard of review, I would say the following: Because the lie as such has no free speech value, strict scrutiny seems inappropriate. The government's reasons for regulating need not be compelling to warrant their regulation. But, given the serious political and structural concerns associated with the regulation of such speech, placing such regulations outside the scope of First Amendment protection or only subjecting them to rational basis review would be inadvisable. It would fail to take those concerns sufficiently seriously. Hence, I would favor a modified version of intermediate scrutiny.

[65] For powerful advocacy of the claim that deliberately false speech does fall outside the scope of the First Amendment, see Brief of Professors Eugene Volokh and James Weinstein as Amici Curiae in Support of Petitioner at 22–34, United States v. Alvarez, 132 S. Ct. 2537 (2012) (No. 11–210), 2011 WL 6179424.

Here is the modification that I have in mind. On its face, the usual recitation of the intermediate scrutiny standard asks whether the regulation substantially furthers an important governmental interest. I have been arguing that some legal regulations of the lie would further an important government interest. But, what troubles me about the usual reading of "governmental interest" is that it focuses entirely on the adequacy of the positive rationale for regulation, e.g., whether it is important and appropriately content-neutral. What is missed by this formulation is official, structured attention to the side effects of the regulation on other mandatory governmental interests—here, whether the particular regulation in question did, in the circumstances, as applied, chill speech or serve as an avenue for governmental abuses. The idea that the concern about stifling (valuable) speech, whether through actual or perceived governmental abuse, is already factored in because some scrutiny is applied seems fanciful. Briefly, my own interpretation of intermediate scrutiny would not take for granted that where there is low value speech (in this case deliberate misrepresentations outside a justified suspended context) and the substantial furthering of an important government interest (in this case, the protection of and/or the affirmation of the significance of reliable warrants), that these facts necessarily compensate for any and all side effects on the climate for speech. I would diffidently suggest a further prong of intermediate scrutiny that expressly asked whether, on its face or as applied, the regulation overburdened (valuable) speech (or other constitutionally protected interests). That test may often be satisfied in practice.

Conclusion

I have not tried to build a decisive case for the legal regulation of lies, but rather to argue that, from a constitutional point of view, whether to grant legal impunity to the lie is not settled by the foundational commitment to *freedom of speech*. Free speech values are not intrinsically threatened by legal regulation of lies. Moreover, a powerful, content-neutral motive for regulation may be to protect and strengthen the effectiveness of our communicative practices and the foundations of a free speech culture.

Acknowledging this compatibility could have practical implications, such as offering grounds to simplify the burdens of proof associated with the regulation of commercial misrepresentation by shifting the evidentiary issues from how audiences were deceived or put at risk of deception to whether or not speakers believed their utterances. Casting aside the freedom of speech objection could also push our deliberation about regulation in new directions, both toward matters of regulatory design and toward the more careful consideration of what other significant values are implicated by legal regulation. In the next chapter, I take up this latter task with respect to regulation of the autobiographical lie. Although its regulation does not inherently encroach on the free speech interests of the thinker, I argue that other substantial values of equality and community counsel against regulation and in favor of legally accommodating this wrongful behavior.

CHAPTER FIVE

Accommodation, Equality, and the Liar

In Chapter Four, I argued that legal regulation of lies need not violate freedom of speech. In particular, I contended that well-crafted regulations need not be content-discriminatory in any normatively significant way, that the permissible regulation of lies does not require a particularized victim of legally cognizable harm, and that lies lack significant freedom of speech value. From a theoretical constitutional perspective, I concluded that freedom of speech poses no inherent barrier to carefully crafted legal regulation of lies, that legal regulation might, if successful, enhance our free speech culture, and that in addition to its effects on particular recipients, deliberate misrepresentations may risk collective, non-particularized damage to the collective fabric of trust.

Nevertheless, it is hard to stomach the idea that we might be held legally accountable for the everyday lies we tell about ourselves, especially those that are not relied upon and are told outside of circumstances of heightened testimonial importance, such as courtrooms, employment applications, tax forms, and fiduciary relationships. The quotidian autobiographical lies I have in mind include the kind told by Mr. Alvarez, the insincere boasts about one's accomplishments, occupations, and travel that some make to new acquaintances or even to colleagues and friends, and even the insincere denials of personal weaknesses and escapades some issue to friends, family, colleagues, and acquaintances. (Some of Lance Armstrong's lies fall in this category, although many of his lies were relied upon or occurred in circumstances of heightened testimonial importance, under oath during official investigations of himself and others.) Even if regulation of autobiographical lies told outside circumstances of heightened testimonial importance would not offend free speech principles, the prospect does not sit comfortably. My claim in this chapter is that this justified discomfort stems not from a justified sense of a violation of freedom of speech or the right to define one's identity, but from the political values of equality and an under-theorized form of accommodation. Some deliberate misrepresentations, such as the autobiographical lies of Mr. Alvarez falsely bragging to have won the Congressional Medal of Honor (discussed in Chapter Four), are objectionable from a public point of view, but nonetheless ought to be legally accommodated as a measure of meaningful social inclusivity and an expression of a tolerant conception of political equality.

In this chapter, I attempt to identify the panoply of values encapsulated by our practices of accommodation to draw attention to the under-noticed social and legal phenomenon of accommodating moral wrongs. I argue that a constrained practice of accommodating some moral wrongs dovetails with a plausible interpretation of political equality, one that demands a high degree of willing compliance with moral principles, but not perfect compliance. I proceed to suggest some guidelines for thinking about when to accommodate moral wrongs and conclude that legal accommodation of autobiographical lies falls within those guidelines.

Accommodation

I plan to build an argument about why, legally, we should accommodate some moral wrongs that we might otherwise have a right to regulate, and then to argue that autobiographical lies fall within that category of moral wrongs. To do so, it will help to trace two sorts of accommodation, one of which is more familiar, while the other, although often practiced, is less explicitly noticed.

"Accommodation," in the sense I will use it, involves a social practice in which we absorb some of the costs of others' free and morally relevant choices in order to acknowledge, create room for, lift barriers to, facilitate, or convey a message about their choices; the social practice of accommodation typically involves some alteration or deviation from our normal approach or reactions to others' free and morally relevant choices. As I will argue, this kind of accommodation takes at least two different important forms and has at least two corresponding, important rationales.

I am not using the term "accommodation" in one of its other common senses. Sometimes we use that term to refer to cases where we alter otherwise reasonable practices to acknowledge that the conditions and practices of others do not fit the prototype around which the practice was constructed. In these cases, we practice what might be called *corrective accommodation*. For example, when we "accommodate" those with disabilities by altering entryways or lengthening exam times for some students, we change our standard practice because, whether from ignorance or for convenience, we have wrongly structured our physical or social environment around an assumption of uniformity that unfairly privileges certain people over others. Entryways built with steps or stairs implicitly presume a certain form of physical ability. Certain examination structures intended to create standard background baselines (time limits or requirements that one read printed documents personally) presume certain abilities that may be extraneous to what is actually being tested. Accommodations for some disabled people, whether through constructing different access routes or offering differently structured exams, are necessary to ensure equal access for everyone and to acknowledge that reasonable limits for some are unreasonable for others.

Although we use "accommodation" to describe these sorts of piecemeal reforms in our practices that reflect the recognition that our standard practices were built around faulty assumptions of false uniformity, we also use the term in another way that does not connote false stereotyping and depends on a separate rationale. Accommodation of this other kind denotes a willingness by third parties or the community to shoulder some burdens associated with another's *choice*, rather than compelling the individual agent to shoulder that burden entirely herself. This sort of accommodation protects an agent's deliberative environment, allowing some significant choices to be made for the reasons most relevant to the activity, rather than for reasons that contingently bear on the activity.

For example, we might view the accommodation embodied in the Family and Medical Leave Act through this lens. Under the Act, employees may take leaves of absences to attend to family responsibilities, such as the needs of a small child or a sick parent. Consequently, their job responsibilities must be shouldered by colleagues or by hiring temporary employees. The theory, albeit one imperfectly realized, is that employers and colleagues should shoulder costs and burdens to ensure that employees may make decisions about family size, family structure, and about how to care for their families without having those decisions dictated or largely dominated by the demands of employers and efficient work environments.[1]

---

[1] Family and Medical Leave Act (FMLA), 29 U.S.C. § 2612(a)(1)-(c) (2006). The Family and Medical Leave Act represents an incomplete form of accommodation, though, because the leaves of absence are unpaid and effectively, therefore, only available to some workers. Id. § 2612 (c). *See also* Julie C. Suk, *Are Gender Stereotypes Bad for Women? Rethinking Antidiscrimination Law and Work-Family Conflict*, 110 COLUM. L. REV. 1, 8–9 (2010)

Some forms of religious accommodation may represent another example. Through religious accommodation, we shoulder (again, imperfectly) certain burdens for certain religious practitioners, such as working a greater share of weekend days or paying unemployment compensation to those whose religious practices render them unsuited for a job. Allowing conscientious objection entails that others bear a greater risk of being drafted and killed in military conflict. I submit that the best justification for this accommodation practice is that it helps ensure that practioners' choices about whether and what to practice turn upon reasons relating to the perceived choice-worthiness of the religious practice and are not predetermined by financial pressures or the fear of prison. Financial pressures and the threat of punishment seem intrinsically extraneous to questions of whether and how one should worship and whether the dictates of conscience are incompatible with some forms of military service.[2] When social circumstances tie these issues together, it is understandable that people will make religious decisions based on financial concerns, but it would be preferable, where possible, to disentangle these considerations to facilitate religious decisions being predominantly based upon perceived religious considerations (or the lack thereof) that bear on the choice. Hence, we may adopt accommodation practices as a method of (partial) disentanglement.

To be sure, neither of these examples are pure ones of choice-protecting accommodation. The Family and Medical Leave Act is, in part, an institutional correction of the flawed assumption that employees are not also dedicated caretakers. Religious accommodation often serves as a correction to institutional structures wrongly designed around a dominant or majority religious practice. The FMLA goes some distance toward making employment more accessible to two-earner families in workplaces where, before, a one-earner family structure was implicitly assumed; religious accommodation goes some distance toward rendering the social

---

("The most common reason for not taking available leave is the inability to afford it"). Eligibility requirements are also difficult for many low-income workers to meet. *Id.* Some state family and medical leave statutes provide for more generous benefits to employees, whether through state funding, lower eligibility requirements, or mandated employer funding. *See* Robin R. Runge, *Redefining Leave from Work*, 19 Geo. J. on Poverty L. & Pol'y 445 (2012) (discussing the barriers to using the FMLA and examining paid leave laws in California, New Jersey, and Connecticut, as well as in several municipalities).

[2] I discuss other examples and the theoretical grounds for this form of accommodation in more depth in Seana Valentine Shiffrin, *Egalitarianism, Choice-Sensitivity, and Accommodation, in* Reason and Value: Themes from the Work of Joseph Raz 270 (Philip Pettit et al. eds. 2004).

environment more hospitable to practitioners of minority religions. Still, these practices also have substantial choice-protecting components. The FMLA partly equalizes the playing field when one compares two-earner families to one-earner families, but it also shifts some of the costs of some people's choices to have and raise children on the childless. Religious accommodation partly equalizes access to social environments when one compares members of dominant religions with minority religions, but the practice as a whole displaces some of the costs associated with choosing to be religiously observant on those who do not make those choices.[3]

From this perspective, the FMLA and religious accommodation practices resemble other accommodation practices in which we absorb costs to insulate others' choices from the deliberative pressures that more rigid cost-internalization practices would exert. Privacy protections represent another such example. Protecting privacy rights over information about one's relationship status, one's credit rating, or one's off-duty behavior may deprive employers, for example, of useful information that would allow them to adjust hiring or work assignment decisions in light of their employees' choices. Insulating citizens from government searches without a warrant may deprive the community of useful information helpful in solving crimes or even of absolving the wrongly accused. Still, we protect many people's choices to keep information private in order, I submit, to insulate them from the potentially distorting influence of others' observation and judgment.

These important forms of accommodation and their deliberation-protecting rationale would not, however, supply a reason to refrain from regulating lies as one method of maintaining the culture of trust. As I argued in Chapter Four, the rationale for legal regulation and the mild pressure or moral reinforcement any well-crafted law would exert need not introduce domineering reasons for truthfulness that are objectionably distant from the most salient reasons to be truthful. Although we may hope the primary reason to tell the truth would be respect for one's interlocutors and for oneself, an interest in the general climate of testimony that the law would protect should not be a distant motivation ei-

---

[3] One may object that some religious practices are regarded by their practitioners as compelled and not as the product of their choices. That's true for some believers and not for others and true for some practices but not others. Some people switch churches and adopt new forms of worship by choice, because other modes feel more welcoming or, on the other hand, desirably stricter. Some people choose particular offices or occupations within their religious community that are not *required* by the terms of the religion, e.g., becoming a priest or a cantor. We still have reasons to accommodate these practices, even when they reflect free choices perceived as such and not (perceived) as compelled activity.

ther. In this way, legal regulation of lying differs from the scenarios I have been discussing in which we accommodate people's choices to avoid the vagaries of socially connected life that may render some considerations more salient than they should be to important deliberations, e.g., those about religious practice or familial decisions. Legal regulation of the lie would not distort deliberation about whether to lie or to tell the truth in the same way as conscription requirements or ungenerous employment conditions may distort religious deliberation or deliberation about family creation and caretaking.

Accommodating Moral Imperfection

Nonetheless, the uneasy prospect of regulating pure autobiographical lies, that is autobiographical lies that do not also deceive, raises the question of whether there is another ground for accommodation, in addition to the deliberation-protecting form that I have just sketched. The case of pure autobiographical lies nicely frames the question of whether we have strong reasons to accommodate others' moral flaws and foibles, even when those flaws impose general externalities and even when a decision not to accommodate them would not skew or distort deliberation.

As I may have signaled simply by raising the question, I have sympathy for the idea. My sympathy does not resonate with the idea of accommodating people's immorality as such, in giving them a break from moral norms or an occasional vacation from accountability to others. It isn't that the pure lie is the sort of minor wrong that we should wink at to demonstrate our less-than-totalitarian nature. Lies are importantly wrong and should be forsworn. Socially and interpersonally, we should be far less casual about lies, as a moral matter, than we are. And, as I have argued, the lie is a legally relevant form of moral wrong, one we have a collective interest in preventing, criticizing, and deterring. Nevertheless, although free speech principles pose no barrier to regulating pure autobiographical lies, declining to regulate them may nevertheless represent a warranted form of accommodation that conveys an important sort of inclusivity and recognition of the sort of agents we are.

I have been assuming that when a speaker lies and either intends or succeeds at deceiving another about a material matter, the consequent speech is regulable as a form of attempted or successful manipulation of another or as an effort to interfere with the listener's rational capacities.[4]

---

[4] For strong accounts of the legal basis for regulating deception as such, see C. EDWIN

Many lies take this form. But many do not. Some lies do not concern material matters but rather inconsequential details, especially unimportant biographical facts. Further, as I have emphasized throughout, lies need not have the effect of deception or be motivated by the intent to deceive. There are still free-speech compatible reasons to regulate such lies given that they denigrate the rational basis of our trust in one another and may degrade the moral culture of trust. But should we regulate them?

As I discussed in Chapter One, often the reasons people lie are more self-regarding than other-regarding, particularly when the lie is unaccompanied by any intention to deceive. The liar may be unable to admit things about himself to others, but may feel the pressure to speak, and so may create autobiographical fiction to cope with the situation. Or, the liar may be unable to admit things about himself fully to himself through public declaration. He may be clinging to an ambiguous form of partial denial. Sometimes, the liar may be nervous or insecure and so manufacture details about the world to give himself the feeling or the appearance of belonging and of confidence.

In the examples I have just rehearsed, the motivations at work involve failures related to personal insecurity, coupled with negligence toward others and insufficient respect for the importance of maintaining the social fabric and its strength. The question I want to ask is whether demanding accountability to others, politically, through legal accountability, for such failures is always warranted. Of course, we rightly ask people to learn to manage their insecurity in ways that reduce the burdens displaced onto others. The self-regarding motivation is not an excuse or a justification for such behavior. But, accommodating such flaws through forbearance from legal rebuke is a way publicly to manifest compassion and understanding for one another's shortcomings.[5] In so doing, we demonstrate the strength of our inclusivity, by showing that we recognize that

BAKER, HUMAN LIBERTY AND FREEDOM OF SPEECH 32–34 (1992); David Strauss, *Persuasion, Autonomy and Freedom of Expression*, 91 COLUM. L. REV. 334, 335, 365–68 (1991) (arguing both that deception involves objectionable manipulation and that "a rational person never wants to act on the basis of false information"). For an argument that the strength of these grounds may depend upon how diffuse the deception is, see Jonathan D. Varat, *Deception and the First Amendment: A Central, Complex, and Somewhat Curious Relationship*, 53 UCLA L. Rev. 1107, 1115 (2007).

[5] In this way, greater equalization of health care premiums and permitting former alcoholics to be eligible for liver transplants may represent two forms of accommodation. *Ex ante*, these practices protect self-regarding consumption and lifestyle decisions from what might feel like draconian social consequences. *Ex post*, these practices may amount to social absorption of the costs of other people's incontinence.

we each have shortcomings, but our imperfections will not disqualify us from full membership, in good standing, in social and political settings.

I will start my argument for legal accommodation of moral failings first with some observations about accommodation within interpersonal morality. It is not merely a counsel of politeness and of prudence that one should forbear from calling attention to every instance of others' errors, even moral errors. Such reticence also represents an aspect of the virtue of toleration. Much toleration involves restraint in the face of others' decisions and commitments of conscience, commitments that the tolerating find alien, distressing, or wrong.

But the virtue of toleration may also apply to others' flaws and errors that may not represent their deep commitments. For example, one may tolerate a colleague when one exercises restraint in the expression of one's complaints about him, even when one's colleague would agree with the substance of one's complaint. Such toleration conveys a compassionate acknowledgment of our shared, flawed humanity and the message that we are willing to continue on together, despite our predictable failures. Normatively, we may expect compliance with the relevant norm and may reasonably judge a violation of it as a violation. Still, refraining from certain forms of rebuke, criticism, and commentary signals a willingness to be patient with others. It signals a (limited) willingness to allow them to recognize and address their shortcomings on their own, at their own pace, as well as an acknowledgment of their ongoing membership in a relationship or in the community that does not depend upon their achieving perfection.

Obviously, there is a difference between showing understanding and acceptance of others' flaws and turning a blind eye to wrongs and to injustice. Compassion should not turn into acquiescence with or apathy towards evil. The idea that not every wrong demands exposure and an accounting may be significant, but, by necessity, this notion must have a limited scope. Moreover, given that there are many venues where we could manifest such compassion, two questions may present themselves: First, should we ever manifest such compassion politically and legally, rather than just personally through interpersonal toleration and forgiveness? Second, is there a limiting principle that identifies when we should accommodate in this way and when we need not?

One may be inclined to think that this form of toleration is appropriate mainly in interpersonal relations. When parties know one another and have a relationship, they may reasonably decide to show tolerance for one another and forbear from standing on their moral rights. Letting things go and accepting people as they are constitute ways to initiate a friendship and to build and demonstrate affection within oneself. But, so the objection may proceed, these are not stances appropriate to or demanded of relations between strangers.

Yet, we do, in fact, witness this behavior in the legal and political sphere, between people who have no relationship to one another other than sharing membership in a political community. Victims decide not to report crimes or not to pursue civil litigation, even when they have a clear case, and even when they lack any relationship to the wrongdoer.[6] Too often, this forbearance stems from flaws in the system. Some victims lack the conviction that they will be safe from retaliation. Others lack the time, energy, information, social support, or the financial resources to vindicate their legal rights and interests. But, these reasons do not exhaust the field. Sometimes, a victim forbears on the grounds that she understands the mistake of the wrongdoer and sees that she might have made a similar mistake herself.[7] The motivation, then, is one of compassion, a sort of recognition of our equal status and operation as flawed moral agents, and an unwillingness to take another to task for the consequences of flaws one harbors oneself.

These are cases of individual forbearance between citizens, not social or collective decisions. But, there are social, collective examples as well. Consider a small potatoes example: library amnesty programs that allow patrons to return late books without penalty and without losing their privileges. One motivation for these programs is that they effectively flush books out of private libraries back into the common stock. On the other hand, screening patrons more carefully, and threatening expulsion or higher fines might be more cost-effective if librarians' aims were simply to guard against excessive book loss. The amnesty approach suggests another motivation: namely, an institutional demonstration of the acceptance of patrons' flaws and mistakes as an aspect of the library's aim to include as many community members as possible.

Legally, there are examples at the civil and criminal level as well. Even among those who file suits in accident cases, there is evidence of a re-

---

[6] *See, e.g.*, David A. Hyman & Charles Silver, *Medical Malpractice Litigation and Tort Reform: It's the Incentives, Stupid*, 59 Vand. L. Rev. 1085, 1089, 1091–92 (2006) (discussing the low rate of litigation among Americans subject to tortious injury generally and in the medical malpractice context).

[7] *See* John C. P. Goldberg, *What Are We Reforming? Tort Theory's Place in Debates Over Malpractice Reform*, 59 Vand. L. Rev. 1075, 1078 (2006) (identifying the recognition that mistakes happen as one reason why people decline to sue despite Americans' reputation to the contrary).

luctance to seek damages from defendants beyond what defendants' insurance would pay, unless defendants act egregiously, are culpably underinsured, or there is a substantial and inequitable gap between how under-compensated the plaintiff would be compared to the enormity of the defendant's assets.[8] This forbearance is not merely the result of individual plaintiffs' decisions, but emanates, in part, from an informal moral convention among members of the bar driven by a sense of how the law should be used.[9] The moral sentiment infusing the convention by plaintiffs' attorneys to advise clients against seeking damages exceeding insurance limits (and to decline to represent clients who insist on seeking greater damages) is that even if the plaintiff has a legal right to a greater recovery, mistakes happen.[10] We are all prone to error; unfortunately, some mistakes have disastrous consequences. Given our shared propensity to negligence, the rationale is that paying and collecting insurance is the proper way to address the damages incurred by negligence.[11] It is too harsh to threaten the defendant's home or car, or to provoke his or her financial ruin in response to an accident or medical error caused by simple negligence.

Within the criminal law, prosecutors who exercise their discretion not to prosecute narcotics offenses and polities that adopt official policies of narcotics decriminalization may, in some instances, be interpreted as accommodating human weakness out of acceptance and compassion, rather than merely conceding to budgetary pressures, evidentiary weaknesses,

---

[8] Tom Baker, *Blood Money, New Money, and the Moral Economy of Tort Law in Action*, 35 L. & SOC'Y REV. 275, 275–89, 295–301 (2001). *See also* Kathryn Zeiler, Charles Silver, Bernard Black, David A. Hyman & William Sage, *Physicians' Insurance Limits and Malpractice Payments: Evidence from Texas Closed Claims, 1990–2003*, 36 J. LEGAL STUD. S9, S39 (2007). Threatening to pursue damages exceeding insurance coverage and showing that the case may support such damages, though, may be used to achieve a settlement and one approximating the limits of coverage. Baker, *supra*, at 292, 314.

[9] Baker, *id.*, at 281–84. In addition to the moral reasons supporting forbearance, there are pragmatic reasons as well, relating to the effort involved and the likelihood of success in extracting greater damages. *Id.* at 289–94. Stephen Gilles interprets Baker's interviews as showing that these practical considerations exert more weight than Baker suggests. Stephen G. Gilles, *The Judgment-Proof Society*, 63 WASH. & LEE L. REV. 603, 666–67 (2006). Absent independent evidence supporting Gilles' more cynical take, I find Baker's nuanced reading more persuasive.

[10] Baker, *id.*, at 284–86. As one plaintiff's attorney observed, "[T]he day any of us can get to the end of the month and say we didn't make a single error, you know, congratulations!" *Id.* at 286.

[11] Of course, the attractiveness of this idea may depend upon general social and institutional practices of encouraging and maintaining adequate insurance coverage and good-faith practices of pay-out on insurance claims.

or the futility of enforcement. Taking this perspective suggests a different discourse about "victimless crimes" and the legal anathema to recognizing the status crime of being an addict.[12] Even if we maintain that the primary affected party is the user, (regular) drug use (and addiction) creates and displaces plenty of externalities onto the community.[13] Rather than thinking of these behaviors as victimless and therefore normatively resistant to regulation, we might instead describe the liberal opposition to criminalizing many forms of regular drug use or the status of being an addict as a form of accommodation triggered by the recognition that the moral failure here usually stems from vulnerability and personal weakness more than it does from predation. We may regard the behavior as a sort of moral failure while nevertheless adopting the stance that the more humane and inclusive approach is not to call the offender on his offense in public, legal fora, but rather to try to help those prone to misbehavior to avoid situations that trigger it and to mitigate the externalities of such misbehavior.

Accommodation and Equality

I have been arguing that, in some arenas, we practice an interesting degree of social and legal accommodation for moral failures. I suspect that this practice does not represent mere expediency but has a deeper justification as a form of recognition and acceptance of some degree of weakness on the part of our fellow citizens. Considering what might justify these examples of accommodation also promises to be philosophically interesting in another way. It may reveal and shed light on an ambiguity in our conception of political equality. To expose this ambiguity, I need to take a detour and provide a little background.

The ambiguity that I have in mind arises within many conceptions of how commitments of equality operate within nonideal theory. Merely to

---

[12] Robinson v. California, 370 U.S. 660, 666–67 (1962) (holding that criminal penalties, especially incarceration, for the status of narcotics addiction constitute unconstitutional cruel and unusual punishment); *but see* Powell v. Texas, 392 U.S. 514 (1968) (declining to extend *Robinson* to invalidate a statute penalizing public drunkenness even as applied to chronic alcoholics).

[13] *See, e.g.,* Josh Bowers, *Legal Guilt, Normative Innocence, and the Equitable Decision Not to Prosecute,* 110 COLUM. L. REV. 1655, 1659 (2010) (referring to "petty crimes that typically lack concrete victims" and produce "diffuse social harms"); Judith S. Brook, Martin Whiteman & Elinor B. Balka, *Parent Drug Use, Parent Personality, and Parenting,* 156 J. GENETIC PSYCHOL. 137, 146–49 (1995) (confirming prior research that parental drug use detrimentally affects parent-child relationships).

add a little precision, I will situate the problem within a framework that is, roughly, Rawlsian, although the Rawlsian framework is essential neither to the ultimate conception nor to the solution to the problem. The problem relates to a question that occupies much of the literature in political philosophy: can we clarify what it means to say of us as members of a political community that we are all moral and political equals, entitled to equal treatment of some sort? Embedded within that enterprise are at least three questions: First, in what way are we moral and political equals, given significant variances in our achievements, behaviors, and abilities? Second, what sort of equal treatment does our status as moral and political equals entitle us to? Third, are there circumstances or behaviors that could alter our status or threaten our entitlements as moral and political equals?

One aspect of the second question, concerning what resources or primary goods one may be entitled to, has recently dominated the literature on equality, largely under the rubric "Equality of What?"[14] Issues related to our duties and responsibilities as equals and whether our discharge of them may affect our status and entitlements have by contrast been somewhat neglected.

The leading, and I think fundamentally correct, answer to the first question ("In what way we are equals given our enormous differences?") is, with some important modifications, the one offered by Rawls. Our status as political and moral equals is grounded in our equal possession and minimal exercise of two higher-order moral powers that we have fundamental interests in developing and pursuing. The first consists in our ability to conceive of, affirm, modify, and pursue a life structured by a conception of the good, i.e., by values and convictions about what matters and what makes for a good life. The second is our ability to understand, contribute to the conception of, and follow justice.[15] Put in different, somewhat less Rawlsian-inflected terms, we are equals in virtue of

---

[14] That literature is too vast to sample or detail responsibly. Interested readers could start with JOHN RAWLS, A THEORY OF JUSTICE (1971); Amartya Sen, *Equality of What?, in* 1 THE TANNER LECTURES ON HUMAN VALUES 195 (Sterling M. McMurrin ed., 1980); Ronald Dworkin, *What is Equality? Part 1: Equality of Welfare*, 10 PHIL. & PUB. AFF. 185 (1981); Ronald Dworkin, *What is Equality? Part 2: Equality of Resources*, 10 PHIL. & PUB. AFF. 283 (1981); G.A. Cohen, *On the Currency of Egalitarian Justice*, 99 ETHICS 906 (1989). Egalitarian skeptics about the axes pursued within this discussion include Elizabeth Anderson, *What is the Point of Equality?* 109 ETHICS 287 (1999); Jonathan Wolff, *Fairness, Respect, and the Egalitarian Ethos*, 27 PHIL. & PUB. AFF. 97 (1998); and Samuel Scheffler, *What is Egalitarianism?* 31 PHIL. & PUB. AFF. 5 (2003).

[15] RAWLS, *supra* note 14, at 504–513.

our each having a life that we should and do care about, one that we can exert agency over and can direct at what we judge to be important, and in virtue of our capacity to act morally and justly by treating others' lives as valuable and, politically, as equally important to our own.

As has been well canvassed, the normative significance of these powers, as well as our interests in developing and pursuing them, do not wax or wane depending upon the talents we possess. The normative importance of my interest in living a fulfilling life is no less than Alice Waters' interest in living a fulfilling life merely because I am the inferior chef; were I to become a better chef, it would not make the importance of my ability to live a rewarding life any more or less pressing. Nor does it seem to matter to the equal importance of my life and Alice Waters' life that many others appreciate her talent at cooking, while fewer appreciate mine. The equal moral importance of my life's going well does not vary depending upon what my talents are or how much others do or do not appreciate them. Not only is it irrelevant whether my talents are highly prized by others or relatively pedestrian, it also does not matter whether I am especially good or merely mediocre at promoting *my own* conception of the good. The normative significance of my interest in living a valuable life does not vary depending on whether I realize my capacity for developing and pursuing a conception of the good to a high degree or with only modest success and savvy. The importance of our lives and of the opportunity to live a rewarding life is equal to one another's, even if some of us are better at living well than others. These ideas propel the conviction in the egalitarian literature that if we pursue this joint cooperative project in order to facilitate our leading fulfilling lives, then because each of our interests in leading a fulfilling life is equal, there is at least a *pro tanto* case for equally distributing, where possible, those goods and resources we produce that constitute opportunities for living a rewarding life.

What is mysterious about this picture is how the possession of the first power, supporting the equal interest in pursuing a rewarding life, relates to the possession and exercise of the second moral power, the capacity for moral agency and justice, as well as how this second power relates to the question of one's entitlements. On the surface, the connection between moral agency and having the status of a *political* equal seems unexceptional. It seems reasonable to maintain that a minimal willingness to behave cooperatively, do one's part, treat others equally and with respect is a prerequisite of eligibility for demanding that one is entitled to equal treatment by others. So too, a minimal degree of moral sensitivity, appreciation for justice, and a willingness to respect the rules achieved through mutual governance seem like reasonable prerequisites for participating in a process of mutual self-governance that in turn expects the compliance of others.

The harder questions pertain first, to what level of ability and compliance we may reasonably expect of one another, and, second, when lapses in our execution of our responsibilities should threaten aspects of our status or threaten what we might call "our good standing." We may fall short in various ways with respect to the second power, while still possessing the interests and capacities associated with the first power. What implications, if any, follow?

One specific set of problems in this territory is familiar. Some severely disabled people may lack the health or the physical or mental abilities to contribute to the cooperative enterprise, even given an expansive view of what constitutes "contribution," and even were our workplaces and public spaces properly configured to be more accessible to the disabled. Other severely cognitively disabled people may not, on some conceptions, meet the minimal requirement of possessing the capacity for moral agency and justice. Yet, in neither of these cases would we doubt that their normative interest in leading a rewarding life is equal to that of the more able or that they deserve to be treated as equal members of the community. How do these convictions square with the idea that the second moral power partly grounds our equality? Even without the possession or exercise of the second capacity, should these disabled persons nonetheless be considered equal cooperative members entitled to primary goods within the cooperative scheme? Or, does their status and treatment fall under some other rubric? Either way, are they entitled to the same share of the benefits and burdens of social cooperation (however that is assessed), or does some other standard of distribution govern their entitlements?

A second set of problems is also familiar but less discussed. Most of us feel fairly comfortable with the idea that some transgressions may legitimately threaten our access to some of the primary goods we otherwise may demand as equal citizens. For example, although the murderer may retain his baseline capacity for moral agency or justice, his behavior may justify limiting his opportunities to exercise certain basic liberties, e.g., of mobility, occupation, choice of residence, and freedom of association. Yet, even for the murderer, these limitations may not be comprehensive. Most believe that all legitimate prisoners should retain a modicum of recognized rights, such as rights of due process, at least minimal rights of freedom of speech (to read, to write, to express political agreement or dissent), rights against cruel and unusual punishment, and rights to at least minimal levels of the material resources that enable a decent life.[16] They are still are entitled to equal protection under the law. And, many believe, that for all but perhaps the worst crimes, the legitimately convicted should have an opportunity to regain their status as political equals in good standing. They should, at some point, be permitted to reenter the community and regain access to the full panoply of entitlements of citizenship, including the right to vote. How exactly the failure to exercise one's second power affects one's status and entitlements seems poorly understood.

Considering these problems together suggests a partial solution. Discussions of the grounding and implications of equality tend to conflate moral and political equality into a single category, to treat the entitlements and responsibilities of equals as a package, while neglecting duties, powers, and responsibilities as a crucial part of the entailment of having equal status. Resisting these tendencies may help to clarify matters.

Suppose we start by distinguishing the category of moral equals from the category of political equals. If we think of moral equals as those about whom the normative importance of their lives going well is equal to that of others, it seems obvious that the severely cognitively-disabled belong in this category, just to focus on one hard case. In light of their moral equality and membership in the community, they are entitled to equal consideration when social decisions are made that may affect their lives. They may also claim equal rights of access to the resources that are necessary for and make possible a fulfilling life.[17]

But, the recognition of their status as moral equals is compatible with doubting that they have the requisite capacities that underwrite a full right to pursue that life autonomously and to make autonomous deci-

---

[16] As discussed at greater length in Chapter Three, however, our use of solitary confinement conflicts with these commitments. Further, although the Supreme Court has affirmed that First Amendment rights do apply to prisoners, the Court applies a more relaxed standard of review for speech restrictions. Turner v. Safley, 482 U.S. 78 (1987). Shockingly, the Court has upheld regulations that, as a behavioral incentive, withhold newpapers, magazines, and personal photographs from "recalcitrant" prisoners for prolonged and even indefinite stretches of time. Beard v. Banks, 548 U.S. 521 (2006).

[17] Because my topic here is not distributive justice, I will bracket the issue of how to assess what the appropriate standard of distribution is for the disabled *qua* moral equals as well as for the more able *qua* moral equals. I also bracket the related question of whether active participation in the joint project of social cooperation forms the basis for a greater share. Although these large questions represent the Gordian knot of problems in distributive justice, it still represents some progress to disentangle them from the question of whether the severely disabled are equal members of the community; this latter question should be unequivocally affirmed.

sions about how to use the resources to which they may be entitled.[18] This is not merely because their prudential competence is compromised. It is also because many basic liberties, including the discretionary power to use economic resources as one sees fit in a joint economic system, may reasonably depend upon one's having the capacity to exercise them responsibly, showing good faith with respect to the effects on the community. Likewise, we may regard them as moral equals while believing they lack the requisite capacities that ground claims to exercise the franchise and, in other respects, to execute the full portfolio of political powers and responsibilities.

More generally, I think we should say that those with the first power, but who are without the qualities that constitute minimal possession of the second power, belong to the community of moral equals, but they are not members of the community of *political* equals, the group of those who possess both powers. Their status as moral equals entitles them to make claims to those goods and liberties grounded in the first power, including the right to be represented by political equals, the right to be afforded equal protection under the law, and other aspects of equal concern and respect that flow from the equal normative significance of their having lives that matter. But, having the further status of a political equal demands, at a minimum, that one have the requisite capacities of moral agency and justice and that one be willing to exercise them. Although its execution is often imperfect, the idea of decoupling equal representation from equal power is commonplace. Children and resident aliens, for example, lack formal political power but count as equals for purposes of apportioning Congressional districts.[19]

Forging a distinction between the status of being a moral equal and being a political equal may help us untangle our views about when poor behavior jeopardizes or, perhaps, suspends one's status as an equal and when, more commonly and more mildly, it places one in poor standing.

---

[18] They may, of course, have the capacities and interests that would ground partial rights of autonomy, namely the right not only to have their treatment guided by their best interests but also the right to have their own perspective on their treatment be heard and given some weight. *See* Seana Valentine Shiffrin, *Autonomy, Beneficence, and the Permanently Demented, in* DWORKIN AND HIS CRITICS 195, 202–03 (Justine Burley ed., 2004); Agnieszka Jaworska, *Respecting the Margins of Agency: Alzheimer's Patients and the Capacity to Value*, 28 PHIL. & PUB. AFF. 105, 135–37 (1999).

[19] *See* Congressional Apportionment: Frequently Asked Questions, U.S. Census Bureau, http://www.census.gov/population/apportionment/about/faq.html#Q2 (last visited Sept. 10, 2013). ("The apportionment calculation is based upon the total resident population [citizens and non-citizens] of the 50 states.")

We might reasonably take the view that those with the capacity for moral agency and justice have some responsibility to exercise that capacity through compliance with legitimate social rules and by using their powers and opportunities responsibly to ensure that the interests of all moral equals are adequately respected and represented. Malfeasance may jeopardize or compromise one's entitlements to the powers, responsibilities, and goods associated with that capacity. One's full good standing may be contingent upon one's minimally compliant behavior as a *political* equal. If one has the capacity to contribute to the project of joint social cooperation but chooses not to do one's fair share, that choice might be relevant to what claims one may then legitimately make to benefits from the social project or to one's retention of control over deciding *how* one will make one's contribution. So, perhaps some rights may attach to one's status and good standing as a political equal who is qualified to make discretionary decisions about the use of what are arguably public resources, powers, and privileges. We might, for example, think malfeasance disqualifies one (for a period) from positions of power or public office (think of character qualifications for the bar or removals from public office) or in more extreme cases, from the freedom to interact freely in public spaces and to use economic resources according to one's own judgment (think of imprisonment, house arrest, fines).

At the same time, one's malfeasance as a political equal does not implicate one's status as a moral equal or the entitlements that follow from that aspect of one's status. This distinction may explain why even those guilty of terrific malfeasance do not lose or waive their right against cruel and unusual punishment, to the minimal resources necessary for health and maintenance, or to minimal rights of freedom of speech, because these rights derive from one's status as a moral equal. This idea unsurprisingly dovetails with the argument in Chapter Three that the fundamentals of free speech rights extend to children and the mentally ill.

Thus far, I have been making three points. First, we should distinguish between one's status as a moral equal and one's status as a political equal. Having the capacities that render one a political equal yields entitlements to a variety of powers and opportunities to exercise those capacities, as well as to duties and responsibilities to show equal consideration for and to represent the full community of moral equals. Second, through dereliction of one's responsibilities as a political equal, one may forfeit, for a period, one's status as a political equal or, in lesser cases, merely endanger one's status as a political equal *in good standing*. Third, even when one does so through spectacularly bad behavior, there are limits to the repercussions of one's compromised status. One does not lose one's entitlements altogether; indeed, even in cases where one's behavior places one is in poor standing, one remains a member of the community and one remains a moral equal.

With these distinctions in hand, let us return the question raised by the social accommodation of moral failures. This issue relates to my second point just above and necessitates an inquiry into what sorts of dereliction should threaten one's status as a political equal (however mildly). The notion that our status as political equals presupposes a capacity for moral agency and justice as well as the active exercise of that capacity remains ambiguous with respect to what degree of compliance with established social norms may be demanded. Given the inalienability of one's status as a moral equal, could unerring compliance be made a condition of being a political equal in good standing, or is that status compatible with significant forms of imperfect moral behavior? Put more precisely, could a just polity condition full status as a political equal on achieving and maintaining a morally perfect record with respect to rules regarding legitimate matters of public concern?

My conviction is that such a standard would be absurd. As I argued in previous chapters, we have duties to make moral progress with respect to our own lives and also to help one another achieve moral progress both as individuals and as a society. To require that this aspiration be completely realized by each person at the brink of adulthood as a precondition of full status as a political equal in good standing is overly exacting and utopian. It is in tension with the understanding that the attainment and execution of moral agency in each of us represents both a process and an achievement toward which we, together, cooperate and contribute. For this joint moral project of cooperation and mutual self-governance to represent a project of *ours*, each of us must be able see ourselves as real members of it and not merely as imposters, worried that we may be exposed and relegated to a lower status. Even as we may reasonably exhort people to achieve a high standard, a reasonable political theory of how *we* are to cooperate together must, in some sense, "take people as they are," and we are all imperfect moral agents. If that is right, then in some noticeable ways, politically, we should mark our acceptance of one another as full members despite some defects in our realization of our second higher-order power.

These points have most urgency when it comes to deciding what sorts of misbehavior should be subject to the criminal law, because criminal convictions so evidently compromise one's public standing. Further, although civil liability may often have a milder effect than criminal liability, the value of accommodating moral imperfection is also relevant to the decision to impose civil liability, at least in those cases where the aim is to identify and hold parties accountable for wrongdoing. Of course, some civil regulations do not attempt to mark moral wrongs but rather aim to provide citizens guidance, coordination points, or a system to identify and collect payments for collective costs. Other civil regulations do, however, single out behavior on the grounds that such behavior threatens an important public good and aim to hold people accountable for publicly relevant wrongdoing as such. To be found responsible as an individual for wrongdoing subject to this procedure of accountability, and possibly, to be subject to remedies that constrain or require certain uses of resources compromises (for a time) one's claim to be a full political equal in good standing.

Some may find this claim about the relationship between civil regulations and good standing exaggerated. I won't dwell on that dispute. My quarry can be tracked without resorting to the language of good or bad standing (although I find it a helpful framing). What ultimately matters is whether we think it appropriate to hold each other accountable, publicly, for each and all of our undeniably relevant failures of public morality.

I think it is inappropriate. The attractiveness of the previously rehearsed examples of social and legal forms of accommodation for moral failures serves as evidence that an alternative is plausible and more reasonable. Through these alternative practices, we signal some acceptance of people's weaknesses as moral agents. The form the acceptance takes is not indifference or complacency about the behavior or the status, but forbearance from particularized forms of regulation or prosecution of the disfavored behavior. In doing so, the community signals its foundational commitment to inclusiveness, demonstrating that one's status as a political equal, in good standing, is not contingent upon unwavering perfection.

Still, and obviously, this accommodation must have limits. The community cannot, as a moral or a prudential matter, show such inclusiveness at every turn. Many, perhaps even most, missteps of legally cognizable significance merit identification and some sort of remedial response. But even in such cases, we must also signal our inclusive stance by ensuring that for most (perhaps all) crimes, punishment may come to an end because there are accessible pathways back to full participation and full status in civil life.[20]

---

[20] Ongoing mechanisms of continuous legal and social subordination of people in vir-

When Should We Accommodate Moral Failure?

So, assuming we should sometimes accommodate through forbearance, but that we should not always do so, where and when should we express this inclusiveness? Because inclusion-motivated accommodation involves forbearance from what one would otherwise have a right to do, it seems plausible that our duty to engage in it takes an imperfect form. Although it may be extremely important to engage in this form of concrete expressive inclusiveness, we need not accommodate at every turn to achieve the expressive end. *Ex ante*, no wrongful actions seem like intrinsically mandatory objects of inclusion-motivated accommodation. Hence it should come as no surprise that there is no clear formula for when we must exercise it. The case for accommodation would be made through rough triangulation rather than mapping a direct route. Why then might we be tempted to think that pure lies represent an appropriate instance for public accommodation?

One triangulation point may be the following positive motivation: if this form of accommodation manifests our conception of political equality, we should practice it, at least sometimes, in ways that are likely to apply to everyone and not just to some of us. If so, even were our practices of rehabilitation, prosecutorial discretion, and judicial mercy more generous,[21] they still would not be sufficiently comprehensive to satisfy the expressive purposes served by demonstrative inclusiveness. Prosecutorial discretion and post-remedial measures of inclusiveness have a rather restricted portfolio of direct beneficiaries, encompassing only those whose infractions are serious enough to involve them in the system in the first place. By contrast, we may demonstrate inclusiveness more broadly by forbearing from regulating an activity that many or most people either engage in or have salient opportunities to engage in. Further, the technique of forbearance from regulating, by contrast with mechanisms of

---

tue of their prior criminal activity (such as the disenfranchisement of felons), even after a sentence concludes and the prior criminal has made good faith efforts to rehabilitate herself and reincorporate herself in the community, betray a lack of commitment to inclusion.

[21] As things stand, police and prosecutorial discretion as well as judicial mercy may be stingily administered because government agents are subject to pressure to generate high arrest rates, high conviction records, and tough sentencing reputations. *See, e.g.,* Bowers, *supra* note 13, at 1693–99 (discussing generally the pressures leading to over-enforcement of petty crimes and the failure to exercise police and prosecutorial discretion); *see also* Rachel Barkow, *The Ascent of the Administrative State and the Demise of Mercy*, 121 HARV. L. REV. 1332 (2008) (connecting norms and practices of the administrative state with the decline of discretion in the criminal law).

discretion, eliminates concerns about discriminatory application. Accommodating a commonplace activity or temptation conveys the message of equality in a concrete way, fittingly, to the entirety of the population. Moreover, including everyone in the scope of some form of accommodation may also, thereby, solidify the social bases of support for the more demanding expressions of inclusiveness involved in limiting incarceration times and attempting to rehabilitate and reincorporate more serious wrongdoers back into the community after their penal terms end.[22] Given the commonplace opportunities and temptations to lie in everyday life, forbearing from regulating the lie fits this desideratum.

Other triangulation points may help to narrow the appropriate territory for practicing this sort of accommodation by identifying where accommodation would be inappropriate. We have strong reasons not to practice such forbearance, especially broad *ex ante* forbearance, where there are particular victims of harm, particular intended victims of harm, or where the damage to public interests is or would be significant (as, e.g., with most environmental wrongs). Where there is no particularized victim of harm, but the externalities fall onto the community more generally, then no injustice is done to a *specific* person by forbearance, although the community as a whole may be wronged. Further, universal (as opposed to discretionary) forbearance seems inappropriate where the motive behind the wrongdoing involves malice to others, substantial negligence, or recklessness. Forbearance in such cases would show too little concern for potential victims. Moreover, these wrongs are less plausibly interpreted as an understandable form of weakness.

These constraints limit the arenas for the exercise of this virtue pretty severely, suggesting that when we find wrongs that meet them, we should consider them as strong candidates for inclusion-motivated accommodation, that is, for accommodation that signals our posture of inclusivity toward one another as imperfect agents. So triangulated, pure autobiographical lies may figure within rather small set of wrongs that fits these criteria. Where the motive of the wrongdoer reflects weakness, insecurity, or fear, rather than animus, manipulativeness, or an objectionable insensitivity to particular people, demonstrating acceptance and inclusiveness may be especially apt.[23] That is, where the problem's origin lies domi-

---

[22] *Cf.* Gillian Lester, *Can Joe the Plumber Support Redistribution? Law, Social Preferences, and Sustainable Policy Design*, 64 TAX L. REV. 313, 315–19 (2011).

[23] Something along these lines may explain the posture of the U.S. Attorney's office toward violations of the federal False Statements Accountability Act. The U.S. Attorney's Manual articulates a policy of prosecutorial discretion declining to prosecute "mere [un-

nantly in a person's inability to reckon well with himself, rather than in his ability to manage himself vis-à-vis others, acceptance of human frailty has a meaningful application. Its limited display does not represent a betrayal or a sidelining of other particular individuals who merit respect. Where the collateral damage is not severe, we may have located an apt venue in which to practice this virtue.[24]

To be sure, not all autobiographical lies will have these features and therefore, not all will be apt candidates for accommodation. Lies offered specifically to particular people, as opposed to general audiences, may impose particularized harm. Even when they are not believed, they may betray a relationship of trust. Often the law may legitimately regard that damage to personal relationships of trust as real but all the same an inappropriate object of legal remedy, a rift better addressed through informal, personal mechanisms. The reluctance to address such intimate harms is not always appropriate though. Autobiographical lies may bear on topics that are of what I earlier called heightened testimonial importance. Such lies may be particularly problematic when they invite particular people to be especially vulnerable, such as lies to sexual partners about one's believed disease status. They therefore may wrong particular people not only through deception but also by making an interlocutor unreliable when it is vital that she should be reliable. Autobiographical lies also may take place in settings of heightened testimonial solemnity, such as court-

---

elaborated] denials of guilt." U.S. DEP'T OF JUSTICE, UNITED STATES ATTORNEYS' MANUAL § 9–42.160 (1997). In part, this policy may embody a method of preventing abusive practices, but in part it may also reflect a recognition that denials of guilt may be a "regrettabl[e] but humanly" understandable reaction to accusation. See Brogan v. United States, 522 U.S. 398, 410 (1997) (Ginsburg, J., concurring) (describing cases in which defendants understandably, if culpably, deny wrongdoing, observing that the federal False Statements Accountability Act may confer overly broad powers on prosecutors, and commending the U.S. Attorney's policy not to prosecute mere denials despite its statutory authority to do so).

[24] Are there other examples of generally applicable practices of forbearance with respect to moral wrongs that affect the public interest but do not have particularized victims? Richard McAdams suggested, in correspondence, that the decision not to require voting by eligible voters may represent such a case. Perhaps it would in a jurisdiction that gave voters the ability to choose "none of the above" and to indicate their belief that the election was flawed or the government was illegitimate. Where voting could not be mistaken for a legitimating action and one's dissatisfaction with the system or the alternatives could be authoritatively registered, the failure to vote does seem to represent a moral failure, whether of laziness or misdirected cynicism, that affects the public by diluting the power of democratic deliberation. Under most contemporary election systems, however, because voters do not have these options and voting may be misused as evidence of legitimation, enforcement actions seem illegitimate and omissions to enforce do not seem like clear cases of accommodation.

rooms or hearings; there too, these arguments for accommodation may be strained.

These considerations may suggest a further distinction between the pure autobiographical lie in social settings and the pure expert lie about non-autobiographical topics, rendering the former more appropriate for inclusion-motivated accommodation than the latter and suggesting that the latter may more appropriately be regulated. All of us are capable of and may be tempted by the autobiographical lie, whereas the expert lie is available only to those who hold themselves out as experts; hence, accommodation of the autobiographical lie better serves the aim of engaging in accommodation with a more universal scope. Moreover, because the expert lie involves the expert affirmatively assuming the role of the expert, this moral failure does not seem as purely a product of weakness but rather involves a greater degree of positive agency. Second, the expert lie threatens a more powerful disruption to the epistemic division of labor and to our trust in the testimonial warrants of others. Socially, we designate ourselves and others as experts to facilitate the epistemic division of labor, to ensure that the less knowledgeable and trained have worthy sources from which to gain significant knowledge, and to signal where those sources are located and where we may reasonably rely on others' asserted knowledge. The expert who abuses this practice and who introduces uncertainty about expert testimonial warrants may be thought to inflict a special sort of harm by involving, but then denigrating, a dedicated communicative mechanism for the division of labor and the cultivation of reliance.

The argument I have been pursuing also supports a distinction between the treatment of pure lies by individuals and pure lies by corporate bodies, particularly business corporations. Just as corporate speech does not represent the revelation of the thoughts of the free thinker and so may not garner direct free speech protection from the line of argument defended in Chapter Three, so too arguments about accommodation only extend straightforwardly to the speech and flaws of individual agents. Individuals, not corporate bodies, are moral equals, and it is the moral weaknesses of individuals, not corporate bodies, that we should acknowledge, manifestly, are compatible with our status as moral equals.[25] We may reasonably impose full liability for corporate lies, both because they are the product of a system of people capable of checking the weaknesses

---

[25] Related arguments would distinguish between self-generated lies by individuals and lies individuals are paid or otherwise solicited to make on behalf of others.

of individual members and, especially in the case of lies told by businesses, because the standard motivations for speech and the concomitant motivations for lies do not stem from the sources that underwrite our interest in insulating speech and accommodating failure. Business-corporate speech is not part of the project of individual self-revelation and the development of mutual cooperative understanding, and the motivations for this lying stem less from weaknesses related to denial and the burdens of self-revelation than from direct and indirect efforts to achieve profits or other related business purposes.

So, although deliberate misrepresentations may not find shelter under the umbrella of free speech protection, there may nevertheless be a principled case for forgoing even well-crafted legal regulation, at least in cases of mere autobiographical misrepresentation by individuals, in order to convey that our conception of equality is inclusive in a particular way. Although we may counsel and expect the moral compliance of our citizens, this is compatible with anticipating and accepting some degree of failure. Failure is as a part of the human condition that we strive against, but we do not require its eradication of as a condition of equal status in our joint moral and political community.

This signal of inclusivity is, it might be noted, rather subtle, occurring through the omission of regulation rather than direct proclamation. In general, hidden signals of *inclusivity* may seem strange, perverse, or even passive-aggressive. But, where the posture of inclusiveness is targeted at accepting the manifestations of others' weaknesses and failings, I am less sure. A subtle signal may convey greater sensitivity than an explicit direction. If a friend gently steers a group conversation away from a topic she knows will embarrass me in a way she knows I will notice but that no one else does, that tactic surely conveys greater sensitivity than if she had explicitly declared, "Let's talk about something else. Seana might be embarrassed if we continue." This may hold true even if I fail to recognize my friend's demonstration at the time and if that failure is no accident. If my friend is masterful, she may circumnavigate the conversation without even my realizing it; I may realize only later when I reflect upon the conversation that she not only spared me from public embarrassment but spared me as well, in the moment, from recollecting the embarrassing episode privately and from feeling anxious about public exposure. My friend here managed to enact a posture of inclusivity by creating the conditions for my feeling comfortable within a group in a way that could be excavated but was not explicitly announced. In this more public case, the demonstration may also occur less directly, by securing in citizens a sense of inclusion, without their being aware of how this was achieved. If our legal actions and omissions generate a climate in which citizens justifiably internalize the sense that their belonging and their equal status is not contingent upon their perfection, then this demonstration succeeds, even if the justified belief is not the product of a deliberate, explicitly conveyed message.

CHAPTER SIX

Sincerity and Institutional Values

Previous chapters have focused on the sincerity, promissory fidelity, and free expression of individuals. I have argued that we have a basic, compulsory responsibility to establish and maintain feasible conditions under which we can understand and carry out our moral duties. This requires us to safeguard the possibility of moral cooperation and moral progress in collaboration with *all* moral agents, even those in poor standing. Creating and maintaining free, open, and reliable channels of communication is an important component of that responsibility. In turn, that responsibility grounds duties of sincerity and promissory fidelity and explains why they have application even within exigent circumstances.

In this chapter, I turn to the specific topic of freedom of speech and sincerity within institutions and institutional roles to explore how these ideas work in institutional contexts. The university will serve as my primary example. My focus will be to show how the mission or end of an institution may both ground requirements for freedom of speech and constraints on misrepresentations, even those misrepresentations whose motive is to flush out the truth.

The freedom of speech issues I will discuss arise from the line of Supreme Court opinions that, in the service of institutional hierarchy and efficiency, have circumscribed the free speech rights of public employees to speak freely about the conditions and nonconfidential content of their employment. These restrictions have been extended to some university contexts by some lower courts. I will argue both that the line of decisions is generally misguided and that the restrictions' extension to the university context involves an additional serious misstep.

The issues concerning sincerity that I will discuss relate to the direct misrepresentations some academic researchers frequently offer to research subjects about the nature, purpose, or features of an experiment, sometimes as part of the experiment itself, and sometimes to protect the integrity of their results from subjects' efforts at confirmation or disconfirmation. For example, researchers may lie to research subjects about their performance on an exercise conducted during the experiment—either downplaying or exaggerating their opinion of the performance—to assess whether the misperception affects the quality of the subject's performance on a subsequent exercise.[1] Or, to insulate the results from influence stemming from the subjects' beliefs about the experiment, researchers may lie about their hypothesis or their general purpose in conducting the study. For instance, researchers studying the influence of wine tasters' price-based expectations of quality on their enjoyment of wine misinformed subjects that the study's purpose was to "study the effect of degustation time on perceived flavors" and that prices were offered only as methods of identification; the researchers also claimed to pour five different wines, but falsely presented two repeat offerings as distinct samples.[2] Although these sorts of lies may have anodyne content, my argument will be that, even so, their use in academic research stands in problematic tension with the values the university is supposed to embody and champion.

My main contention is that the university has distinctive epistemic ends that in turn provide an independent basis for academic freedom, as well as a special source of criticism of the use of misrepresentation as a tool of academic research. Although I concentrate heavily on the university, I will illustrate how the argument's structure applies to other institutions such as the police, who frequently lie to subjects of interrogation as a method of eliciting the truth. Along the way, I aim to develop some further issues about justified suspended contexts to motivate some distinct arguments for sincerity, grounded in particular institutional ends and functions.

Turning our attention to institutions introduces some fresh philosophical challenges to requirements of sincerity and freedom of speech. One may be tempted by what I call "institutional exceptionalism"—the idea

[1] David Pittinger, *Deception in Research: Distinctions and Solutions from the Perspective of Utilitarianism*, 12 ETHICS & BEHAVIOR 117, 134 (2002) (describing a variety of false feedback experiments).

[2] Hilke Plassmann et al., *Marketing Actions Can Modulate Neural Representations of Experienced Pleasantness*, 105 PROC. OF THE NAT'L ACAD. OF SCIENCES 1050 (2008). This study is critically discussed in Collin C. O'Neil and Franklin G. Miller, *When Scientists Deceive: Applying the Federal Regulations*, 37 J.L. MED. & ETHICS 344 (2009).

that valuable institutions create special, bounded contexts of communication and behavior in which we may suspend adherence to some of the normal moral presumptions that govern interpersonal contexts, including the moral presumption of sincerity, in order to pursue other valuable ends.[3] To capture the advantages of market competition, we tolerate (and some encourage) aggressive forms of negotiation and competition in business dealings that would be inappropriate elsewhere; to cultivate and enjoy the advantages of physical competition, we permit (and some encourage) physical aggression and violence in sports settings that might constitute assault in other arenas. Likewise, one may be tempted to extend this idea more generally to suggest that given the distinctive valuable ends we pursue through organized, compartmentalized institutions, if it facilitates the achievement of these ends, there may also be reason to relax both requirements of sincerity as well as free speech protections for individuals within institution settings.

Another motivation for such exceptionalism is that institutions do not have the mental and emotional lives of individuals that ground some ethical duties. Indeed, this constituted part of my claim in Chapter Four that we need not extend the same freedom of speech protections to business associations as we do to individuals. In the case of sincerity, part of the argument for the strong duty of sincerity arises from our special need to grapple with the opacity of other minds given our moral need to understand each other's mental contents. Because institutions lack those sorts of mental contents and because they do not suffer from a metaphysical sort of opacity (only a bureaucratic sort), these arguments for duties of sincerity may appear to lack straightforward application in the institutional domain. This may then appear to create some room to use insincerity within well-delineated institutional settings to pursue some significant ethical goals.

I disagree with the general claim that institutions and players within institutional roles have special permissions to engage in deliberate misrepresentations and am unconvinced by the specific case for academic

---

[3] *See, e.g.,* MEIR DAN-COHEN, HARMFUL THOUGHTS 247–49 (2002). Similar ideas have been debated with respect to the range and content of duties of promissory fidelity in business contexts. *See, e.g.,* Daniel Markovits & Alan Schwartz, *The Myth of Efficient Breach: New Defenses of the Expectation Interest,* 97 VA. L. REV. 1939, 1954 (2011) (arguing that "perform or pay" may be a morally appropriate form of promissory commitment within "commercial transactions in open, cosmopolitan societies"); Seana Valentine Shiffrin, *Are Contracts Promises?, in* ROUTLEDGE COMPANION TO PHILOSOPHY OF LAW 242, at 247, 251 (Andrei Marmor ed., 2012) (criticizing the view that the moral norms of promising differ substantially in business contexts).

lying that I will examine here. Some of my resistance stems from the fact that I am not utterly convinced that the arguments for individual sincerity lack application in institutional contexts, in part because individual persons in noninstitutional capacities are often the recipients of institutional speech, and in part because individuals carry out institutional behaviors and may be implicated in those tasks.[4] But here I want to put those points aside and instead develop two sorts of institution-specific rationales against lying: one appeals to the tension between the particular epistemic ends of the university and lies within it, the other appeals to the special symbolic function that universities (and other institutions) may perform through pronounced compliance with challenging norms like the free speech protection and the prohibition against lying. To develop these rationales requires delving a little deeper into the question of how suspended contexts may permissibly be formed. My discussion will try to explain why notice, agreement, a good purpose, disclosure, and later revelation all may be insufficient to inoculate intentional misrepresentation.

I start by reviewing my basic case against lying and then delve into some further issues about suspended contexts that are raised by misrepresentations within institutional contexts. In particular, I criticize the idea that mere declarations that one is suspending the context of truthfulness are sufficient to justify doing so. I illustrate the defects of this idea through a discussion of the doctrine of puffery in contract law.

From there, I turn to my main argument that an institution's epistemic ends may preclude lies in their service. To introduce this argument, I start with the example of the police and explain why, properly understood, the internal institutional ends of the police condemn their regular practice of lying. I then proceed to offer a lengthier, more circuitous argument about academic freedom and misrepresentations in the university. Here, the argument structure is more complex. It twice engages the issue of institutional exceptionalism, first through a discussion about academic freedom, which involves grappling with arguments that freedom of speech operates differently within institutional contexts than outside them, and then by offering an argument against academic misrepresentation. Finally, I offer an independent argument about how the symbolic posture of institutions such as the police and the university may supply further reasons to abstain from misrepresentation.

---

[4] I discuss this point in Seana Valentine Shiffrin, *The Divergence of Contract and Promise*, 120 Harv. L. Rev. 708, 747–48 (2007).

Lies and Suspended Contexts

As I contend in Chapter One, the lie's primary moral defect is that it subverts the reliability of a special, uniquely precise mechanism for the conveyance of our mental contents. Reliable, sincere speech enables sophisticated forms of self-understanding, knowledge of others and of the world, moral agency, and personal relations of trust. The relation between communication and these foundational compulsory ends explains the strong presumption of sincere communication as well as our responsibility to strive for accuracy.

As I argue in Chapter Three, this relation also supplies the foundations of freedom of speech. Affording opportunities for the sincere externalization of one's mental contents and access to others' mental contents, and enabling the dynamic interchange between them is an essential social condition of freedom of thought, the development of the capacities of the thinker, and the development of moral agency. It therefore is an individual human right and among the prerequisite social conditions for a just society.

Despite this strong, morally charged presumption for engaging in and protecting sincere expression, we are also morally capable of creating what I call *justified suspended contexts* that disable the normative presumption of sincerity. One enters a suspended context when one goes to see a nondocumentary film or picks up a novel. Normatively and epistemically, one does not reasonably expect the propositions uttered to represent the truth directly. It is understood that the authors do not aim to convey their mental contents but rather may advance propositions they may not believe because they are pursuing another purpose through communication. Although mutual understanding and mutual enlightenment are central mandatory ends that oblige us to cultivate and exercise reflexes of sincerity, communication is also central to the pursuit of other valuable goals, whose realization may be disserved through expectations and practices of unexceptional, sober, literal sincerity. The importance of play, relaxation, the exercise of the moral and theoretical imagination, and the distinctive effectiveness of the indirect conveyance of truths through metaphor and other nonliteral representations may explain why the presumption of literal truthfulness is legitimately suspended within humorous and fictional contexts. The importance of demonstrating hospitality and a welcoming atmosphere may explain the suspension of the truth presumption involved in etiquette. The importance of creating and maintaining privacy may explain a nuanced suspension with respect to certain personal topics.

But, although justified suspended contexts are pervasive and crucial to our flourishing and our pursuit of morally significant ends, their proliferation must not, in operation, effectively displace the *presumption* of truthfulness. Further, it is an insufficient justification for the generation of a suspended context that it is generated to further the pursuit of a good end. Likewise, it is an insufficient justification that its generation is disclosed or even that it is agreed to.

One's experience with suspended contexts might incline one to think otherwise, to think that unilateral initiation, accompanied by publicity, suffices for their permissible creation. After all, I can break into a joke or begin reciting a soliloquy; in so doing, I utter propositions I do not believe, and I do so in all innocence and with moral impunity. Albeit without this exact philosophical frame fully in mind, I *intend* to create a justified suspended context.[5] Although that is an understandable interpretation of our experience with fiction and joking, that experience may be misleading if taken as a theoretically illustrative paradigm case.

---

[5] Not all suspended contexts are created intentionally or permissibly, as the previously discussed cases involving communications with the famous Murderer at the Door (Chapter One) or the more common mugger (Chapter Two) show. The murderer initiates a content-specific justified suspended context by seeking information that it would be impermissible to supply because supplying it would facilitate a crime; one may permissibly misrepresent the location of the intended victim. The mugger initiates a content-specific justified suspended context by demanding information in a manner that renders silence or refusal either unsafe or revealing. One may permissibly misrepresent about these topics in response to such demands because the context does not carry the truth presumption for the victim. Although the misrepresentation satisfies the publicity constraint because, e.g., the murderer has reason to know his plan is immoral and therefore has reason to know that information appearing to further it should not be presumed truthful, it is not the murderer's intent to create the justified suspended context. Indeed, its creation is impermissible. What really occurs is that the murderer creates a justified suspended context with respect to the victim's representations; the murderer has not himself created a justified suspended context with respect to his own representations. So, this example also brings out the fact that suspended contexts may be asymmetrical: the truth presumption may operate for one participant but not for another. The murderer has created a justified suspended context for his interlocutor with respect to certain content-based representations, but the murderer himself still labors under an obligation to tell the truth. Further, the murderer cannot suddenly eliminate the suspended context by declaration. To reestablish the symmetrical truth presumption about charged topics connected to his criminal plans, he would have to renounce his threat and/or his criminal plans persuasively and effectively. Doing so might involve making sufficient amends.

The power to create justified suspended contexts must be more complex and constrained. Truth-telling is an essential, nonnegotiable activity. We cannot pursue our other ends to such an extent that truth-telling stops being reflexive or agents often find themselves in reasonable and serious doubt about whether assertions are presented to be trusted. We have to leave substantial space for the presumption to operate as a default. Although fictional and other "entertainment" contexts serve crucial purposes, enabling oblique exploration of perceived truths and the exercise of the imagination, constant immersion in them is a personal vice as well as a cultural liability. Similarly dangerous is overindulgence in the postmodern penchant for constant cynicism and wordplay. Such overindulgence can put substantial obstacles in the way of straightforward communication, which in turn disable its reflexive use and wither audiences' expectations of its reflexive use. Hence, the boundaries of suspended contexts must submit to some definition, even if their edges remain somewhat blurred. Their range and invocation must be cinched so that their operation does not threaten the dominance or availability of the presumption of sincerity. Not only should we cultivate reasonable habits and expectations of reflexive truth-telling, we should also guard against transforming what could be meaningful, substantive avenues of discourse into communicative no-man's lands.

Puffery

The doctrine of "puffery" in commercial sales serves as an example of how suspended contexts may be misused and obstruct meaningful communication. Advertisers and vendors who make specific factual representations about their products may be legally liable for fraud or warranty violations if those representations are false. But, under the "puffery" doctrine, those speakers are legally immunized with respect to their more general expressions of opinion. They are not legally responsible for the truth of those opinions. More troubling, they are not legally responsible for their sincerity either, even when those opinions are not believed by the speaker or are recklessly issued without foundation and investigation.[6]

---

[6] *See, e.g.*, RESTATEMENT (SECOND) OF CONTRACTS, § 168, § 168 cmts. b & c, § 169 (1981) (statements of opinion concerning the value and worth of what is being sold are generally not assertions for the purposes of the duty not to misrepresent, and recipients of opinions generally may not rely on them unless they stand in a special relationship to the speaker). If the speaker does know facts incompatible with the opinion, though, that may generate liability. *Id.* § 168(2)(a).

Bayer may declare it sells "the world's best aspirin that works wonders" and need not demonstrate its belief in or any foundation for that comparative assertion.[7] Never mind whether it is the best aspirin or not, never mind if Bayer was culpably self-deceived about its own product's qualities. The doctrine has further consequences, namely that Bayer may publicize its comparative claim without conducting a single internal comparison test to support its having any opinion about the matter. Likewise, Standard & Poor's, a credit-rating service upon which pension funds rely to decide where to invest, may tout its "integrity, reliability, and credibility." Further, it may advertise that its decision-making was "transparent and independent," and complied with "best practices," producing "independent and objective analysis," without having to give any substantive reply to allegations that all these claims are fraudulent because Standard & Poor's purposely used outdated information for profit, courted rather than avoided conflicts of interest, and indiscriminately doled out high ratings.[8] Barclays Bank may claim that it is a "responsible global citizen" that does "business ethically" but lack even minimal legal responsibility for the truth of these claims, such as having to make a showing that they monitor the global consequences of their actions or have an internal ethical code that guides decision-making.[9] The puffery doctrine not only protects inaccuracy, but also shields insincere but seriously forwarded claims that are made without any basis, however misguided, for the speaker's making such a claim sincerely. The puffery doctrine insulates all these claims from minimal accountability on the grounds that we should expect sellers to be prone to exaggerate the virtues of their wares and that general adjectives do not admit of clear standards of satisfaction. Therefore, we are supposed to think that general adjectives would not influence a reasonable listener.

---

[7] *In re* Sterling Drug, Inc., 102 F.T.C. 395, 752, 757 (1983).

[8] *See* Boca Raton Firefighters & Police Pension Fund v. Bahash, 506 F. App'x 32, 36–39 (2d Cir. 2012). Hearteningly, a similar puffery defense was rejected by a federal court in California. United States v. McGraw-Hill Co., Inc., No. 13–0779, 2013 WL 3762259, at *7–8 (C.D. Cal. 2013) (distinguishing *Boca Raton* on the basis of the government's more detailed pleadings and the difference between shareholder interests and investor interests).

[9] Gusinsky v. Barclays PLC, 944 F. Supp. 2d 279, 289-290 (S.D.N.Y. 2013) (holding in a case involving Barclays Bank's alleged manipulation of LIBOR rates that statements pertaining to "being a responsible global citizen" and "doing business ethically" were puffery and therefore could not be the basis of a fraud claim), aff'd in part, vacated in part sub nom. Carpenters Pension Trust Fund of St. Louis v. Barclays PLC, No. 13-2678, 2014 WL 1645611 (2d. Cir. Apr. 25, 2014) (affirming lower court's ruling on puffery).

These arguments are, I submit, misguided. Of course some breathing room might be advisable to allow expressive outlets for contained bursts of spontaneous exaggeration by sincere, enthusiastic sellers. So too, the law should ensure some breathing room for the sort of playful jests and humorous exaggerations that make commercial advertisements clever and more tolerable. These considerations would, however, yield only a limited defense for exuberance or evident humor. The scope of that defense would fall short of encompassing the permissive doctrine that we have, one that protects the sort of well-considered, deliberate corporate advertising campaigns that brag in all seriousness (without any evidence that would support a sincere, even if misguided, claim) that a "diet pill" will help one "lose weight fast."[10] Although the generality of these claims may defy crafting any reasonable standards to verify their truth, it is quite simple to identify conditions under which those claims are false or irresponsibly made. If the pill is entirely untested or if internal memos show that the manufacturer had doubts about their claims, we could charge the seller with deliberate insincerity—even if we are loath to hold the seller accountable for any particular benchmark of speed or weight loss. The permissive atmosphere generated by the puffery doctrine therefore outstrips its justifications.

The legal permission to "puff" and the liberal use of this opportunity generates communicative clutter for no redeeming purpose. At the same time, it protects opportunities to try to manipulate unguarded consumers with insincere exhortations. Moreover, by insulating sellers from expectations of sincerity, the doctrine generates a sort of communicative badland that obstructs meaningful communication. It hampers the ability to have a reliable, informative exchange between informed parties about the seller's sincere and careful estimation of the general and relative quality of the seller's wares. Consumers have no reason to believe what sellers say given the proliferation of sellers who engage in puffery. Indeed, the legal expectation is that consumers will approach general expressions of opinion with caution and distrust; the doctrine goes so far as to instruct the consumer that, insofar as she is reasonable, she should ignore general statements by advertisers. Sincere sellers therefore cannot decisively transmit their sincere beliefs to consumers in general terms. That obstacle represents a loss both to sellers and consumers, for we must assume that

---

[10] *See* David A. Hoffman, *The Best Puffery Article Ever*, 91 Iowa L. Rev. 1395, 1404–06 (2006) (discussing examples of successful invocation of the puffery defense against legal claims of fraud or warranty claims, et alia).

many sellers have well-informed opinions about their products' relative value or their internal practices.

It is true that the puffery doctrine pertains only to general representations. All the same, even quite general information may be otherwise unavailable to consumers. A consumer may have no easy way of knowing whether Barclays Bank makes efforts of any significant kind to gauge the consequences of its behavior on global markets or to comply with ethical codes. By insulating utterly irresponsible and groundless claims, the puffery doctrine precludes the consumer from having confidence in Barclays' general representations about the matter. This forces Barclays either to make more specific representations and commitments than they may be comfortable with, whether because of privacy or flexibility concerns, or to fail to be able to convey believably a true, but general, fact about their ethical practices.

Further, the puffery doctrine encourages inflationary rhetoric. It may deter sincere estimations by sellers that their product is (merely) "good," out of a fear that consumers will understandably interpret this as an admission of inferiority. Rather than sellers' speech serving as a meaningful occasion for the transmission of sincere, responsibly formed opinions, the puffery doctrine licenses sellers' irresponsible and even disbelieved celebratory expressions about their products. When such sellers defend their puff by appealing to the idea that no reasonable consumer would believe such claims, this suggests that they must be attempting to penetrate some chink in the consumer's epistemic armor and to influence the off-guard consumer through sheer pressure or other forms of nonrational suggestion.[11] The generation of an epistemic suspended context here seems to serve some private interests that are hard to defend. At the same time, its generation stymies the realization of public interests in communication about a significant aspect of our joint economic life and possibly contributes to the atrophy of the reflex of sincerity. Hence, their generation and the legal doctrines that protect their generation seem unjustified.

Individual Duties of Sincerity

The risks that our habits and expectations of sincerity will fade and that the channels of meaningful communication will fall into decline

[11] There is some evidence that puffery succeeds in influencing consumer beliefs, despite the law's position that the reasonable consumer should be impervious to puffed claims. *See id.* at 1435–39 (discussing studies showing a relatively high level of consumer susceptibility to puffery).

caution vigilance when creating epistemic suspended contexts. The dangers they pose weigh against their casual generation as well as their creation to serve private purposes, especially minor ones. Further considerations reinforce these principles and suggest that a transparent acknowledgment of one's practice is an insufficient condition for the permissible generation of a suspended context. On many occasions, individuals may have a direct duty to engage in (true) revelatory speech. An effort to suspend the context may transgress that duty. For example, a doctor has a duty to a patient to reveal the doctor's diagnosis and the patient's test results. Declaring upfront that she may pull a prank or make things up would not make her failure to engage in truthful speech permissible, though it might make her ethical transgression apparent. One concern in this domain, captured by strictures against deception, is to avoid implanting false beliefs in patients. Another concern, often overlapping, is to effectively convey true propositions. This latter aim manifests both positive obligations to engage in revelation and obligations to communicate truthfully. Mere declarations and transparency about one's insincerity, where sufficiently focused and specific, can operate as methods to avoid transgressing the negative duty to refrain from implanting false beliefs because transparency empowers at least those listeners who are attentive, flexible, and responsive to engage in effective self-protection. By making a clear declaration of one's intention to create a suspended context and addressing that declaration to a competent and perceptive interlocutor, one may avoid (responsibility for) *deception* of one's interlocutor, but that is not the same as effectively suspending one's duty to engage in truthful communication. The doctor cannot shrug off her duty to speak truthfully by declaring an intention to shirk it; all she can do is avoid the further collateral damage of successful deceit. If she declares her intention to play loose and fast with the truth, she fails to serve as an available and reliable resource of medical information, although she has a duty to serve as such a resource.

Although the point may be more pronounced in the case of professionals and others with special role duties, it is not limited to them. Something would be morally awry if a friend, business associate, or even a store clerk prefaced each or most conversations with the disclaimer that what they said wasn't necessarily to be believed or even that, as the fancy struck, they might misrepresent, though they would eventually correct the record. So too, announcements that a friend planned to treat the truth-telling context as suspended with respect to a topic that comprised part of the basis of the friendship, e.g., her feelings or their mutual boat-building project, seem off-limits. A business associate could not acceptably declare that conversations about deliveries, meeting times, or agendas were suspended contexts as far as his speech was concerned. Such declarations would not only make a mockery of the conversations but would show disrespect for the interlocutor, the important purposes served by communicative interaction, and, in many cases, for the relation the parties have toward each other.

Of course, such conversational prefacing could be performance art that permissibly and vividly brought home the importance of truthful communication. The stranger who informs you that he feels no responsibility to speak his mind openly on Tuesdays if and when the topic is tortillas may underscore the importance of making room for whimsy. A good friendship *could* involve silent companionship without discourse or efforts at direct revelation. I'm not bent on disagreement. Still, I suspect that these cases are parasitic outliers. Like much art, their meaning and justification derives from their unusual, instructive contrast with the important, default common practice.

My hypothesis is that the default common practice demands that when we are in or initiate contact with one another, we owe some information and some access to one another. Although we may keep certain facts private, we cannot interact while holding ourselves and our knowledge remote—whether this is accomplished by entirely unreliable testimony or merely by silence. We have some standing background duties to remain epistemically available and believable. These duties preclude lying but also provide resistance against the profligate generation of suspended contexts that create pockets of unavailability and unreliability. If that is right, then to justify a detour from the presumption, the suspended context must serve a normatively substantial end. It cannot be generated at whimsy or just by declaration. The presumption of truthfulness is not a mere default of convenience but is a normatively sticky default; its presumptive operation underwrites the basis of the accumulation of knowledge and the possibility of close, moral relations with one another.

Further, even where there is a normatively substantial end that would be served by a suspended context, its generation must not work to undermine, threaten, or sideline the duties of revelation, honesty, and reliability that we have toward one another, duties whose form may of course vary, depending on whether we are mere strangers to each other, associates, friends, or within a professional relationship of care.

Institutions and Duties of Sincerity

Related constraints govern institutions and their ability to create permissible suspended contexts by declaration alone. Care must be taken to ensure that the creation of suspended contexts within institutions does not exert such strong influence on the culture at large that these contexts deteriorate the general presumption of sincerity. Further, their operation cannot work on the individuals within such institutions so as to compromise their habits, expectations, and the personal honest relationships that facilitate their effective participation in our culture of presumptive truthfulness.

Finally, the use of the suspended context must not work to undermine the valuable ends to which the institutions are dedicated, to frustrate the epistemic goals and duties embedded within those ends, or to disable our ability to achieve other compulsory ends. Consider, for example, newspapers and encyclopedias that plant false articles to prove that other sources "steal" their material.[12] Their *aims* may well be justifiable, namely to embarrass and deter free riders and, more importantly, to ensure accuracy by preventing and exposing unattributed copying that imparts false impressions of independent confirmation. Pursuing those ends by deliberately planting false articles, however, works to undermine the point of such accuracy—namely, that newspapers may be taken at their word. The practice is therefore in tension with their larger aim of serving as a reliable epistemic resource.[13]

The Police

In what follows, I want to focus on this last point. I want to consider how the epistemic ends of particular sorts of institutions place particular con-

---

[12] Shyamkrishna Balganesh, *"Hot News": The Enduring Myth of Property in News*, 111 COLUM. L. REV. 419, 444 (2011); ISAAC CLARKE PRAY, MEMOIRS OF JAMES GORDON BENNETT AND HIS TIMES 135 (1855); Henry Alford, *Not a Word*, NEW YORKER, Aug. 29, 2005, at 31 (describing a deliberately false biography in the *New Columbia Encyclopedia* of 1975 about Lillian Virginia Mountweazel [a nonexistent person] and identifying "esquivalience" as the fake word planted in the New Oxford American Dictionary); cf. Mrinal Pande, *Check Please*, INDIAN EXPRESS (Apr. 9, 2010), http://www.indianexpress.com/news/check-please/602256/ (reporting a newpaper's April Fool's prank of planting false stories to catch plagiarism by rival media).

[13] A related stance propels the admirable frustration and contempt of Jim Fingal, a fact-checker, in his colloquy with John D'Agata, an "essayist." D'Agata's article on a Las Vegas suicide regularly invented details and altered facts for dramatic and syntactic resonance, yet deployed a fact-laden style to impart a feeling of verisimilitude, as chronicled in JOHN D'AGATA & JIM FINGAL, THE LIFESPAN OF A FACT (2012).

straints on their use of deliberate misrepresentations to achieve those ends. Before turning to my main interest, the university, I want to rehearse another example of how an institution's mission may include its serving as an epistemic resource, and how this in turn constrains its generation of suspended contexts to pursue other aspects of its mission. Although newspapers are more obviously an epistemic institution than the police, a particular version of this problem attaches to misrepresentations by government officials generally and by the police in particular, because the police serve as one of the major points of direct contact between citizens and the government.

My worries about police misrepresentation do not stem from idle hypotheticals. Lies by the police are everyday, officially sanctioned practices. Lying to interrogation subjects is a commonplace, recommended police procedure, whether about material facts relating to the case, the evidence the police have, or the moral gravity of a crime.[14] Interrogators are advised to vilify the victim to induce the suspect to let down his guard and confess. For example, the interrogator might speculate (falsely) that an unwilling sexual partner was a tease, probably wanted things to get rough, and that the purported forced encounter was understandable.[15] The leading criminal interrogation manual recommends that the interrogator "sympathize with the suspect by affirming that, in the circumstances, anyone would have engaged in the criminal behavior"; "minimiz[e] the moral seriousness of the offense" to reduce the suspect's guilt-related inhibitions; "suggest a face-saving motive for the commission of the crime, which he knows is not true"; and "[i]n some cases . . . falsely imply, or outright state, that evidence exists that links the suspect to the crime."[16] In sex offense cases, as a form of sympathy and minimization of the crime, the manual recommends that the interrogator should

---

[14] Fred Inbau et al., Criminal Interrogation and Confessions 241–68, 293–98, 427–29 (4th ed. 2004) ("Many of the interrogation techniques presented in this text involve duplicity and pretense"). *See also* Richard A. Leo, *Police Interrogation and Social Control*, 3 Soc. & Legal Stud. 93, 106–08 (1994); Richard A. Leo, *From Coercion to Deception: The Changing Nature of Police Interrogation in America*, 18 Crime L. & Soc. Change 35, 43–47 (1992); Anne M. Coughlin, *Interrogation Stories*, 95 Va. L. Rev. 1599, 1605–06, 1642–51 (2009).

[15] Coughlin, *supra* note 14, at 1642–51.

[16] Inbau, *supra* note 14, at 241–47, 427–29. The authors recommend that lying about what evidence has been collected should be avoided, however, because investigators may lose credibility if the suspect gathers that they are bluffing. *Id.* at 429. *See also* Deborah Young, *Unnecessary Evil: Police Lying in Interrogations*, 28 Conn. L. Rev. 425, 427–28 (1996) (mentioning the advice of training manuals and seminars).

falsely represent that, in the past, a friend, relative, or even the questioner himself engaged in similar coercive behavior.[17]

Misrepresentations about *legal* rights usually encounter constitutional hurdles, but not always insurmountable obstacles.[18] Still, not all legal misrepresentations are constitutionally barred from giving rise to admissible confessions and other evidence. In Nebraska, for instance, the police misrepresented whether sexual conduct with a minor was a crime to prompt a confession, which a state court ruled was not invalidated by the misrepresentation.[19] In Indiana, to elicit a confession, police officers allegedly misrepresented that the suspect's purported conduct would only constitute manslaughter and not murder and reinforced that misrepresentation by showing the suspect the Indiana criminal code; a federal court denied the defendant habeas relief and held that the alleged legal misrepresentation would not render the confession involuntary.[20]

In the U.S., a great deal of police misrepresentation is, it seems, commonplace and officially sanctioned. One serious complaint about this practice is that some evidence suggests that police lies play a substantial role in eliciting false confessions.[21] These allegations are serious and very

---

[17] See INBAU, *supra* note 14, at 241–43; *see also* Coughlin, *supra* note 14, at 1646–51.

[18] The constitutional approach to lies that elicit confessions is to ask whether the misrepresentation renders the confession involuntary. *See, e.g.*, Moran v. Burbine, 475 U.S. 412, 421 (1986) (holding that for a confession to be admissible, the waiver of the right against self-incrimination must be voluntary, not the product of "intimidation, coercion, or deception"). *See generally* 2 WAYNE R. LaFAVE ET. AL., CRIMINAL PROCEDURE § 6.2(c) (3d ed. 2007). Misrepresentations about facts, including about what evidence the police have, are not thought to render consequent confessions involuntary per se and are frequently upheld as constitutional through an analysis asking whether given the "totality of the circumstances," the confession was voluntary. *See, e.g.*, Frazier v. Cupp, 394 U.S. 731, 739 (1969) (upholding a confession obtained through a misrepresentation by the police that the suspect's cousin had confessed and thereby implicated him); Lucero v. Kerby, 133 F.3d 1299, 1311 (10th Cir. 1998) (upholding a confession following a police misrepresentation that the suspect's fingerprints were found at the crime scene); *see also* United States v. Lall, 607 F.3d 1277, 1285 (11th Cir. 2010) (holding a confession involuntary in a case in which the police assured a suspect that information provided would not be used to prosecute and that the suspect did not need an attorney and remarking that "police misrepresentations of law [as contrasted with police misrepresentations of fact] ... are much more likely to render a suspect's confession involuntary").

[19] State v. Walker, 493 N.W.2d 329, 334 (Neb. 1992) (finding that a police officer's misrepresentation that consensual sexual contact with a minor would not constitute a crime did not invalidate the defendant's confession). *See also* Commonwealth v. Colby, 663 N.E.2d 808, 810 (Mass. 1996) (holding that an alleged police misrepresentation that polygraphs were admissible in Virginia would not invalidate a confession and noting no qualitative difference between misrepresentations of law and misrepresentations of fact).

[20] Conner v. McBride, 375 F.3d 643, 653 (7th Cir. 2004).

[21] Misrepresentations may play a role in eliciting false confessions, whether because the

troubling. If lies in interrogation promote inaccuracy, they seem utterly unsustainable. Here, though, I want to offer another argument that is independent of the substantial concerns about the unreliability and inefficacy of the practice. Assume (as against all likelihood) that, where deployed, direct misrepresentation is more episodically effective at gleaning important and accurate information than direct interview methods. I would still contend that these lies, while understandable, are wrong. The police have institutionally grounded reasons not to lie, even effectively, to achieve their valid and admirable purposes. The practice of lying is in tension with the role the police play and should play in our scheme of epistemic moral cooperation.

That role might be elaborated as follows. So far, I have been emphasizing that successful moral agency involves epistemic cooperation. To know the specific contents of our moral duties, we need information from others about themselves that we could not glean on our own. Further, given the complexity of moral circumstances, we often need help identifying and understanding the mid-level moral principles that govern our situation. Finally, many of our moral duties are triggered (and sometimes determined) by joint decisions or collective actions, whether those that generate a circumstance calling for response, those that generate a worthwhile convention, or the joint decisions comprising law. To recognize our moral obligations and opportunities, we need a supportive, reliable epistemic environment.

If we are indeed engaged in epistemic moral cooperation and take advantage of some divisions of labor, it would make sense that we would locate some sources as epistemic authorities, that is, sources we can and should be able to rely upon for information and judgment about our moral, political, and legal duties. Ultimately, as individuals, we are each responsible for our moral agency—for getting it right and understanding why it is right. Still, given the challenges of maintaining moral agency and the complexity of our modern moral and political circumstances, sincere sources of information and judgment may play valuable roles as reality

---

suspect begins to believe the false narrative about his guilt, because the suspect operates under the misunderstanding that even the authorities consider that little is at stake, or because the suspect thinks his (true) claims of innocence are futile but that a confession may reduce his sentence. *See* Brandon L. Garrett, *The Substance of False Confessions*, 62 STAN. L. REV. 1051, 1097–99 (2010) (describing police misrepresentations about the evidence in their possession and the role it may have played in eliciting false convictions); *but see* Laurie Magid, *Deceptive Police Interrogation Practices: How Far Is Too Far*, 99 MICH. L. REV. 1168, 1190–97 (2001) (contending that the evidence that police deception elicits false confessions is inconclusive and anecdotal).

checks and calibration points, while also constituting a source of common culture. This is especially important in the legal domain.

Politically, those in charge of putting our joint moral commitments into action and enforcing them—namely, state officials—are well placed to serve as points of triangulation, expositors, and repositories of our best information about the law and its moral and political underpinnings. We need salient common sources of information to help us locate the relevant moral and legal facts and to identify the content of the joint perception of those facts. We also need to know that officials *believe* these to be the relevant facts, if those officials are to merit the role of a legitimate political (not merely epistemic) authority. Thus, state officials, at least in a democracy, must aspire to be relevant epistemic authorities on the law and on at least that aspect of morality embodied in law. We *should* be able to rely on their transmissions about the content of law, legally relevant morality, and legally relevant facts.

These ideas would render police misrepresentation—even to a wrongdoer—especially morally problematic. If their role partly involves serving as a reliable epistemic repository, then the police subvert their own role when they misrepresent the content of the law, the moral severity of an offense, or the evidence they have collected. There is no gainsaying that the end that mendacious police interrogators pursue is substantial, namely the identification of the culpable and, though less prominently touted, the exoneration of the innocent. Nonetheless, the practice subverts what seems to be a compulsory end of the government, and of the police specifically: to act as a source of reliable and trustworthy moral knowledge—an epistemic repository—about the law, its application to relevant situations, and its underlying justifications. They have that duty even to persons of interest, perhaps especially to guilty parties who are, *ex hypothesi*, struggling with moral and legal compliance issues. Because their epistemic responsibilities are bound together with and frame their investigatory aims, the police cannot argue that the mere significance of the end justifies the suspension of the truthfulness presumption.

One may object that when interrogating, the police are not acting within their role as epistemic sources. They are collecting, rather than disseminating, knowledge; and so the standards of reliable dissemination do not apply.

I find this position unsatisfactory. For the police, collecting and offering knowledge are necessarily intertwined and not liable to strict compartmentalization. In attempting to discover information about a crime, the police engage in moral and legal representations. They rely upon their status as legal authorities to convey the importance and seriousness of the situations about which they collect information. They further rely on their status as legal authorities to convey the protection they can and must offer those questioned. They represent that a particular behavior constitutes a crime that is sufficiently serious to merit a citizen's cooperation, even if it is against that citizen's personal interest. The police rely upon these representations as well as their general credibility to cajole, persuade, and intimidate citizens into supplying information truthfully and voluntarily. The success of the untruthful statement within interrogation depends upon its being presented as truthful and upon the perception that the police are trustworthy agents discharging their public duties. Moreover, information-gathering encounters serve to reinforce the status of the police as well as the significance of legal compliance. Because the mission of the police requires that they be taken at their word about legal matters in important circumstances, the use of the lie in one such circumstance undermines their justified credibility in other structurally similar circumstances. The police are at all times engaged in educating citizens about the law and its situational application, as well as in observing and documenting compliance and noncompliance. That being the case, in important ways, all situations in which they operate are structurally similar.

Academic Freedom and Academic Misrepresentation

I have briefly touched upon the subjects of media, commercial, and police misrepresentations, but I do not pretend to have done more than scratch the surface of the issues they present. My remarks aimed simply to introduce some examples of how one might begin to doubt the general invocation of institutional exceptionalism to justify deliberate misrepresentation. Although institutions may not have the same mental properties that underpin some of the arguments against lying, they may have specialized epistemic ends, internal to their missions, that are incompatible with the use of episodic misrepresentation to achieve those or other ends. To pursue this idea further, I now turn to resist some institutional exceptionalist arguments deployed to justify restrictions on freedom of speech within public employment contexts, and the university in particular, and also used to justify the use of the lie as a research technique at the university. I will start by proposing a partial, incomplete conception of the (public) university that emphasizes some salient characteristics germane to building a principled case for academic freedom and then offer a reply to those threats to academic freedom that draw on institutional exceptionalism.[22] Finally, I will turn to the academic lie. I contend that the nature of our enterprise and the justifications for academic freedom give rise to a distinctive institutional case against using deliberate misrepresentations as a method of research.

The Mission of the University and the Underpinnings of Academic Freedom

Suppose we conceive of the university as a special sort of collaborative epistemic repository for humanity, a repository that aims to generate, cultivate, appreciate, disseminate, and preserve our best, sincere understandings of the domains of important human knowledge and the means, methods, and history of collecting them, both for the sake of knowledge and for many consequent purposes, long- and short-term. Although the university serves its members' individual interests in self-expression, the pursuit of which is integral to the university's success, the university has also a collaborative social function that is not reducible to being a site where individual members of the public separately and privately pursue their interests in self-expression, knowledge collection, and intellectual development as they might in public spaces like Central and Hyde Parks. It aims to be a cooperatively constructed site at which knowledge and understanding are pursued and honestly disseminated by responsible, independently minded investigators, each dedicated to getting it right and each, it is recognized, liable to begin and end investigations with distinctive judgments, ones that may be irreconcilable with the judgments of others. Because we depend upon one another epistemically to understand our own thoughts and to gain a reliable grasp on our complex surroundings, part of the process of getting it right must involve sharing one's

---

[22] My focus will be on the public university because it provides a clearer example of an institution that aims to and is bound to serve the public at large. Private universities often fit this model, although some of them, on some issues, straddle the boundary between a university and a private expressive association dedicated to the benefit of specific citizens as well as the study and promotion of particular ideas and points of view. I intend my argument about academic freedom to have the same force for private universities, but my position has the implication that private universities may single out, loosely, certain topics or areas of study for special attention but should not, as part of their mission or identity, insist on or promote particular viewpoints as required or favored positions for university members. This implicitly critical stance of the posture of many private universities would require more argument than I offer here.

methods and one's research to allow for sincere questioning, criticism, appreciation, and growth.

Unlike other collaborative institutions dedicated to ideas, such as the think tank or advocacy organization, a university deliberately rejects the organizing aim of speaking with a single voice. For the university, investigation is valued for itself and not to vindicate or advance any particular cause or view. An enforced or expected consensus around a position would not, therefore, represent a form of compromise necessary to achieve a central mission of the institution. Rather, a policy of mandated consensus would subvert the academic mission.

Where members' investigations are pursued and exchanged with honesty and integrity, persistent differences will be epistemically interesting and perhaps significant. Where their investigations converge, that convergence will be epistemically interesting, in ways it would not have been if arriving at a consensus was preordained or its achievement was a background organizing constraint. The social value and meaningfulness of research hinges upon a culture of diverse minds engaging in responsible, independent, candid, sincere, and mutually responsive methods of investigation. The enterprise of the university will therefore bear a grudging relationship to hierarchy and take a hostile stance toward permanent power relations with respect to the recognition of knowledge and the conditions of its production. Consequently, civil controversies will be predictable features of the university setting and often signs of health and proper functioning.

This anti-hierarchical stance underpins academic freedom with respect to the content of teaching, research, university governance, and outside activities. To form and maintain a flourishing community of independent, but mutually enlightening, study and research in an environment of scarce resources and attention, members must make decisions, both individually and for the institution, about what topics are worth pursuing, what scholarship is qualitatively excellent and worthwhile, and which people and what institutional structures contribute well to such a community. These judgments must themselves be independent and sincere, or else the institution will risk instituting a form of pre-ordained coordination about ideas *indirectly* through the selection of its members. Because the epistemic value of what it produces depends upon members' independence and the absence of enforced cooperation and compromise around an official point of view, it is important that these judgments should not be deployed whenever conceivable, but only to facilitate the construction and continuation of an epistemic repository constituted by a community of independently minded investigators. Further, these judgments must be subject to scrutiny and criticism from any corner; one's support or criticism should not be dismissed merely because of one's place in a hierarchy.

Finally, such decisions should not, *arbitrarily*, be made permanent. Judgments allocating structures of power and establishing substantive priorities that determine the conditions of pursuing and disseminating knowledge (e.g., the comparative size of the humanities budget) should be understood, on principle, to be only provisional, periodically up for questioning and reconsideration. In a university setting, permanent, unquestionable decisions would only cement some members' perspectives and conflict with the conviction that understandings may evolve and that the worth of an idea or the permission to voice it is not contingent upon one's status, friends, or the idea's popularity.

By contrast, the tenure process permits the qualitative judgments that constitute the community, but it also provides insulation to the faculty from the possibly contaminating concern that sincerity, coupled with difference, will result in expulsion or demotion. An appointment's permanence is designed not to reify a particular qualitative judgment, therefore, but to safeguard individual sincerity. It is a form of permanence that is not arbitrary.

This understanding of the university yields resources to respond to newly emerging threats to academic freedom. To be sure, academic freedom faces many of the same threats as ever: namely, political and patronage pressures to conform the content of teaching and research to others' external agendas.[23] Arguably, indirect demands to attract and to appease funding sources, whether from the state or private donors, have become more acute in recent years, particularly as public funding of higher educa-

---

[23] *See, e.g.*, James Risen, *Ex-Spy Alleges Effort to Discredit Bush Critic*, N.Y. TIMES, June 16, 2011, at A1 (reporting allegations that the CIA attempted to personally discredit a university professor who wrote a critical blog about American foreign policy in the Middle East); AM. ASS'N OF UNIV. PROFESSORS, ACADEMIC FREEDOM AND TENURE: LOUISIANA STATE UNIVERSITY, BATON ROUGE (2011), *available at* http://www.aaup.org/NR/rdonlyres/28F1CE64-5ABE-4FB0-829C-3D9C9807A44D/0/LSUJuly2011Report.pdf (reporting two separate incidents at LSU, one in which a professor was retaliated against for his research on the cause of flooding during Hurricane Katrina, and another that saw a professor removed from her class due to the grades she assigned); Pat Flynn, *Academic Freedom Flap Boils Over: UCSD Faculty Irate, Demands Action After Dean Ordered Professor Not To Publish Research*, SAN DIEGO UNION-TRIB., May 26, 2011, at B-1, *available at* http://www.utsandiego.com/news/2011/May/25/ucsd-faculty-says-professors-academic-freedom-brea (reporting that a dean warned a professor not to publish material that contradicted the work of a colleague).

tion has sharply declined.[24] In addition to these rising pressures, at least two new sources of menace have emerged over the last twenty years.

New Threats to Academic Freedom

First, the power of Institutional Review Boards (IRBs) has ballooned in ways that impinge upon the free pursuit of independent research.[25] Before embarking on their research, academics who conduct research on human subjects must gain approval for their research protocols from IRBs. These oversight committees were originally instituted to protect research subjects from the sort of harm and exploitation committed by infectious disease researchers from the 1940s through the 1970s, including both the Nazis in the concentration camps and also U.S. researchers at home and abroad. Prime catalysts for instituting reform and oversight included studies in which researchers deceptively inoculated prisoners with gonorrhea and syphilis or injected mentally disabled children with hepatitis, and the Tuskegee experiments in which researchers purporting

[24] *See, e.g., This American Life: Game Changer* (Public Radio International radio broadcast July 8, 2011), *available at* http://www.thisamericanlife.org/radio-archives/episode /440/transcript (describing university practices of promoting research results about natural gas extraction from shale to gain state and industry favor and related university practices of suppressing environmentally significant research by a public health professor about significant side effects associated with such practices for fear of alienating state and industry support); *see also* Larry Abramson, *Colleges Receive Gifts, But Are Strings Attached?*, NPR (May 13, 2011 3:00 PM), http://www.npr.org/2011/05/13/136285599/colleges-receive -gifts-with-strings-attached (describing allegations that the Florida State University allowed the Koch Foundation substantial influence in selecting faculty members and curriculum in exchange for a 1.5 million dollar donation); Kent S. Miller & Ray Bellamy, *Fine Print, Restrictive Grants, and Academic Freedom*, ACADEME, May-June 2012, at 17 (discussing Koch Foundation and BB&T Foundation's donations and expectations of influence on curriculum and hiring at Florida State University); Risa L. Lieberwitz, *Confronting the Privatization and Commercialization of Academic Research: An Analysis of Social Implications at the Local, National, and Global Levels*, 12 IND. J. GLOBAL LEGAL STUD. 109 (2005) (exploring the influence of commercial interests and corporate influence over faculty research and the contamination of the university's public mission).

[25] *See, e.g.,* Judith Jarvis Thomson et al., *Research on Human Subjects: Academic Freedom and the Institutional Review Board*, ACADEME, Sept-Oct. 2006, at 95, 95–96, *available at* http://www.aaup.org/AAUP/comm/rep/A/humansubs.htm; JUDITH JARVIS THOMSON ET AL., AM. ASS'N OF UNIV. PROFESSORS, REGULATION OF RESEARCH ON HUMAN SUBJECTS: ACADEMIC FREEDOM AND THE INSTITUTIONAL REVIEW BOARD 1–3 (2013), *available at* http://www.aaup.org/file/IRB-Final-Report.pdf (reporting obstacles to research imposed by IRB requirements and violations of freedom of speech and recommending that research that either imposes a minimal risk of harm on subjects or consists entirely of speech activities be exempt from IRB requirements); Philip Hamburger, *Getting Permission*, 101 NW. U. L. REV. 405 (2007); Philip Hamburger, *The New Censorship: Institutional Review Boards*, 2004 SUP. CT. REV. 271.

to treat patients deliberately withheld effective cures for syphilis for decades from a group of rural African-American men in order to study the progression of the disease.[26] Sociological research asking or inducing subjects to engage in abusive behaviors toward others also served as an impetus to the adoption of federal requirements that recipients of federal research money use institutional review boards to check the possibility of abuse.[27]

Although IRBs perform an important checking and protective function to ensure that historically serious abuses do not recur, their jurisdiction has expanded alarmingly to include research that poses no physical or substantial psychological threat to subjects, but merely involves speech, such as the administration of simple questionnaires. This raises both the prospect and the reality of placing barriers to communication and of suppressing speech-based research because the (anticipated) content of the speech or the effects of initiating conversation encounter disapproval from colleagues, administrators, or the public.

Second, the Supreme Court's recent jurisprudence on freedom of speech for public employees has been dismal, culminating in *Garcetti v. Ceballos*,[28] a case that held that freedom of speech posed no obstacle to the discipline of a deputy district attorney for authoring an internal, civ-

---

[26] *See* National Commission for the Protection of Human Subjects of Biomedical and Behavioral Research, *The Belmont Report* (1979) (available at http://www.hhs.gov/ohrp /humansubjects/guidance/belmont.html); CARL H. COLEMAN ET AL., THE ETHICS AND REGULATION OF RESEARCH WITH HUMAN SUBJECTS 3–51 (2005).

[27] *See* Coleman et al., *supra* note 26, at 48–50 (describing the Milgram experiment and the Stanford prison experiment).

[28] Garcetti v. Ceballos, 547 U.S. 410 (2006). *Garcetti* completed an important triumvirate of cases involving public employee speech. *Pickering v. Board of Education*, 391 U.S. 563 (1968) signaled an openness to a highly tolerant speech culture by holding that public employees could not be disciplined for off-duty speech about matters of public concern unless it disrupted job performance. It was followed by *Connick v. Myers*, 461 U.S. 138 (1983), which, though consistent with *Pickering*, moved toward a narrower approach than *Pickering* by holding that on-duty speech by a public employee about the internal politics of the district attorney's office was not a matter of public concern and therefore did not register as a First Amendment issue. *Garcetti* built on this misstep by further holding that on-duty speech about a matter of public concern but within the scope of the speaker's employment also falls outside of the First Amendment's free speech scrutiny. *Borough of Duryea v. Guarnieri*, 131 S. Ct. 2488 (2011), cemented the Court's indifference to retaliation against public employee speech by finding that the First Amendment's petition clause offered no relief to an employee who filed a complaint about an employment matter that was not deemed a matter of public concern. *See also* Judith Areen, *Government as Educator: A New Understanding of First Amendment Protection of Academic Freedom and Governance*, 97 GEO. L.J. 945, 974–76 (2009); Robert M. O'Neil et al., *Protecting an Independent Faculty Voice: Academic Freedom After* Garcetti v. Ceballos, ACADEME, Nov.-Dec. 2009, at 67, 75–78 (2009), *available at* http://www.aaup.org/AAUP/comm/rep/A/postgarcettireport.htm.

illy worded memorandum conveying concerns about police misrepresentations within a search warrant application and therefore recommending dismissal of a case. Some lower federal courts have extended *Garcetti* to deny public university professors First Amendment protection against retaliatory discipline for disfavored speech critical of administrative decisions, including the allocation of grants or promotion decisions.[29] Underpinning both newer threats is a version of institutional exceptionalism. It centers on the idea that academic freedom only protects against the inappropriate regulation of ideas in research and teaching and does not extend to preclude or constrain the hierarchical regulation of administrative and managerial structures within the university.

INSTITUTIONAL REVIEW BOARDS

The difficulties with this posture are evident when we consider the increasing prevalence of requirements that researchers satisfy a mere "administrative" hurdle to protect safety by supplicating for IRB approval before pursuing human subjects research, even when the research merely involves communication with others, such as via interviews and surveys. Notably, the IRB process subjects a university member's research proposal to review, without appeal, by other academics, often outside their field, and sometimes by lay people, who may delay or obstruct the researcher's ability to pursue an intellectual project. If the value of the university inheres in its being a collaborative enterprise of harvesting and disseminating knowledge by facilitating consensual interaction between *independent* researchers who exercise their sincere judgment, then that value is jeopardized by un-nuanced requirements that researchers gain the approval of their colleagues to engage in inquiry through a procedure that is not subject to appeal. If my threshold ability to pursue a question depends upon your agreeing that question is worthwhile and in my sub-

[29] *See, e.g.,* Hong v. Grant, 516 F. Supp. 2d 1158 (C.D. Cal. 2007) (holding that statements made by a professor regarding department governance fell under *Garcetti*'s exception for employment-related speech, and thus were unprotected by the First Amendment), *aff'd* on grounds university officers are protected by sovereign immunity, 403 F. App'x 236 (9th Cir. 2010); Renken v. Gregory, 541 F.3d 769 (7th Cir. 2008) (upholding summary judgment against a public university professor who alleged retaliation after he criticized the university's use of grant money); Ezuma v. City University of New York, 665 F. Supp. 2d 116 (E.D.N.Y. 2009), *aff'd*, 367 F. App'x 178 (2d Cir. 2010) (granting summary judgment against a professor who alleged retaliation based on his support for a colleague's sexual harassment claim and his questioning of the department chair's qualifications). *But see* Demers v. Austin, 746 F.3d 402 (9th Cir. 2014) (finding an exception to *Garcetti* for teaching and academic writing and interpreting academic writing broadly to include commentary on organizational matters that affect the substance and methodology of academic inquiry).

mitting to your *demands*, rather than your suggestions, about how that question should be investigated, then the independence of my judgments is burdened. The approval requirement also introduces the opportunity for considerations irrelevant to the intellectual inquiry to constrain what knowledge is pursued. As the one-time chair of the University of Chicago IRB for the biological sciences shockingly admitted, in the spirit of defense and not concession, "Universities are sensitive to political influences that compromise their corporate interest. Institutional Review Boards can forestall the public image problems and protect the institution's reputation by weeding out politically sensitive studies before they are approved."[30] Exactly. Although the university has moral interests in ensuring that its facilities and powers are not irresponsibly deployed to cause people harm, those interests should be pursued in ways compatible with its equally fundamental end of respecting intellectual freedom as the constitutive method of collecting and celebrating knowledge.

EMPLOYEE SPEECH AND INSTITUTIONAL EXCEPTIONALISM: *GARCETTI*

A similar problem besets the increasingly powerful idea, both outside and inside the university, that the efficient management of institutional structures permits substantive requirements of agreement, and that these requirements are compatible with our other core commitments to freedom of speech because those commitments apply only in other domains. That idea drives *Garcetti* and is beginning to infect university culture, through its contestable premise that governance matters are separate from academic endeavors and therefore exempt from free speech guarantees. As part of the circuitous path back to academic misrepresentation, I want to address what is wrong with this division. The error in this way of thinking of the relationship between free speech and institutional structure, especially university structure, also illuminates the mistake we make, I think, in authorizing misrepresentation in research.

Start with the general idea driving *Garcetti*, that free speech guarantees do not apply within a bureaucratic structure because free speech may hamper organizational effectiveness. What motivates *Garcetti*, partly, is a narrower, reasonable idea—that employers, even public employers, should have a relatively free hand in evaluating workers' performance and in making employment decisions based on the quality of that perfor-

---

[30] Jonathan Moss, *If Institutional Review Boards Were Declared Unconstitutional, They Would Have To Be Reinvented*, 101 Nw. U. L. Rev. 801, 804 (2007).

mance. Where the work being evaluated involves speech, the task will inevitably involve content-based evaluations of speech. I accept the general proposition that activity that is disruptive to the workplace or that constitutes subpar work performance, including speech, may reasonably be subject to workplace evaluation and discipline. But the decision as to what counts as disruptive or inadequate work performance should be influenced and constrained by our free speech commitments.

A commitment to individual free expression should prevent state officials from reprimanding employees merely for their sincere, civilly expressed opinions about the conduct of government affairs, even about—*especially* about—subject matter that falls within the scope of the speaker's employment. Why especially? Employees are likely the people who know the most about the relevant issues at their worksite and about its products. Their concerns may find their most immediately relevant, competent audience on site, so their individual interests in worksite expression are particularly pressing. This site-specific expertise, plus the fact that the internal governance of government workplaces is intrinsically a matter of public concern, forms the crux of the infirmity of *Connick v. Myers*, the precursor to *Garcetti*, which declared that speech restrictions could be levied on public employees speaking about internal workplace matters because these were perversely deemed not to be matters of public concern.[31]

If we are committed to the importance of individual self-expression, while remaining fully alive to the fact that individuals differ and often react strongly to their differences, then we have to accept that it is a natural outgrowth of free, robust, candid expression that some people will be upset, concerned, thoughtful, and mentally occupied on occasion about what others have to say; they may talk about others' speech, either to evaluate it or excoriate it. A certain amount of time-consuming controversy comes part-and-parcel with the freedom of citizens to make their thoughts known and to hear and try to understand others. This may, concomitantly, reduce the efficiency of some governmental operations, measured in a particular way, compared with the efficiency that might be achieved if they were run on a strict hierarchical basis. Getting things done quickly, with maximum levels of pleasantness and apparent consensus, may be harder when people present their sincere views rather than parrot a party line. But these criteria of measurement are too narrow. The

---

[31] 461 U.S. 138 (1983). For an extended, persuasive critique of *Myers*, see STEVEN H. SHIFFRIN, THE FIRST AMENDMENT, DEMOCRACY, AND ROMANCE 74–80 (1990).

free circulation of information and opinions provides significant legitimacy and accuracy gains that should also count as forms of success, alongside speed and pleasantries, within a public enterprise.

In making these points, I aim to respond to some of Robert Post's frequently voiced themes about the different forms of speech regulation suited to the "managerial domain," which he puts to the service of justifying the approach of *Myers*.[32] One difficulty with the invocation of the need of management structures to justify restrictions on public employee speech is that Post's conception of efficiency in governmental operations seems to presuppose criteria of success that valorize smooth and quickly executed hierarchical relations. However well- (or ill-) suited that conception might be to the business world, it does not seem sensitive to the general nature of government operations within a democracy (with the exception of emergency situations of the kind encountered by fire departments, hazardous waste crews, and their ilk). The criteria of success more reasonably applicable to them should include the desiderata that decisions are accurate, substantively legitimate, fair to the public they serve, and undertaken with an effort to ascertain the needs and perspectives of those affected by them, including the employees who execute them.

The mere fact of doubts or dissension, along with the associated effects of reactions to them *as such* (e.g., response, discussion, and the natural moderate tensions associated with the airing of difference), cannot be treated as relevantly disruptive, "efficiency-reducing," or incompetent to a discipline-worthy degree if, at the same time, we embrace freedom of speech and the more democratic criteria of success just articulated. In a free speech culture, part of management's task is to channel difficult outbursts or dissident expression so that, while they may naturally produce choppy waters, they do not mature into an unmanageable storm that disables colleagues from adequate job performance. Dissent or agreement registered in ways that overwhelm thoughtful management may qualify as workplace disruption reasonably subject to discipline, but the mere fact that the *content* of the expression is unwelcome or provocative to others, including supervisors, should not.[33]

---

[32] *See, e.g.*, Robert Post, Constitutional Domains: Democracy, Community, Management 260 (1995); Robert Post, *Recuperating First Amendment Doctrine*, 47 Stan. L. Rev. 1249, 1273 (1995) (endorsing *Connick v. Myers*).

[33] One method that might reasonably prove cause for discipline would be repeated, persistent speech in a manner that becomes harassing and thereby interferes with workers' ability to perform other job functions. I take it that that isn't really a content-based objection.

In many cases, the government has obligations to engage in truthful speech about its activities, both because of its constituent ends and to enable accountability. Hence, discipline of employee speech within the scope of employment is all the more disturbing when the speech is disciplined *because* it is factually true. It is beyond bizarre that the First Amendment demands that falsity must be proven in most libel cases,[34] but that actual, relevant, non-confidential, non-garbling, factual truth does not constitute a decisive First Amendment defense against the disciplining of a public employee *qua* employee for disfavored speech.

It should serve as a *reductio* of the *Garcetti* line of cases that a recent appellate court, reviewing a police officer's termination for his refusal to retract his own truthful eyewitness report about a colleague's physical abuse of a suspect, held his speech was protected under the First Amendment only because his speech could be construed as delivered *qua* citizen and not *qua* official.[35] The idea that the officer's truthful speech was protected (only) because he spoke in the capacity of a citizen seems a convoluted rationale given that he witnessed the incident only due to his employment status. Likewise, although it delivered a welcome result, the Supreme Court's recent unanimous decision in *Lane v. Franks* unfortunately invoked this rationale in holding that the First Amendment protects a public employee from employer retaliation for giving truthful, compelled testimony about corruption, a matter of public concern, even when the employee's knowledge was gleaned through the employment. In *Lane*, the Court placed emphasis both on the facts that the employee's speech at issue was *sworn* testimony and that the testimony was offered as a citizen and not as part of the employee's ordinary job responsibili-

---

[34] *See, e.g.*, New York Times v. Sullivan, 376 U.S. 256, 267–83 (1964); Philadelphia Newspapers, Inc. v. Hepps, 475 U.S. 767, 775–76 (1986).

[35] Jackler v. Byrne, 658 F.3d 225, 240–42 (2d Cir. 2011). Because filing factual reports was part of his job duty, as the lower court remarked with more of a sense of paradox than the sense of ridicule that seems warranted, "Jackler's refusal to alter his report was done in his capacity as a police officer . . . . Ironically, it is because he was a public employee with a duty to tell the truth that his insistence on fulfilling that duty is unprotected." Jackler v. Byrne, 708 F. Supp. 2d 319, 324 (S.D.N.Y. 2010). It is tragicomical that, given *Garcetti*, to find for the fired officer the appellate court had to claim that the First Amendment problem lay not with firing him for filing a truthful report but with attempting to compel him into perjury. *Jackler*, 658 F.3d at 242. *See also* Dahlia v. Rodriguez, 735 F.3d 1060 (9th Cir. 2013) (en banc). Dahlia found that a police officer's reports of police abuse were protected by the First Amendment when, but only when, the officer's reports did not go up the chain of command and, thus, could be construed as falling outside of his job duties. Judge Pregerson's sensible and more coherent concurring opinion argued instead that a police officer's reports of police abuse should be protected by the First Amendment whether such reports are required by the job or not and whether they are filed within the chain of command or not. *See id.* at 1080.

ties.[36] Although the Court did not reach the question whether the First Amendment would also extend to protect truthful, but disfavored, testimony when testifying falls within the scope of one's employment duties, as is common for police officers, coroners, and many social workers, it would be perverse and arbitrary to draw a sharp distinction between these categories. Not only would a distinction disserve the public interest in eliciting the truth from public officials and in protecting the reliability of sworn testimony, but it would also force public employees more deeply into untenable moral conflicts in which employment and loyalty are pitted against sincerity and truthfulness; within a First Amendment culture, the government, even when acting as an employer, should not be allowed to place these needs and virtues in opposition but should be required to reconcile them. Furthermore, although there are unique legal risks associated with perjury, sworn statements do not uniquely implicate employees' interests as people in speaking truthfully and sincerely. A sincere truthful complaint of corruption or police abuse to one's superior should gain the same protection as sworn testimony in court about the same matter—whether that testimony is compelled or volunteered and whether it is offered pursuant to or outside of one's official duties.

The more straightforward rationale for protecting public employees' speech is that government employees *qua* employees enjoy rights of free speech with respect to the duties and conditions of their employment unless that speech is substantially disruptive of an important governmental function or constitutes inadequate job performance. Furthermore, the concepts "disruptive" and "inadequate" must be interpreted charily to realize this speech-friendly approach.

That is, the fact that the speech is relevant, competently and civilly delivered, and factually true should operate as a complete defense to a *content-based* claim of disruption or inadequacy, except when factually true speech breaches a legitimate demand of confidentiality (or privilege) or when it garbles the government's speech. With respect to garbling, some employee speech may immediately, by itself, disable, disrupt, or subvert the relevant government speech or activity, and so may be reasonably subject to discipline consistent with free speech. Think for example, of the police officer who reads the Miranda warnings to a citizen just arrested but, without losing a beat, adds, "They make me say all that stuff, but it's a pile of malarkey. You should just tell us what happened

---

[36] 134 S. Ct. 2369 (2014).

right now, without delay."[37] That demonstration of disagreement may garble the government message that the citizen's rights will be respected; a reasonable listener may take the officer's coda as a prelude of forthcoming abuse and an unwillingness to respect those rights. The government, however, has a strong, legitimate interest in its own speech: in speaking clearly and in having that officer, *qua* government employee, deliver its message. But we should understand this category narrowly. I would distinguish, for example, the police officer who publicly opines, "A referendum has passed that decriminalizes marijuana; that's the public policy and I will stand by it, but personally, I regard this policy as a disaster."[38] Because the officer makes explicit the difference between her personal and the official stance and affirms she will abide by the public position, her speech does not garble the government's message.

GARCETTI AND ACADEMIC FREEDOM

Apart from my general opposition to *Garcetti*, a special problem bedevils that decision's extension to the public university setting. So far, I have argued that *individual* interests in expression should be recognized in on-duty, job-related speech. Now I want to argue that the (public) university's function and its special epistemic ends generate unique concerns

---

[37] The mandatory reading of the Miranda warning does not demand insincerity on the part of this officer; the demand that one not garble the government message in this case demands only contextual reticence about the officer's attitudes toward the practice of giving the warnings. The warnings themselves do not represent the speaker as affirming the importance or normative appropriateness of the rights of representation and against self-incrimination and the means to their satisfaction. There are, I believe, strong thinker-based reasons to attempt to ensure that government speech is worded in ways that do not demand direct insincerity or its appearance on the part of officials, even when they speak on behalf of and represent the government. Further, the case might differ if after the reading, the official says, truthfully and sincerely, to warn rather than to intimidate, "It says an attorney will be provided for you, but I should warn you that the guy who hangs out at the courthouse is an incompetent lush. It would behoove you to find someone else." That official's speech, where true, should be protected. The qualification in effect dilutes the government's message, but the culprit is the state's failure to ensure representation that respects the suspect's rights, rendering the diluted message more accurate than the intended message.

[38] Context and position matter when assessing whether individual speech garbles a compulsory government message. A prosecuting attorney, even a deputy district attorney, who voices sincere, reasonable concerns about the validity or sufficiency of evidence against a defendant partly discharges her role as an attorney of the court in doing so, given the presumption of innocence and general obligations of the state to use its considerable power carefully, even if her superior disagrees with her assessment. A federal public defender who publicly makes known his doubts about the innocence of a colleague's client, even as an act of private conscience, may thereby undercut his role as an advocate in ways that garble the government's message and its stance that every person merits a rigorous defense.

about *Garcetti* and bolster a claim that the public university should be treated as special within First Amendment jurisprudence.[39] Although a university differs from a park in some ways I have mentioned, like the park, it operates as a public forum in which independently minded speech is invited for its own sake, for the sake of its members, and for the sake of the broader community. Because it solicits speech and knowledge for its own sake and is also devoted to enabling the development and exercise of our capacities to think and reflect as mutually influencing but autonomous agents, a core First Amendment function, the university should be regarded as a publicly established center for the fostering and enriching of First Amendment activity. To invite free speech as way to develop knowledge and then to impose measures of content-restriction unnecessary to, and in tension with, the forum's function seems inconsistent with guarantees of and rationales for freedom of expression.

Thus, I take issue with Robert Post's general line of argument, an extension of his position on *Myers*, that "[t]he classroom is not a location in which the value of democratic legitimation is at stake," and more generally that "[a]cademic freedom is covered by the First Amendment not because of the value of democratic legitimation, but because of the value of democratic competence."[40] Post aims to make the point that the classroom and the university generally differ from the public square in that faculty must make content-based determinations of quality to assess students' performance and these assessments then may determine students' status at the university; those determinations involve the exercise of disciplinary authority, rather than the toleration and equality for all that is required in contexts that underscore the value of democratic legitimation.[41] In this way, faculty members promote democratic competence by developing disciplinary expertise amongst themselves and their students and contributing to the common stock of disciplinary knowledge. These

---

[39] In *dicta* in *Garcetti*, the Court gestured in this direction (although only with respect to teaching and research). "There is some argument that expression related to academic scholarship or classroom instruction implicates additional constitutional interests that are not fully accounted for by this Court's customary employee-speech jurisprudence." Garcetti v. Ceballos, 547 U.S. 410, 425 (2006). Justice Kennedy was attempting to assuage Justice Souter's well-founded concern that *Garcetti* would be extended to the university. *See id.* at 438–39 (Souter, J., dissenting).

[40] ROBERT POST, DEMOCRACY, EXPERTISE, AND ACADEMIC FREEDOM 70, 83–84 (2012). Post is critical of interpreting *Garcetti* to allow university administrators to dictate the content of faculty research and teaching, but he is silent on the issues raised by *Garcetti*'s application in the lower courts to student and faculty free speech with respect to internal administrative affairs and faculty governance at the university. *Id.* at 93–96.

[41] *Id.* at 33–34.

are fair points, but Post goes too far in intimating that opining on a ballot measure and voting in an election uniquely epitomize the important forms of and sites of contribution to democratic legitimation. A classroom (and a university) embodying a full-blown commitment to freedom of speech plays a role in exemplifying, reinforcing, and training citizens in democratic values of toleration and openness to criticism that a dictatorial classroom does not. Both may produce the same level of disciplinary competence that contributes to a well-informed citizenry, but the former instills disciplinary expertise within an environment that remains as open as possible to input from all comers and to criticism. It thereby operates as a forum and exemplar of democratic legitimating activity, whereas the dictatorial classroom, however powerful it is at instilling the disciplinary competence that serves democracies, is in tension with democratic values.

If we further regard the public university as serving as a showcase for First Amendment values, then protecting the speech of its members serves the symbolic function of modeling our commitment to free speech and demonstrating the strength of the state's willingness, in its own institution, to bear the same sorts of costs for that commitment that the public in general commits to absorbing for the First Amendment. Thus, there are distinct First Amendment reasons to extend guarantees of academic freedom to members of the public university, by which I mean guarantees that members will not be obstructed from participating in university life, whether it be in the areas of research, teaching, or university governance, because they express their sincere, even if unpopular, judgments.[42]

Thus, I have claimed that both having to gain permission to do basic research and being deterred from evincing sincere opinions about the conditions under which we seek knowledge are antithetical to standard, individualistic free speech values. Moreover, they are antithetical to the rather special commitments the university makes to reject the presupposition of a univocal perspective and, positively, to prioritize and symbolize the values of knowledge and inquiry with integrity. These values fuel a hostility to hierarchical efforts to control access to information, to make authoritative declarations about what views indepen-

---

[42] Further, they should be insulated from suffering negative employment (and educational) repercussions as a response merely to the fact and content of the expression of their candid, responsible, supported, sincere opinions. In light of this understanding of the university's function, these guarantees should extend not merely to research and teaching activities, but also to university governance and to constrain or preclude many forms of IRB oversight.

dent researchers should adopt, and to restrict commentary on knowledge claims and the conditions of their pursuit, even when those
hierarchical efforts are motivated by the aim of efficiently obtaining and
maintaining knowledge.

Academic Misrepresentation

For these reasons, I also contend that the underlying foundation of academic freedom is hostile to the use of academic misrepresentation as a
research tool. Yet the practice of such misrepresentation is commonplace.
Likewise, direct misrepresentations figure in the standard experimental
repertoire of the experimental psychologist.

The use of the lie to research subjects is approved by the American
Psychological Association Code of Conduct when the researcher determines that the research will not cause the subject physical pain or severe
emotional distress,[43] the deception is justified by "the study's significant
prospective scientific, educational, or applied value," and "effective nondeceptive alternative procedures are not feasible."[44] Psychology faculty
regularly enroll subjects in research and directly lie to them about the
experiment and its contents. Standard examples involve lying to subjects
about the question pursued by a study or the identity of the objects, tasks,
or people encountered during the experiment.[45] A recent study of two
prominent psychology journals found that between a third and a half of
the studies they published used deception as an investigatory technique.[46]

---

[43] This component of the Code rules out the most famous of the deceptive experiments,
the Milgram experiment, in which participants were directly misled into believing they were
administering increasingly more painful, eventually seemingly tortuous, electric shocks as
sanctions to other research subjects who purportedly answered exam questions inaccurately. The subjects' recognition that they were capable of such brutality was tremendously
distressing to them. Stanley Milgram, *Behavioral Study of Obedience*, 67 J. OF ABNORMAL
AND SOC. PSYCHOL. 371 (1963); STANLEY MILGRAM, OBEDIENCE TO AUTHORITY: AN EX-
PERIMENTAL VIEW 44–54 (1974).

[44] American Psychological Association, 2010 *Amendments to the 2002 Ethical Principles of Psychologists and Code of Conduct*, 65 AM. PSYCHOLOGIST 493 (2010). The American Sociological Association's Code of Ethics contains similar guidelines. American Sociological Association, "Code of Ethics," *asanet.org* 1997, http://www.asanet.org/images
/asa/docs/pdf/CodeofEthics.pdf.

[45] Franklin G. Miller, John P. Gluck, Jr., & David Wendler, *Debriefing and Accountability in Deceptive Research*, 18 KENNEDY INST. ETHICS J. 235, 236–37 (2008).

[46] Ralph Hertwig & Andreas Ortmann, *Deception in Experiments: Revisiting the Arguments in Its Defense*, 18 ETHICS & BEHAV. 59, 64–67 (2008). Unfortunately, Hertwig and
Ortmann do not always distinguish between lies and indirect forms of deception, so one
cannot isolate the specific percentage of cases using direct misrepresentation; but they note

One common example is the Trier Social Stress Test, a standard research protocol for assessing stress used in numerous psychological studies around the world.[47] Subjects are asked to perform a public speaking exercise while researchers aim to distract and irritate them. To make the speaking sufficiently stressful, researchers tell the subjects that the speeches are being filmed and will later be reviewed by an expert. In fact, the camera has no film and no expert evaluates the speeches.[48]

Although the Trier test is routinely approved by IRBs, it is not clear how it passes the requirement that nondeceptive techniques be infeasible. Those paired lies are completely gratuitous; even if the suggestion of observation were essential to create the appropriate sort of stressful environment, neither lying nor deception is necessary to achieve that goal. The researchers could actually film the speeches; they could hire an expert to screen them. Presumably, they do not do this because observation would cost more money without advancing their research aims. But that doesn't mean that the study is not possible or even practicable without lying. It suggests that, in practice, "feasible" is taken to encompass cost considerations. In practice, it suffices as a justification for lying to research subjects that to tell them the truth would be more expensive than to lie, at least with respect to "harmless" lies.

In the more ethically interesting cases, the lie told to research subjects is more integral to the research question under investigation. Elizabeth Loftus's research figures among the more notable examples of academic misrepresentation, both because of the genuine significance of her results and the bold, personal lies she tells. Loftus demonstrated the potential unreliability of memories (and the hazards of eye-witness testimony) by showing that it is possible to implant false memories by lying to subjects about their past. In a famous study, she collected information about subjects' childhood and then presented them with written biographical ac-

---

that in one of the journals they studied the direct provision of false information about stimulus material, about the identity of participants, and about the subjects' performance were very common methods of deception, used 62 percent, 24 percent, and 30 percent of the time when deception was used. *Id.* at 66.

[47] Clemens Kirschbaum, Karl-Martin Pirke, & Dirk Hellhammer, *The 'Trier Social Stress Test'—A Tool for Investigating Psychobiological Stress Responses in a Laboratory Setting*, 28 NEUROPSYCHOBIOLOGY 76 (1993); Brigitte Kudielka, Dirk Hellhammer, & Clemens Kirschbaum, *Ten Years of Research with the Trier Social Stress Test—Revisited*, in SOCIAL NEUROSCIENCE: INTEGRATING BIOLOGICAL AND PSYCHOLOGICAL EXPLANATIONS OF SOCIAL BEHAVIOR 56, 57 (Eddie Harmon-Jones & Piotr Winkielman eds., 2007).

[48] *See also* Ralph Hertwig & Andreas Ortmann, *Deception in Psychological Experiments: Two Misconceptions and a Research Agenda*, 71 SOC. PSYCH. Q. 222, 224 (2008) (reporting that many deceits "are typically driven by convenience rather than necessity").

counts, containing primarily veridical anecdotes interspersed with false stories about their having become lost in a shopping mall as a child; after these false stories were reinforced by mendacious family members recruited for the study, the research subjects over time began to claim they had direct memories of these fictional events.[49] Her more recent research embeds direct lies in credible materials to induce subjects to believe that, in their past, foods such as strawberry ice cream, pickles, or hard-boiled eggs had made them ill and thereby elicits a fresh aversion to those foods.[50]

These practices are often propelled by good motives, to be sure. Direct misrepresentation is commonly used in human subject research on the grounds that: it is necessary to mislead research subjects to obtain reliable, unbiased results; the research is important; nonclinical researchers do not owe research subjects any fiduciary duties and indeed are engaged in a (hierarchical) collaboration to seek knowledge;[51] and that the misrepresentation is designed to be temporary, so debriefing procedures should soothe any ethical qualms.

It is contested whether these techniques are, on balance, episodically effective even within the confines of their contexts at eliciting accurate information and avoiding contamination through subjects' awareness of the purposes of the studies. Although one might have expected psychologists to be acutely sensitive to the hazards of manipulating trust, surprisingly, it is experimental economists who balk at direct deception, because they worry that it contaminates the pool of research subjects by incubating distrust.[52]

Although there is plentiful room for debate about the matter, I do not care here to question the efficacy of these techniques. For argument's sake, I will assume that, on some occasions, direct misrepresentation is more episodically effective at gleaning important and accurate information than truthful experimentation. Even allowing for greater creativity in research design, complete abstention from direct misrepresentation

[49] Elizabeth F. Loftus, *Lost in the Mall: Misrepresentations and Misunderstandings*, 9 ETHICS & BEHAV. 51, 54–55 (1999); Elizabeth F. Loftus & Jacqueline E. Pickrell, *The Formation of False Memories*, 25 PSYCH. ANNALS 720 (1995).

[50] Daniel M. Bernstein, Cara Laney, Erin K. Morris & Elizabeth F. Loftus, *False Memories About Food Can Lead to Food Avoidance*, 23 SOC. COGNITION 11, 26–27 (2005).

[51] Bryan Benham, *The Ubiquity of Deception and the Ethics of Deceptive Research*, 22 BIOETHICS 147, 153 (2008).

[52] Hertwig & Ortmann, *supra* note 46, at 60; Hertwig & Ortmann, *supra* note 48, at 222; Dan Ariely & Michael I. Norton, *Psychology and Experimental Economics: A Gap in Abstraction*, 16 CURRENT DIRECTIONS PSYCH. SCI. 336, 337 (2007).

might preclude the acquisition of certain forms of knowledge. Hence, adhering to demands of sincerity may involve serious epistemic losses. But that sort of missed opportunity is not unique or special. It is part and parcel of moral, democratic life. In general, showing respect for others' bodily integrity, their intellectual independence, and their other autonomy rights involves costs that might not be endured if we used more hierarchical or abusive methods of organization and inquiry.

I do not aim to rehearse or vindicate the general arguments for respecting moral and democratic commitments even when those commitments entail sacrificing some valuable opportunities to achieve other forms of social good. My more modest objective is to show that these commitments are implicated by our communicative practices within the university setting. Far from the university being insulated from the demands of sincerity and freedom of speech, the university and its research endeavors are both subject to these demands and should serve as a showcase for the values these demands protect.

Specifically, appealing to the salutary consequences of misrepresentation to justify these techniques seems in tension with a conception of the university as an institution where meaningful conditions of knowledge generation, preservation, and dissemination demand a principled openness to entertain input from all corners and to report perceived knowledge sincerely. This posture of openness is essential to ensuring the possibility of discovering and confirming truth, to inculcating the skills necessary for students to continue these investigations, and to give citizens sufficient grounds for confidence in the university's results as sincere, responsible conclusions about matters of individual and public concern. This conception of the university seems to exclude lying to research subjects, even if those misrepresentations will be later corrected.

First, the contrary position sends a distinct message that university members' commitment to sharing its perceived, sincere hypotheses about the truth may not guide its communications when something more significant seems to be at stake. This willingness to misrepresent reduces the basis others have to trust whether the university's other declarations are reliable; one may reasonably wonder whether, on similar grounds, sincere reporting has been suppressed to pursue other, unrevealed aims. The fact that the greater end that misrepresentation serves is knowledge generation, is less a justifying than an exacerbating feature, for the pursuit of knowledge generation should not be an exceptional circumstance at the university. Its agents are always, continuously investigating.

Second, the position that direct misrepresentations about the purposes, methods, and conditions of research are acceptable suggests that the input of certain members of the university community, namely research subjects, may be blocked, via a misrepresentation, at the time when such input would be salient, during or prior to the research. Those closest to the conditions of producing knowledge should have an opportunity to assess, criticize, and contribute to the reasons that drive the structure of knowledge generation and production in which they are involved and the experiments to which they are subject. Lies to research subjects put that sort of timely contribution out of reach for those very people.

Third, lies to research subjects generate a troubling inequity of epistemic burdens. Successful, responsible research and valid results usually depend upon research subjects divulging their sincere responses and reactions to questions and experimental situations. Some research requires the subject to trust the researcher by revealing confidential, embarrassing, or otherwise revelatory information about herself. It would compromise many research results if subjects elected to misrepresent information they felt was unnecessary to reveal or if they judged that misrepresentation would serve their own important ends. So, the idea that the researcher, while soliciting the subject's trust, regards herself as authorized to misrepresent information seems to undercut the basis for the subject's trust. Further, it either seems to establish an inequality of epistemic burden (one party must represent truthfully, but the other need not) and to affirm a maxim of representation that, if adopted by research subjects, would compromise the integrity of the research.

One may object that rigorous debriefing of research subjects should address these worries by revealing the nature of the communicative context to the subjects. I am unconvinced this resolves all of the relevant ethical pitfalls of misrepresentation. Debriefing may, in theory, tackle the issue of researchers imparting false beliefs and deceiving subjects.[53] But

---

[53] In practice, there is reason for concern. In light of the university's mission to facilitate the accumulation and appreciation of knowledge, it should trouble both potential research subjects and researchers that at least some misrepresentations appear to be sticky and resistant to correction. Some research suggests that subjects who are warned prior to reading that a fictional passage contains some embedded false factual propositions nevertheless have a higher rate of belief in the false propositions than those not exposed to the fiction. See, e.g., Elizabeth J. Marsh, Michelle L. Meade & Henry L. Roediger III, *Learning Facts from Fiction*, 49 J. Memory & Language 519, 534–35 (2003) (demonstrating subjects' general susceptibility to believing information read in fictional stories, and then to later falsely thinking that those beliefs were held prior to reading the belief-implanting fiction);

that practice alone, even if entirely successful, does not address the concern that the willingness to misrepresent facts, purposes, and aims in the service of obtaining and verifying knowledge calls into question virtually every representation of the academic.[54] Knowing that someday, when the inquiry is deemed to be over, any misapprehension will be corrected is insufficient to warrant confidence in an academic's representations, for a listener has no way of knowing which side of the temporal line she occupies. That concern seems heightened given that many researchers observe behavior and interactions outside the spatial and temporal boundaries of the lab or their official contact with research subjects.[55]

To address that concern, the context of misrepresentation and its starting and ending points would also have to be clearly delineated in advance. Where the research genuinely pursues important results, the misrepresentation is intrinsically necessary to pursue that knowledge, and the subject is warned about the possibility of and temporal boundaries of misrepresentation and debriefed at a time and date certain, then perhaps the discrete and compartmentalized misrepresentation is justified. Perhaps this is not so different from inviting a listener to read fiction or watch a film, although the fictional components are less evident here than in most fictional contexts.

A consistent practice of this sort would represent a substantial improvement over the status quo. But some dissimilarities with fiction still rankle. With fiction, the reader may immediately adopt a posture of epistemic remove and "consume" it as metaphor or fable or fairy-tale without undermining its point; the reader may simultaneously regard it as

---

Elizabeth J. Marsh & Lisa K. Fazio, *Learning Errors from Fiction: Difficulties in Reducing Reliance on Fictional Stories*, 34 MEMORY & COGNITION 1140, 1147–48 (2006) (reporting that subjects had a difficult time monitoring errors in fictional readings even when they were told the stories were unreliable); Markus Appel & Tobias Richter, *Persuasive Effects of Fictional Narratives Increase Over Time*, 10 MEDIA PSYCH. 113, 127–29 (2007) (finding a "sleeper effect" in persuasion in fiction, meaning that beliefs obtained by reading fictional works congeal as time passes).

[54] *Cf.* Leslie K. John et al., *Measuring the Prevalence of Questionable Research Practices with Incentives for Truth-Telling*, 23 PSYCH. SCI. 524, 526–27 (2012) (inferring from a survey of nearly 6000 research psychologists, 2155 of whom participated, that "nearly 1 in 10 research psychologists has introduced false data into the scientific record").

[55] *See, e.g.*, Paul Condon, Gaëlle Desbordes, Willa Miller & David DeSteno, *Meditation Increases Compassionate Responses to Suffering*, 24 PSYCH. SCI. 2125, 2125–26 (2013) (studying behaviors of unaware research subjects in waiting rooms before they entered the training sessions for which they signed up). *See also* Hertwig & Ortmann, *supra* note 46 at 66 (describing the, admittedly less common, research technique of keeping subjects unaware they are being studied or watched).

false and engage fully with it for the purpose for which it is offered. The reader is not estopped from attempting to ascertain and investigate what parts of the fiction are purely fancy.

By contrast, when the misrepresentation really is intrinsically necessary, the subject cannot, consistent with the purposes of the research, adopt a posture of active questioning or remove while she is exposed to it; the subject needs to believe what is said or, at least, not actively call it into question.[56] The warning must be disregarded or framed in such general terms that it cannot affect the subject's active engagement with the false propositions presented as true. So, at the most relevant moments of interaction, the researcher acts on a maxim that affirms presenting the false as though it were true with the aim that it be taken as true for the researcher's purposes of furthering knowledge. Although the context is delineated, affirmation of that maxim seems in tension with a foundational commitment to sincere expression as an ethical and meaning-bestowing constraint on the pursuit of knowledge.

Of course, not all suspended contexts are like fiction in which the listener may simultaneously engage and consciously suspend belief. Friends misrepresent to enable surprise parties; e.g., a friend might say "The movie starts at 7. On the way to the movie, we need to pick something up at Jack's," when there is a party at Jack's house and no true plan to see a film. Unsurprisingly, I am skeptical about these misrepresentations. They seem to me rather fraught and questionable, although I recognize that others see them as edgy but ultimately innocent.[57]

Whatever the correct assessment, it is not obvious that the putative justification for the surprise party misrepresentation is merely that the intention is not to permanently deceive and that the truth will be disclosed shortly. Rather, the ethical case (whether successful or not) for the direct misrepresentation depends, I suspect, on the fact of a close, trusting, and ongoing relationship of care between the parties, in which the contours of when one party may act as the other's representative for her benefit have been established in the explicit and implicit ways friends forge these boundaries and permissions. In the research context, the misrepresentation is not designed to serve the particular listener's benefit,

[56] I put aside the exceptional case where what is being studied is active, transparent distrust, e.g. subjects' reaction to being lied to where they know they are being lied to and they know the liar knows they know this.

[57] Benham, *supra* note 51, at 155 (arguing that "joking deceptions may actually strengthen certain relationships").

and it is not delivered by someone who has such a relationship or particularized set of understandings.

Further, if the inequity between the researcher and subject with respect to the implicit epistemic permissions to comment and react is discomfiting, the warning and debriefing model does not alleviate that discomfort at a critical moment of interaction between the parties. I do not claim that the researcher and the research subject are or should be treated as full epistemic peers. The researcher's greater expertise may justifiably give her access to resources, opportunities, and decision-making powers that the research subject reasonably lacks. The difficulty is not that the researcher and her subject lack equal power with respect to experimental design. So too, the difficulty is not that the university administrator and the generic faculty member do not have equal administrative power with respect to when the academic calendar should begin and what departments should get what funding. But, in the case of academic freedom and university governance, what seems like an objectionable inequality is the posture that only certain members *should* be able to comment freely on certain subject matters; therefore others do not merit sincere representations, which in turn thereby circumvents the possibility of their contributing to the discussion. Among the conditions of confidence in the university's results is that the university does not obstruct, prohibit or punish, *ex ante*, sincere contributions from any corner, even while it may reject them on substantive grounds and affirm their contraries. Likewise, what seems objectionable about the research misrepresentation is that it represents an effort to obstruct a participant's offering her sincere reactions at a key moment of action and decision, when the participant is being acted upon. It thereby denies that form of equality to research subjects.[58]

Institutions as Symbols

I will conclude by offering a final argument against lying by appealing to the symbolic significance of the police and the university. In a well-

---

[58] My stance on the wrong of disabling input from any corner requires qualification in the case of confidentiality. I agree that the names of reviewers, the names of research subjects, and the disposition of certain individual's cases and complaints may be kept confidential and, therefore, that commentary by community members about them may be permissibly obstructed. This seems consistent with my general stance both because those facts are not the proper subject of general public investigation (whereas the same cannot be said for research studies or protocols) and because the protection of privacy is another structural element to ensure the safety of sincerity.

functioning democracy, the police do not merely keep the peace, nor do they merely keep the peace through threats, force, and other methods of deterrence. They serve as moral epistemic authorities and that is part of how they keep the peace. They also symbolically represent our moral commitments and the rule of law by holding themselves to high standards of integrity. Unfortunately, I am merely speaking theoretically, but this theoretical role does work in explaining our particular form of outrage and betrayal when actual police officers act badly or direct subordinates to lie on their behalf. The university collects, preserves, and disseminates knowledge and reproduces our ability to do so, but at the same time, the university serves, for the culture, as an operative symbol of the importance of knowledge and its free pursuit with integrity.

Institutional symbols, I submit, have importance because they are not empty or cheap. They operationalize devotion to a value and underscore how precious that value is, despite the obstacles and costs associated with its achievement. The maintenance of a free university, for example, shows that a commitment to truth and to wide-ranging debate and dissension as preconditions of worthwhile knowledge, is not merely an abstract position, but is a possible way of life that can be sustained across generations and can withstand public, messy debates. Institutions offer both a possibility proof of the ability to abide by such values over time in social circumstances and serve as an aspirational model, offering a counter to social temptations to cynicism and corner-cutting.

But to function in this way, as symbols of steadfastness to a demanding commitment, I suspect that the manifestation of devotion to the relevant values must be fairly bold and straightforward, i.e., easy to read, not demanding subtle interpretations. Generally, symbols function well when they are, so to speak, in large typeface.[59] My diffident suggestion, then, is that if these institutions are the public face of moral uprightness and devotion to truth for its own sake, then that has implications for institutional casuistry. The analogy would be to the notion in law that justice must not only be done but be seen to be done. The implication is that even when a general requirement may not reach a particular domain and

[59] Enrique Peñalosa, former mayor of Bogota, strived to build towering schools and libraries in Bogota so that, through architecture, the importance of these institutions would be made salient to citizens in much the same way as the physical prominence of cathedrals conveyed their social significance to the citizenry. Enrique Peñalosa, *The "Urban" in International Economic Development: Lessons from a Colombian City*, UNIV. CHI. INT'L & AREA STUDIES MULTIMEDIA OUTREACH SOURCE (April 20, 2004), http://chiasmos.uchicago.edu/events/penalosa.shtml.

adherence to it would be in some sense discretionary, that nevertheless, it should be adhered to in order to ensure that signal strength is not diminished and that nonadherence is not misinterpreted as a less than full commitment to the general requirement. So, even were it true that, strictly speaking, the interrogation room and the laboratory might be considered as domains outside the scope of the presumption of sincerity, to treat them as justified suspended contexts would dilute the symbolic strength of our perceived commitments to the social, noninstrumental importance of knowledge and the preservation of reliable and free mechanisms for its transmission. Even when it is carefully compartmentalized, a willingness of university researchers to bypass the truth when it proves inconvenient, or may involve sacrificing access to some knowledge, undercuts the symbolic valorization of truthfulness that aims to bolster the cultural strength to abide by the presumption of sincerity despite its substantial personal and institutional costs.

I began this chapter by advertising a challenge to institutional exceptionalism with respect to free speech and truth-telling. I have ended with an endorsement of institutional exceptionalism, but with a distinctly different valence, requiring higher rather than lower fidelity to free speech and truth-telling. Some social institutions, like the state and the university, do not merely deliver goods and services but have special commitments to moral ends that in turn affect how they may pursue those ends. Further, these institutions serve symbolically as beacons for those values, in light of which they may labor under higher, rather than lower, standards.

Hong v. Grant (2007), 205n29
hostile audiences and freedom of
speech, 126, 129–30
Hyman, David A., 165n6

immoral agents. *See* duress; Murderer
at the Door
immoral promises, 34–35
Inbau, Fred, 195n14, n16
indecency and obscenity, 106n48
individual duty of sincerity, 191–93
individual versus corporate speech,
98–102
Indonesia, criminal penalties for defamation in, 92–93n24
inflationary rhetoric, 191
initiated promises in response to duress, 50–51, 53–54, 60–65, 67, 71,
73–78
Institutional Review Boards (IRBs),
203–4, 205–6, 213n42, 215
institutions, 3–4, 182–223; duties of
sincerity, institutional, 194; exceptionalism, institutional, 183–84,
199–200, 206–11, 223; freedom of
speech, 182, 183, 221–23; individual duty of sincerity and, 191–93;
police, internal institutional ends
of, 185, 194–99; presumption of
truth, importance of maintaining,
188; puffery, 188–91; suspended
contexts and, 185, 186–88, 194;
symbolic function of institutions,
185, 221–23
Internet defamation, 92–93n24
Iran hostage crisis, 68–69n31
IRBs (Institutional Review Boards),
203–4, 205–6, 213n42, 215

Jackler v. Byrne (2011), 209n35
*Johanns v. Livestock Marketing Asso-
ciation* (2005), 96n29
John, Leslie K., 219n54
justified suspended contexts, 16–19,
28–29, 32–36, 38, 40–43, 146,
149, 151–53, 155, 183, 186–88,
223. *See also* suspended contexts

Kaczynski, Ted, 77
Kagan, Elena, 125n21
Kaminski, Margot, 122n14
Kant, Immanuel: on activity as deception, 20; on duress, 49–50; on importance of truthfulness, 5–6, 9,
27–29, 89n13; *Lectures on Ethics*,
5, 6, 9; modern reconstructions of
arguments of, 29, 40; on Murderer-
at-the-Door arguments, 5–6, 8, 26–
28, 35–36, 40, 43; self-defense,
Herman's Kantian argument for, 73
Kasky v. Nike (2002), 132n28
Kendrick, Leslie, 123n17, 125n22
Kennedy, Anthony, 125n21, 135, 136,
212n39
kindness or sympathy in response to
duress, 61–62, 66–68
Koch Foundation, 203n24
Korsgaard, Christine M., 29n39

Laird, James D., 96n30
Lall, U.S. v. (2010), 196n18
Lane v. Franks (2014), 209–10
lawyers and legal advocates: prosecutorial discretion, 166–67, 176;
public speech of, 211n38; representations made by, 142
legal enforcement of initiated promises made under duress, 64–5,
68–71
legal regulation of autobiographical
lies, 3, 119, 157–81; defining accommodation of some moral
wrongs and, 158–62; equality and
accommodation, 3, 158, 167–75,
180–81; limitations on accommodation of moral failure, 176–81;
moral imperfection, accommodating, 162–67
legal regulation of lying and freedom
of speech, 3, 116–56; compelled
disclosure, 133–35; content-discrimination, 124, 125–32, 135;
criminal versus civil penalties for,
123–24; disproportionate remedies, 122; First Amendment issues,

content-based approach to lying to, 32–37; deliberate misrepresentation of one's own moral location to, 43–46; disagreements over acceptability of lying to, 5–6; distinguishing wrong of lying from wrong of deception, 2, 8, 19–26; emergency-propelled thinking, dangers of, 44–46; false promises to, 34–35; justified suspended contexts and, 16–19, 32–33, 38, 40–44, 187n5; Kantian position on lying and, 5–6, 8, 9, 27–29, 35, 40, 43; Murderer Next Door and, 8, 26, 30, 36, 40; pathological liars, 14–15, 17–18; problem of total communicative isolation of, 30–32, 37–38, 74–75; qualified absolutism of stricture on lying and, 1–3, 6–8; reciprocity arguments regarding, 17–18, 30–32; redemption, allowing for possibility of, 37–38; reentry into moral community of, 38–44; self-defense approaches to, 29–30

narcotics decriminalization and prosecutorial discretion, 166–67
New York v. Ferber (1982), 129
New York Times, publication of Unabomber manifesto by, 77
New York Times v. Sullivan (1964), 209n34
noise regulation, 135, 137
nondiscursive communication and free speech, 81, 84, 93, 103, 113–15

Obama, Barack, 76n38
obscenity and indecency, 106n48
O'Neil, Collin, 22n30
Ortmann, Andreas, 214–15n46, 215n48
Owens, David, 56–57

Pande, Mrinal, 194n12
particularized harm caused and legal regulation of lying, 135–39

pathological liars, 14–15, 17–18
Peñalosa, Enrique, 222n59
"penumbra" theory, 111, 112n58
"perform or pay," 184n3
perjury, 13–14, 131, 209n35, 210
persuasion, 63, 74–75
Philadelphia Newspapers, Inc. v. Hepps (1986), 209n34
Pickering v. Bd. of Educ. (1968), 204n28
Pink, U.S. v. (1942), 69n31
plea bargains, 57n22
Pledge of Allegiance, compelled recitation of, 94–96
police: as institution, 185, 194–99; legal rights, misrepresentations about, 196; lying and deception used by, 31n44, 195–97; Miranda warnings, restraints on delivery of, 210–11; symbolic function of, 221–23
political compromise, 143–44
political resistance and false speech, 148, 149–51
political versus moral equality, 171–75
Post, Robert, 84n6, 107n51, 208, 212–13
Powell v. Texas (1968), 167n12
Pregerson, Harry, 209n35
presumption of truthfulness/sincerity, 11; exceptionalism, institutional, 184; importance of, 2, 5–6, 9–12, 25–26, 27–29, 187–88; individual duty of sincerity, 191–93; institutional duty of sincerity, 194, 223; social interdependence and, 1, 9–12. *See also* suspended contexts
private censorship versus state action doctrine, 106–7, 108–11
promises: actions that cannot be valid objects of, 53n16; in business, 184n3; false promises to immoral agents, 34–35; made under duress (*see* duress); to perform intrinsically wrong actions, 53; persuasion versus, 63

CPSIA information can be obtained
at www.ICGtesting.com
Printed in the USA
JSHW030423130121
10887JS00002B/181